CULTURE, PLACE, AND NATURE

STUDIES IN ANTHROPOLOGY AND ENVIRONMENT

K. Sivaramakrishnan, Series Editor

CULTURE, PLACE, AND NATURE

Centered in anthropology, the Culture, Place, and Nature series
encompasses new interdisciplinary social science research on
environmental issues, focusing on the intersection of culture,
ecology, and politics in global, national, and local contexts.
Contributors to the series view environmental knowledge and
issues from the multiple and often conflicting perspectives of
various cultural systems.

NATURE

THE END OF ECOLOGY IN SLOVAKIA

PROTESTS

EDWARD SNAJDR

UNIVERSITY OF WASHINGTON PRESS   SEATTLE AND LONDON

THIS BOOK WAS SUPPORTED IN PART BY THE DONALD R. ELLEGOOD
INTERNATIONAL PUBLICATIONS ENDOWMENT.

University of Washington Press
P.O. Box 50096, Seattle, WA 98145 U.S.A.
www.washington.edu/uwpress

Library of Congress Cataloging-in-Publication Data
Snajdr, Edward.
Nature protests : the end of ecology in Slovakia / Edward Snajdr.
p. cm. — (Culture, place, and nature)
Includes bibliographical references and index.
ISBN 978-0-295-98855-9 (hardback : alk. paper)
ISBN 978-0-295-98856-6 (pbk. : alk. paper)
1. Environmentalism—Slovakia.   2. Environmental policy—Slovakia.
I. Title.
GE199.S56S63   2008   333.72094373—dc22   2008020389

Unless otherwise noted, all photographs are by the author.

CONTENTS

FOREWORD

THE STUDY OF SOCIAL MOVEMENTS HAS LONG BEEN A CENTRAL area of scholarly inquiry. Such movements range widely from political protests by and for indigenous peoples to aspirations of northern middle classes for cleaner air and water, safer playgrounds, and healthy food. Social science inquiry into social and political mobilization has enriched the literature on international environmentalism, and environmentalism has in turn widened cultural understanding, both topically and theoretically, by bringing to the fore questions about emotional attachment to places and about how values and beliefs concerning multigenerational well-being shape political agendas.

Environmental questions have compelled scholars to examine mobilization at many levels of social organization, as well as to investigate the interplay across these levels in establishing purposes, shaping struggles, and creating modes of cultural representation that infuse activism with meaning. The rethinking of staple formulations of social-movement analysis necessitated by environmental cases is presented here elegantly by Edward Snajdr.

Snajdr takes on important issues concerning the formation of political ideals and the emergence of varied forms of political consciousness in moments of historical transformation, as exemplified in the rise and decline of environmental movements in Slovakia, both before and after the Velvet Revolution and the end of totalitarian communist government in Czechoslovakia in 1989. *Nature Protests* begins with a puzzle: why did environmental activism dissipate and subside, failing to inform the mainstream of democratic political agendas after the end of communism in Slovakia? As Snajdr shows, the dialogues around what is nature and why it should be preserved not only shape an ethic of altruism and an attitude of self-discovery but present, in practical terms, lessons for direct democracy. The combination results in a spiritually realized ethic of care about human health, natural beauty, and the freedom to imagine different ways of living in the city or in the countryside.

As civil society sprang to life in Slovakia and Bratislava, ecological thinking was submerged in the establishment of a multiparty democratic polity, as necessary contention and debate fragmented the pioneer environmentalists and downgraded their cause in response to pressing local demands and to the geopolitical concerns of separation from the Czech Republic, engagement with the European Union, and the definition of a Slovak nation. As a result, in post-socialist Slovakia there arose an ethnicized environmental consciousness, in which "natural elements" like the Danube and its valleys were not embodiments of environmental qualities like fresh water but, rather, landscapes to be claimed for the history of Slovak identity.

Slovakia's separation from the Czech lands was followed by a violent introduction to the fast-paced capitalism of post-Communist globalization and its unbridled exploitation of ethnic divisions, unstable markets, and weak new democracies. In this tumult, Snajdr reflects, ecology (as an issue and as a worldview) was dimished in the hurly-burly of public debate—sixty-eight political parties sprang up in Slovakia in four years after 1990—and the turmoil of adapting a small country to a world capitalist order. We are left to ponder nothing less than the political future of environmental consciousness in burgeoning democracies.

K. SIVARAMAKRISHNAN
Yale University
May 2008

ABBREVIATIONS

CPA   Center for Public Advocacy

CSOP   Czech Union for Nature Conservation

HZDS   Movement for a Democratic Slovakia

MV   City Committee, SZOPK

NGO   nongovernmental organization

NNKK   Return to the Landscape Foundation

OP   *Nature Protection* (*Ochranca Prírody*), SZOPK periodical

OV   District Committee, SZOPK

SDL   Party of the Democratic Left, branch of former Communist Party

SNS   Slovak National Party

STUŽ   Society for Sustainable Living

SZ   Green Party (Strana Zelených), federal party

SZA	Slovak Green Alternative, republic-level party
SZOPK	Slovak Union of Nature and Landscape Protectors
SZS	Slovak Green Party (Strana Zelených Slovensko), republic-level party
SZM	Slovak Union of Youth
ŠtB	Office of State Security (Štatné Bezpečnosť), Slovak secret police
UV	Central Committee, SZOPK
VPN	Public Against Violence
ZO	Basic Organization, SZOPK

ACKNOWLEDGMENTS

THE RESEARCH FOR THIS BOOK WAS MADE POSSIBLE BY GRANTS from the National Science Foundation, the International Research and Exchanges Board (IREX), and the Fulbright Institute for International Education (IIE), as well as by support from the American Council for Collaboration in Education and Language Study (ACCELS) and the Thomas Kukučka Memorial Scholarship through the Slovak Studies program at the University of Pittsburgh. The Office for the Advancement of Research at John Jay College also provided a grant in support of publication.

A number of people and organizations have been helpful to me in the fieldwork for this project and in the writing of this study. I should like to express my thanks and gratitude to all of them. In Slovakia, Juraj Podoba provided personal guidance and inspiration for the project. During my fieldwork the Ethnology Institute of the Slovak Academy of Sciences provided me with office space and its director, Dušan Ratica, gave generously of his time and resources. All of the members of the Ethnology Institute welcomed me with a stimulating research environment and warm hospitality. Nora Hložeková, Viera Zimová, and Maria Paniaková, who comprised the staff of the Fulbright Program in Slovakia in 1994–1996, deserve special thanks for their energy, organizational skills, and availability to offer and deliver assistance whenever I asked. In Bratislava, so many people befriended me and opened their lives to me. I am indebted in particular to Ľubica Šipošová, her mother Ľuba, her father Zdenek, and her brother Zdeno; Jana Kečkešova; my Slovak "coach," Beata; Jaromir "the Musician"; and Martin and Rado. They all shared their lives and their friends with me. I could not have completed my fieldwork without the companionship and good cheer of Paul Mego and Patti Tanski-Mego.

In the environmental movement, thanks must go to Mikuláš Huba, Juraj Rizman, Juraj Krívošik, Rasto Prochazka, Juraj Mesík, Juraj Zamkovský, Palo Široky, Matuš, Poĺko and Sylvia, and all the *aktivisti* who gave so much of their time, their homes and their thoughts and concerns. I must also thank Andrea Chorvátova, for helping me with access to Green Party archives, for *Closely Watched Trains*, and for many conversations about ecology and life in general.

In Pittsburgh, the Russian and East European Studies Program at the University of Pittsburgh, under the direction of Ronal Linden, Bob Donnurummo, and Juliet (Jacobson) Hunt, provided me with a Foreign Language Area Studies Fellowship and a remarkable learning and networking environment. In the Department of Slavic Languages and Literatures, Martin Votruba and Sylvia Lorinc delivered outstanding language training and instruction in Slovak. Mary Rusinow graciously shared her home and garden with me at critical moments of data analysis.

In New York, I should also like to thank Ric Curtis, Chair of the Anthropology Department at John Jay College CUNY, for nurturing a particularly supportive academic environment in which to complete the writing of this book. The Faculty Fellowship Writing Program of the City University of New York allowed me time away from the classroom to complete the project and access to keen (and candid) input from CUNY colleagues including Valli Rajah, Alyson Cole, Patricia Mathews Salazar, Michelle Rief, and Karlyn Koh. Stephen Steinberg, who led this engaging seminar for new faculty at CUNY, deserves special thanks for revitalizing my interest in the project and for encouraging me to "tell the story."

Many other people have read and commented on various versions of the book including Robert Hayden, who was my thesis advisor at Pittsburgh, Andrew Strathern, David Hudgens, Paul Mego (both in the field and after), Charles Dunbar, Chris Svec, David Doellinger, and Padraic Kenney. I must also thank two scholars and teachers who have passed on but who continue to inspire me: Arthur Tuden, who encouraged me to think critically about ecology and culture; and Dennison Rusinow, who led me through East European history with knowledge, good humor, and friendship.

I would like to thank Culture, Place, and Nature series editor K. "Shivi" Sivaramakrishnan for his helpful editorial remarks as well as two anonymous readers for their thorough, generous, and insightful comments and suggestions. Special thanks must also go to Lorri Hagman, senior editor at University of Washington Press, for all her guidance; to Rachel Scollon for her editorial work; and to Marilyn Trueblood for production assistance.

I greatly appreciate the support of my family who helped me in various ways during research and writing: my late father, Edward Snajdr; my mother, Sallee Poole, and her husband Pete; my remarkable in-laws Angel and Sam Trinch; and my wonderful sisters and brother, Suzanne, Elizabeth, and Eric. Finally it is difficult to measure how this work reflects the contributions and support of my wife, Shonna Trinch. She not only read and re-read various versions of the text but also provided the inspiration, engagement, and friendship that make scholarship and life meaningful. This book is dedicated to her and to Rocky and Lucia, our two children, who make every day precious.

Brooklyn, New York
June 2008

Nature Protests

Introduction

ON EARTH DAY, APRIL 22, 1989, SEVEN MONTHS BEFORE Czechoslovakia's Velvet Revolution, the Bratislava City Branch of the Slovak Union of Nature and Landscape Protectors (Slovenský Zväz Ochrancov Prírody a Krajiny, SZOPK) issued to the public what was, at the time, a rather bold proclamation.[1] "We are ill and must be cured," the Union's document charged. The group of volunteer conservationists warned that it was "necessary to reverse the present trends" and bravely called for a "change in values, full information and independent control of the condition and development of the environment" (SZOPK, MV 1989). The imperative tone of this Earth Day demand seemed to belie the repressive climate of Czechoslovakia's communist regime, which even by late 1989 exhibited almost no signs of cracking. Other events in Eastern Europe and the Soviet Union had by then suggested communism's impending collapse. During that same April, roundtable talks between the Polish labor union, Solidarity, and the regime in Warsaw resulted in a historic agreement to hold free elections. Less than a year before, in May 1988, the Hungarian communists had initiated a national discussion of change. Even Mikhail Gorbachev, the leader of the Soviet Union, allowed partially open elections to the Congress of People's Deputies in March 1989. And despite the fall of the Berlin Wall on November 9, Czechoslovakia's communists still clung to power. Only after mass demonstrations and strikes in late November of 1989 did the regime finally give in.

Yet as early as 1987, beginning with the daring publication of *Bratislava/nahlas*, an illegal and electrifying report detailing the environmental devastation of Slovakia's capital city, Slovak greens began to rally dissident writers, religious activists, students, and ordinary citizens to the cause of nature. SZOPK's Earth Day proclamation marked what appeared to be a burgeoning green revolution in socialist East Europe.[2] By the late 1980s, from Leipzig to Budapest and from Krakow to Kiev, ecology gained prominence as a subject among various currents of regime opposition. But in Slovakia, more than in any other socialist society, environmentalism became a central and growing challenge to communist power. During the Velvet Revolution, Slovakia's environmental movement numbered in the tens of thousands, and its key activists took the helm of the public demonstrations in Bratislava calling for change.[3]

After Czechoslovakia's communist regime collapsed, however, Slovakia's green movement quickly shrank to only a handful of members. Activists who were once lauded as heroes of freedom and tolerance were portrayed by the post-socialist state as "enemies of the nation," and the pollution they had fought to wipe out remained or even worsened. Why did Slovakia's ecology movement, so strong under socialism, fall apart so rapidly? How did environmentalism develop in Eastern Europe as such an articulate challenge to totalitarianism and then suddenly dissolve into a muddled and marginalized collection of nongovernmental organizations (NGOs)? Can environmentalism survive at all in a post-socialist world, or does the collapse of communism perhaps signal the end of ecology?

We will see first how environmentalism became a message that stood in opposition to socialism. In part, it is a story of unlikely subversion, beginning with the fact that the regime allowed volunteer nature activism in Slovakia to develop a set of cultural dialogues about lifestyle, landscape, identity, and freedom. These dialogues first appeared in recreational efforts, under the rubric of nature protection, to preserve folk architecture as cultural monuments. Through this unassuming work, weekend and amateur conservationists began to articulate a larger arena of pollution, societal decay, and state neglect. Their efforts to expand ecological activism opened up a critical forum, attracting a wide range of anticommunist forces that utilized the versatility of nature protests as a surrogate to challenge Czechoslovakia's totalitarian regime. More than in any other case of the fall of communism in East Europe, Slovak environmentalism played a decisive political and discursive role in consolidating the elements of *civil society*.

Civil society is "the independent self-organization of [public life], voluntarily engaged in the pursuit of individual, group or national interests" (Weigle and Butterfield 1992:3).[4] The emergence of this sector of society and its influence on communism's downfall is a story of significant variations in different East European states (Pollack and Wielgohs 2004; Ramet 1995). In Poland, for example, Solidarity and the Catholic Church were key currents of resistance. The peace movement in East Germany mobilized many groups of people, including students, religious groups, labor organizations, and artists. In contrast with these cases, Hungarian reform communists virtually gave up the Party's power from within by collaborating with a broad coalition of nascent civic groups. In Romania, striking miners sparked a mass civic revolution which ended violently with the back-alley execution of the country's leader, Ceaușescu. During Czechoslovakia's rapid but bloodless Velvet Revolution, the playwright Vaclav Havel and Charter 77, the dissident human rights group, were the heart and soul of Civic Forum, the public movement that wrested power from the regime in the Czech Lands. In Slovakia, ecological activists became the founders and organizational engine of Public Against Violence, Civic Forum's Slovak counterpart.

From the story of how greens broadened their activism in Slovakia and became prominent leaders in the Velvet Revolution, we also learn about the ideology, architecture, and power of state socialism and how these comprised an *environmentality* of communism. Arun Agrawal defines *environmentality* as the relationships among knowledge systems, power applications, institutional structures, and people as these apply to the environment and to environmental politics (Agrawal 2005:8). He employs this analytic synthesis of political ecology and Foucauldian *governmentality* to examine and understand "the long processes of changes in environmental politics, institutions and subjectivities" regarding "localized environmental regimes" of forest protection in a North Indian village (Agrawal 2005:229).[5] This conceptual model, I would argue, is also useful in examining relationships between governmental power regimes in totalitarian states and local cultural and political practices and processes that both support and play against official notions of nature, space, and place. In the context of Eastern Europe, we see a particular environmentality emerge during several decades of state socialist hegemony, one in which regimes became owners, users, protectors, and abusers of both natural and human resources. Through ideology, education, economic development, and repression, party-states sought to create and control humans as environmental subjects. Yet, as I will show, within the framework of communist environmentality, the system ironically overlooked the sphere of nature activism, which it allowed in the form of independent volunteer conservation groups. These volunteer activists capitalized on the power of ecology to unite multiple voices of cultural resistance, which imbued the concept of environmentalism with new meanings and values.

At the same time, this book is an account of the vulnerabilities and limits of ecology as a unifying idea. Here, Agrawal's analytic approach also provides us with a useful framework to explore rapid and extensive shifts in power structures, institutions, and ideological perspectives within a variety of political and cultural transitions, of which post-socialism is only one example. These shifts may result in competing and dynamic environmentalities within and between local and global arenas, creating conditions in specific historical periods and cultural contexts that I call *post-ecological*. During such shifts, environmentalism falls out of sync with transforming political and cultural relationships. Competing ideologies of identity, economy, and power reformulate nature and its symbols and create new environmental subjects. Where *ecology* is a modern political formulation (Worster 1977) that posits integrated and interdependent relationships between people and their environment, *post-ecology* is a period in which environmentalities are in flux.

If the communist regimes in East Europe and the Soviet Union came to be viewed as "enemies of nature," their quite sudden demise has created a post-ecological moment. This moment has brought the more fragile aspects of nature's discursive versatility as an idea and as a cultural subject into sharp relief. Post-socialism inevitably and ironically allows people the freedom to redefine nature and to perceive it to be threatened in new ways. With the fall of communism in Slovakia, not only did greens lose a clear target, but the return of nationalism to the political arena unexpectedly refigured some forms of environmentalism as foreign concepts and as challenges to cultural and political independence. At the same time, international environmental groups have tried to influence the direction and focus of indigenous activism. As we will see, alongside disillusioned conservationists struggling to promote global ecology, the spectrum of Slovak environmentalism after communism includes chauvinistic ethno-activists selling nature to foreign tourists and angry ecoterrorists fighting fascism with historical theater. All of these forms that currently comprise Slovakia's post-ecological condition have been shaped not only by persistent pollution but perhaps even more by anxieties about change and uncertainty in a post-socialist world.

In addition to being a saga about combating ecological devastation, the rise and fall of environmentalism in Slovakia is a drama involving conflicting ideas about nature, nation, and the state. These ideas have emerged from Slovak society's dynamic history, beginning after the First World War, when Slovaks were freed from decades of near-feudal subjectivity under Hungarian rulers during the Habsburg Dual Monarchy.[6] In 1918, Slovaks joined with Czechs to form the Republic of Czechoslovakia and enjoyed a period of democratic governance. Slovakia, however, was a junior partner in the young democracy, and its economy remained heavily agricultural. In 1939, Slovakia became an independent state under the leadership of Jozef Tiso, at first supported and then overtaken by Hitler's Nazi Germany.[7] Not long after the Second World War, a reconstituted democratic Czechoslovakia quickly yielded to complete communist control, a fate it shared with the rest of Eastern Europe. Slovakia continued to transform under state socialism. Alexander Dubček, a Slovak reform communist, along with party liberals and dissidents, led a brief period of openness in 1968. In less than a year this Prague Spring, as it became known, was shut down by the invasion of Soviet and Warsaw Pact troops. Gustav Husák, loyal to Moscow, replaced Dubček and instigated a long period of political repression, euphemistically termed *normalization*. The only enduring outcome of Dubček's leadership was Slovakia's elevated status as a federal partner with the Czechs in the socialist state. In late 1989, during the Velvet Revolution, the communist regime collapsed. Three years later, at the beginning of 1993, Slovakia and the Czech Republic separated, becoming independent states.

Reflecting this complex history, the country's current population of 5.3 million includes a substantial Hungarian (Maďar) minority (10 percent), who share with Slovaks a predominantly Catholic heritage. In addition to very small Czech (1 percent) and Ruthenian (0.6 percent) communities, Slovakia includes a large and more or less undocumented number of Gypsies or Roma. Estimates of the Roma population range from as few as 80,000 to as many as 400,000 people, a number roughly equivalent to the size of Slovakia's capital, Bratislava. During the Soviet period, this diverse population suffered repression at the hands of one of the most hard-line regimes in the Eastern Bloc, which restricted religion and travel, but also tempered ethnic politics. After the so-called Velvet Divorce, when

Slovaks and Czechs split their state in 1993, ethnic tensions between the Slovak majority and Hungarian and Roma minorities, as well as the pace of economic and democratic reforms, remained central to Slovak political debates. The 1990s was a decade dominated by the arguably authoritarian but highly popular rule of Vladimir Mečiar, who revived Slovak nationalism and who placed the state on a path toward independence from the Czechs. During this period it was an open question whether Slovakia would join those states of the former Eastern Bloc that had moved toward democracy, or slip deeper into the authoritarianism that gripped countries to the east such as Ukraine, Moldova, and Russia. In contrast to their Czech counterparts, who joined NATO in 1999, Slovaks did not enter this alliance until five years later. Under new leadership at the end of the 1990s, Slovakia, along with the Czech Republic, Hungary, Poland, and four other formerly communist states, joined the European Union in 2004.

I link the experience of Slovak nature activism with these broader political and cultural dynamics by drawing equally on the tools of anthropology and history. During field research in Slovakia carried out from 1993 through 1995, I conducted participant observation and ethnographic interviews and examined archival data reaching back to the 1960s in order to capture the continuities and disjunctures of life during and after state socialism. On the one hand, environmentalists shared much with the broader culture of communism: standing in line for scarce consumer goods, suffering limited access to information from Western countries, and enduring the threat of surveillance by government authorities and Party operatives. On the other hand, many activists considered themselves to be different, not only because they attempted to live in a manner unique to their own society but because they were passionately engaged in trying to change that society. These individuals therefore inhabited an ethnographic landscape that cannot be defined geographically but rather conceptually and performatively by the issues and activities that the subjects themselves took up. Like other ethnographies of post-socialism (Borneman 1992, Dunn 2004), my research into this landscape departs from more traditional anthropological studies in the region from the communist period, which tended to be limited to distinct village communities (Arensberg 1954; Halpern and Kerewsky-Halpern 1972; Hann 1980; Salzmann and Scheuffler 1974; Verdery 1983).[8] The field site of environmentalism was diverse and dynamic. Although most of the people I interviewed lived in Bratislava, many did not. Some environmentalists held public demonstrations, while others only wrote essays, articles, and press releases. A few activists traveled extensively to do their work, around the country or, in some cases, across the globe. Thus while much of my field work took place in Bratislava, where most environmental organizations were headquartered, the sites and experiences of activism spanned the whole of the country: from brigades into remote mountain ranges to protests on the sloping banks of the Danube, from work in tiny crowded offices off urban side streets to heated confrontations with security personnel beneath the looming cooling towers of nuclear power plants. Marches, blockades, historical renovation projects, and even funeral memorials together comprised the ethnographic landscape of Slovak environmentalism.

To work in this rather complicated setting, I joined a new environmental organization that formed during the beginning of my field research in the mid-1990s. Although this strategy of participant observation allowed me access to people involved in both the past movement and its post-socialist derivatives, it also committed much of my time to a specific wing of the activist community. To balance this situation of what Lisa Markowitz (2001:42) calls studying "up and over," that is, demarcating the ethnographic field among organizations intensely engaged with the national and international network of NGOs, I also sought other venues for data collection and participant observation. As an ethnographer at the Ethnology Institute of the Slovak Academy of Sciences, with the explicit goal of documenting the history of Slovakia's ecology movement, I conducted interviews with older activists, academics, politicians, and lay persons, and collected documentary sources about activism and conservation.[9] As both historical ethnographer and participant activist, my goal was to reconstruct the many sides of Slovak environmentalism's thirty-year history.

Perhaps not surprisingly, most experiences of the Velvet Revolution—a time of confusion, anticipation, exhaustion, and euphoria—and the role of green activism within it were not recorded. When the pace of change slowed, some people placed their recollections and assessments in a variety of printed matter, including organization literature, meeting minutes and notes, and official and private correspondence. By locating and reading these sources, I prepared to compare them with activists' personal accounts. In a sense, some of the interviews I conducted yielded assessments of assessments, a critical blend of hindsight and nostalgia, no doubt influenced by contemporary political events. After all, from 1989 to 1995 Slovaks had lived under six governments, and personal perspectives of the communist past and the post-socialist transition had, in a few cases, undergone significant revisions. The local press, consisting primarily of *Sme* (We Are), *Slovenská Republika* (Slovak Republic), *Narodná Obroda* (National Revival), *Práca* (Work), *Pravda* (Truth), and the Slovak weekly *Zmena* (Change), provided insight into Slovaks' changing views on ecological issues, politics, and culture.

In addition to capturing the voices of Slovakia's ecology movement by observing, reading about, or participating in protests and demonstrations, my task also required analytically contextualizing this diversity as an ethnography of environmental politics in the public sphere. To achieve this, along with combining historical and ethnographic methods, I integrate recent anthropological and sociological approaches to the study of social movements with recent frameworks in the field of political ecology. Together these perspectives can help us analyze the complexity of local social movements within an understanding of broader political relationships between culture, nature, and place.

ANTHROPOLOGY AND POLITICAL ECOLOGY: ENVIRONMENTALISM AS CULTURAL DIALOGUE

Anthropologists have long understood that humans relate to the environment through their cultural values and societal norms and see their societies reflected in nature as well as emerging from it. While subsistence practices and technology levels may limit the human/nature relationship (Lee 1979; Netting 1981), how people envision their lives as part of the natural world always passes through a cultural filter (Tsing 2001; Turnbull 1968). Nancy Turner (2005) and Eugene Anderson (1996) suggest that some cultural systems are implicitly in harmony with nature, whether or not its members are aware of this balance. Other societies vary widely in their symbolic and social construction of environments. For example, some societies construct their environments as timeless natural resources (Hays 1987), others as ordered spaces of philosophical inspiration (Glacken 1967), and still others as untamed wilderness for exploration (Oelschlaeger 1989). In fact, most societies seldom think about nature in terms of its limits.

Yet emerging from these societies are people who do think about the limits of nature and who are subsequently labeled, and who label themselves, *environmentalists*. Environmentalists have been broadly defined as people who have a "concern to protect the environment, wherever and in whatever form it exists" and who thus attempt to change or break away from prevailing cultural values (Milton 1996:33). As such, scholars have commonly understood environmentalists as comprising a type of *social movement*. Herbert Blumer defines a social movement as a collective enterprise to "establish a new order of life" (Blumer 1969:37). Traditional social movements of the nineteenth century emerged around the mobilization of labor, political representation, or religious freedom, drawing from relatively homogeneous groups based on class or ethnicity. In the mid- to late twentieth century, so-called new social movements concerned with issues such as feminism, civil rights, and sexual rights, among many others, began to appear, "focused on bringing about change through changing values and developing alternative life-styles" (Scott 1990:6). These collectivities were not always directly or explicitly political but were nevertheless characterized and understood using analytical tools that assessed group access to (or isolation from) political processes (Tourain 1981), or their success or failure in mobilizing material resources and gaining public support (Mayer and McCarthy 1979).

Recent work by anthropologists and sociologists recognizes that both new and old social movements remain grounded in and shaped by culture. This research draws on discursive frameworks to move our understanding of social movements beyond once-dominant theories of class struggle and rationalistic models of resource mobilization. In formal, linguistic terms, *discursive* refers to the process of communication or a verbal exchange which requires a producer and a receiver of expressed information, in short, a conversation (Bakhtin 1986[1952]). Dell Hymes (1986 [1972]) contextualizes this process of discourse within and between what he calls *speech communities*, where members share "ways of speaking" along with other cultural norms. In a broader, more interdisciplinary sense, *discursive* has come to mean expressions directed by local cultural and historical conventions and represented through iterative behaviors which comprise particular world views (Foucault 1994 [1972]). Contemporary scholarship has incorporated both of these meanings of discourse to examine how social and political institutions and practices are the product of and operate within dialogical fields of power relationships. From this discursive framework, social scientists have begun to consider the cultural nuances of context, local and transnational activism, and modes of power in explaining the genesis, development, and fate of various social movements. For example, anthropologists have examined how social movements have organized around culturally situated issues of gender equality, ethnic and indigenous autonomy, and religious freedom in various global frameworks of market flows, development politics, and human rights debates (Nash 2005; Alvarez, Dagnino, and Escobar 1998). In sociology there has been a resurgence of interest in the role of emotions in defining, mobilizing, and sustaining specific activisms (Flam and King 2005; Goodwin, Jasper, and Polletta 2001). For example, Julian Groves (2001) highlights the centrality of emotion in the growth and intensity of personal and collective animal rights activism, and Nancy Whittier (2001) interrogates the functional dimensions of passion and pain among victims and advocates struggling to increase public awareness about the crimes of pedophilia and incest.

By foregrounding the discursive aspects of social movements, we also see how they create communities of collective experience and shared rituals.[10] Similar to what Etienne Wenger (1999) and Lave and Wenger (1991) call *communities of practice*, members of a social movement create a shared capability over time. But as discursive formations, the dynamics of social movements may also be shaped by outsiders who respond to members' collective ideas, actions, and behaviors. For instance, the gay community in the U.S., comprised of people espousing specific beliefs about behaviors and lifestyles related to many facets of sexuality, must also operate as a fundamentally dialogical formation, relentlessly engaged with mainstream conceptualizations of cultural norms of sexual identity and practice, all within the public sphere through which the community itself is also defined (Warner 2000). By contrast, the skinhead movement propagates and claims to protect what its members consider to be mainstream norms, but in a public manner stylistically different from the mainstream culture, including open intimidation and the use of violence (Blazak 2001; Hagan, Merkens, and Boehnke 1995). Both of these groups are clearly more than "counter-cultures" or "sub-cultures" because, although they can be conceptualized as opposing a broader cultural or class system (Piven and Cloward 1977), they depend on an engagement with that system for their identity and distinctiveness. Finally, as discursive formations, social movements do not require stable or even large memberships to make an impact on culture or society, and may at times assume an imagined, even mythical character, imparted in part by mainstream society, through which a movement's message and thus the movement itself is sustained.[11]

Like the participants of other social movements, environmentalists are not only concerned with concrete issues such as nature conservation or the eradication of pollution. They also devise and perform rituals with which they not only challenge the rest of society but also reinforce and confirm their identities as part of a collective. At the same time, the cultural and political sources of such rituals reveal the complex positionality of the movement's members. Thus, one is never only an environmentalist, but perhaps also a Catholic, a feminist, or a fascist. Indeed, from a discursive perspective, environmentalists may be characterized by outsiders not as advocates, but as proselytizers, even terrorists.[12] Martha Lee recognizes these discursive positionings in her ethnographic study of the radical and controversial American environmental organization Earth First! She argues that

> social protest movements do not appear, fully formed, on barren soil; they are instead deeply rooted in the culture from which they emerge. From their genesis, they bear the mark of that culture's assumptions about political life, and their development depends upon the way in which that soil nourishes it (Lee 1995:1).

Lee examines Earth First! as a modern American "millenarian movement," which touts a contemporary apocalyptic environmental doctrine but that sees its roots in Jacksonian democracy. Lee finds that despite the group's political desperation, based on a fatalistic vision of the future, Earth First! remains faithful to an extremely moral, if exaggerated, American paradigm of democracy and direct action. The group's wilderness philosophy is significantly influenced by American conservationism and yet rejects its heritage of participatory volunteerism to embrace an equally American and more romantic tradition of sabotage and guerilla intervention. Lee's vivid ethnography reminds us that environmentalism can be built upon different and often competing assumptions about political life, about worldview, and about community.[13]

From this broader perspective on environmentalism, known as *political ecology*, we can begin to investigate links between beliefs about the environment and political ideology, between cultural identity, its configuring symbols, and public performances. As Stephen Yearley (1996) suggests, the global environmental movement is far from monolithic and includes several discursive formations and currents emerging from and engaged within diverse cultural and political contexts. For example, environmentalism in North America has evolved in a dialogue with both capitalist society and democratic participatory politics. Elite volunteerism to save wilderness areas during nineteenth-century industrialization shifted to working class grassroots activism as labor movements formed in the twentieth century (Cohen 1981; Devall 1970; Hays 1958; Ladd, Hood, and Van Liere 1983; Mazur 1975; Thomas 1983).[14] Ecological activism in Latin America and in Asia has been significantly shaped by the social and economic side effects of well-intentioned, but somewhat misguided, international development and assistance projects (Escobar 1999; Gonzalez 1972; Khator 1991; Viola 1988; Wali 1989).[15] What Bron Taylor (1995) calls Third World "ecological resistance movements" have concentrated as much on cultural preservation, in a dialogue with post-colonial economic dependency, as they have on protecting biodiversity, endangered lands, or vanishing species. In sharp contrast to the developing world, the diverse green movement in Western Europe has gained momentum not only from increased environmental consciousness in post-industrial culture, but also through the political successes of green parties willing to conform to the discursive norms and pragmatic compromises of parliamentary systems, even as they have tried to change these (Kitschelt 1989).

Political ecologists have not only traced changing environmental values alongside growing public activism (Lowe and Rudig 1986), but have critically examined the relationships among local ecologies, specific power/knowledge regimes, and technologies of government within historically contingent political economies (Blaikie and Brookfield 1987).[16] Recent scholarship in political ecology has followed Richard Peet and Michael Watts's (1996) call to incorporate a discursive framework in understanding reformulations of nature according to specific historical and cultural power/knowledges and technologies of government. For example, among the first to explore the concept of governmentality in the field of environmental history, K. Sivaramakrishnan (1999) examines the power relationships involved in the historical process of forest management and state making in colonial Bengal. Also working in South Asia, Haripriya Rangan (2001) has interrogated the discursive and political contexts of the mythologization of the Chipko, or "tree-hugger," movement in the Indian Himalayas as these relate to global environmental activism as well as to modes of administration and policy in the region. James Fairhead and Melissa Leach (1996) investigate the disjuncture between expert knowledge and village practices and its implication for compromising sustainable land use in Guinea.

Drawing from all of this work, Arun Agrawal (2005) synthesizes the diversity, scope, and depth of the process of making environmental subjects and subjectivities through the concept of *environmentality*. Agrawal's model, which uses the example of decentralization strategies in forest conservation of a North Indian village, abandons oppositional pairings such as state against society. Instead, he explores how the relationships among and between people, power regimes, knowledge systems, and institutions create new conceptualizations of local ecosystems. For Agrawal, *environmentality* is not just an orientation to nature, but a set of contingent relationships emerging from both the limits and the possibilities generated by historically situated economic, political, ideological, and technological practices. Within this framework, nature and place, in addition to being "settings," are also fundamental cultural subjects, defined and redefined through shifting human relationships. These relationships include both technologies of the state, by which landscape represents power (Scott 1998; Hughes 2005), and modes of resistance to these technologies (Scott 1985).

Agrawal's model has significant comparative value for other contexts. Moving beyond India, for instance, Cotten Seiler (2006) examines the environmentality of social technologies and capitalist consumption of mobility and place in the development of the interstate highway system in Cold War–era U.S. society. Through what he calls *automobility*, Seiler shows how the state creates a new environment which ironically facilitates and transforms older relationships of culture based on race. In contemporary Mexico, Cori Hayden (2003) shows, through an analysis of the bioprospecting industry, how an emerging environmentality of neoliberalism and biotechnology forces local residents to sell nature in order to save it. Through the framework of environmentality we can also examine the totalizing models of governmentality in state-socialist East Europe and their effects on relationships between people, nature, and the state. At the same time, this approach may yield new understandings about the significant and rapid changes in politics, economy, and culture brought forth by those states' demise and what is now generally referred to as *post-socialism* (Verdery 1996).

SHIFTING ENVIRONMENTALITIES: THE CASE OF EAST EUROPE

It is now well known that the heavy industrial development and urbanization that unfolded during state socialism created severe ecological devastation in many areas of the former Eastern Bloc and Soviet Union. While very little information reached Western observers before the collapse of communism, some evidence managed to slip through the Iron Curtain by the late 1980s. The nuclear accident at Chernobyl in 1986 did not just shock Westerners with the immediate and dangerous impacts of nuclear waste and radioactive fallout. It also provided the most striking portrait of a system whose leaders were not only negligent in terms of safeguarding against major environmental health threats, but also determined to mis-represent the extent of these maladies for political reasons.

Inside East Europe and the USSR, however, ecology as an issue seem-ingly remained buried under political repression and censorship. Even after the disaster at Chernobyl, evidence of the seriousness of the region's environmental problems continued to be strenuously concealed by the regimes, and information on individuals and groups that mobilized around ecological issues remained sporadic and sparse (Weiner 1988). It was only after the collapse of these regimes that the full extent of the envi-ronmental crisis was exposed. Images of the blackened faces of children in industrialized northern Bohemian villages (Thompson 1991), accounts of severely deformed fetuses in laboratories in Ukraine and Russia, and studies of poorly contained chemical leaks in various locations through-out Eastern Europe surfaced only after totalitarianism crumbled (Fesh-bach and Friendly 1992). These environmental horror stories confirmed suspicions in the West that communist regimes were not only economi-cally inefficient and even dangerous to human lives, but that they also selfishly kept environmental dangers from the public for the sake of main-taining a hold on political power. The mounting evidence suggested a unique environmentality of communism.

After the dramatic fall of communism, the wave of new political par-ties and organizations fueled the hopes of some Western observers that a new ecological era had arrived. For example, Hillary French, in a *World-watch* paper, characterized East European green movements as "green revolutions" (French 1990). Michael Waller suggested that human rights gave dissident groups the political teeth to shape environmental issues as public challenges, and saw in environmentalism a common denomi-nator with which to measure the opposition's discourse against state-socialist regimes (Waller 1989:303). Likewise, Patrick Marshall (1991) argued that Eastern Europe offered the West new models for responding to ecological maladies, and a new system that placed environmental pol-itics high on the agenda of the new states. Indeed, early public opinion surveys in East Europe indicated such a development, showing ecology at or near the top of a long list of social concerns. In the new democratic political arena, green parties took the stage—some prominently, some fleetingly—in virtually all of the countries of Eastern Europe.

Yet by the mid-1990s, environmentalism seemed to have lost its footing. Was ecology simply a praetorian surrogate for expression in a repressive system? According to Sabrina Ramet (1995), in political systems that do not fulfill the needs of a population, social institutions have a tendency to become politicized. She characterizes this phenomenon, following Samuel Huntington, as *praetorianism*, a syndrome where traditional institutions, such as the Church, labor unions, or students, take on political roles when "'normal' channels are unavailable for certain purposes" (Ramet 1995:179). These institutions then serve political functions that diverge from their intended or perceived roles. Along with traditional institutions, like the Catholic Church or labor unions, several nontraditional organizations also assumed a praetorian political character. For example, once their work was interpreted and advertised by communist authorities as subversive (Dowling 2002:137; Ramet 1995:128–29), the Jazz Section of the official Czechoslovak Musician's Union became one of the sites of political resistance in Prague. Environmental movements in Central and East Europe no doubt emerged as discursive movements serving a praetorian function. Barbara Hicks (1996), for instance, notes how in the 1980s, alongside Poland's Solidarity labor movement, the Polish Ecology Club grew as a social movement. Jane Dawson (1996) also explores the praetorian overlap of green ideologies with other political goals, suggesting that many antinuclear movements became surrogates for opposition against the Soviet state.

The political power gained by environmental activists under state socialism, however, and particularly in Slovakia, was more than the endpoint of a praetorian moment. It was also the result of publicly exposing the grim realities of pollution and poor health, and through this exposure recognizing the fundamental weaknesses of a notably repressive political system. As these alarming threats were revealed, the authorities had no ready-made answers or credible excuses like the ones they had relied on in other realms of social and political life. When consumer goods ran short, regimes could (and frequently did) borrow resources to prop up an inefficient economy. In terms of demands for other reforms, empty directives and proclamations in the state press were used to confuse and to placate a simmering public. The condition of the environment, however, was hard to conceal. Ironically, and most notably in Slovakia, an independent conservation movement was allowed to grow within what appeared to the regime to be a framework of Marxist-Leninist environmentality. Instead, environmentalism turned out to be one of the soft spots in the underbelly of communist hegemony.

But this was the old world. Ecological politics in post-communist East Europe now involves more than the challenge of anticipating and responding to major changes in the rules of what F. G. Bailey (1969) has called the "competitive game." The collapse of communism has also resulted in a substantial refashioning and repositioning of relationships among economies, institutions, technical knowledge, public spaces, even history and memories, all with important implications for nature activism.

ENVIRONMENTAL ACTIVISM IN A POST-ECOLOGICAL AGE

Donald Worster has called the twenty-first century the Age of Ecology, where ecology is essential "if humankind is to save itself from destroying the biological underpinnings of civilization" (Oelschlaeger 1989:208). In this age, it is assumed that the environment will (or at least should) play a fundamental role in configuring human relationships and in guiding political action. I suggest, however, that this age, if it ever existed, has come to an end. Certainly one could point out that the terrorist attacks of September 11, 2001 and the resulting global war on terror have firmly displaced ecology and ecological justice at the turn of the century. I would argue that events in East Europe after the fall of communism put this process in motion a decade earlier. Far from being the Age of Ecology, the twenty-first century is an era of what I will call *post-ecology*.

By post-ecology I mean a period in which environmentalism no longer is capable of uniting disparate discourses and groups under the umbrella of ecological justice. This does not mean that ecology, as a movement, idea, or ethics, has disappeared. However, a post-ecological condition is one in which other ideologies usurp, appropriate, exploit, and diminish specific environmental worldviews to serve other ends. James Fairhead and Melissa Leach (1996) suggest just such a condition in their critique of the relationship between environmental experts and villagers in Guinea, a setting where issues of official expertise and policy development run counter to, and perhaps aim to destroy, implicit, local practices of sustainability. In addition to the forces of market capitalism and democracy, as well as ideologies of nationalism and security, environmentalists themselves are reproducing this process through their actions. For example, Kevin DeLuca (1999) shows how *image politics* has replaced social change as the substantive standard by which activists in the global environmental movement measure their progress in the political arena. Regardless of whether policy is created or changed, activism has increasingly focused on the media event. In this way environmentalism reifies itself as a discursive space struggling in a marketplace in which capitalism and nationalism have, in many cases, consumed green ideas, actions, and values.

In East Europe, socialism's fall coincided with the high-water mark of environmental activism as a unifying social movement. Post-socialism has ushered in new and persistent environmental problems, including important questions about nuclear energy, particularly the use of Chernobyl-type reactor designs in plants under construction; the control and exploitation of limited water resources; and the continuing use of low-grade coal. These problems are exacerbated by political, economic, and social transformations as the region moves to market capitalism and joins the European Union.

Returning to our focus on Slovakia, we will see how environmentalists capitalized on the idea of ecology as an integrated political space to expose how official policy failed to reflect real conditions. We will also examine how the collapse of communism has initiated the formation of new environmentalities. In this formation, once-isolated activists engage with new kinds of praetorianism that alter the purpose and the message of ecology in the post-socialist transition.

Addressing this process as history and ethnography, the researcher must ultimately decide where to begin and where to end the narrative. The exciting and unexpected events during the Velvet Revolution are no doubt important. Many of the ideas and experiences of these revolutionaries during this extraordinary time were fundamental in the way they have shaped the present situation of environmentalism. But this study is mainly concerned with what came before and with what happened after the three weeks of the dramatic collapse of the regime in Czechoslovakia. Much of life from the past system resonated into the transition, creating the contradictory and inverted relationships of a post-ecological condition.

To trace these inversions and to account for these contradictions, the chapters that follow unfold more or less chronologically. Chapter 1 presents the broader ideological and cultural framework of communist environmentality from which Slovakia's conservation movement arises. I identify this framework as a set of contradictory relationships between the socialist state and its citizens. The state is at once polluter and protector of the environment, and its citizens both venerate nature and collude in its neglect. From these contradictions emerges szopk (the Union), a volunteer grassroots organization devoted to wildlife conservation and the restoration of folk architecture. Chapter 2 explains how even under the watchful eye of the Communist Party, the Union and its members pushed the boundaries of this safe, yet paradoxically subversive, space of ecology under socialism, attracting dissidents and citizens alike to the cause of environmentalism. In chapter 3 I show how the growing green movement's successful confrontations with the state amounted to some very powerful acts of cultural demystification. From the illegal publication of *Bratislava/nahlas*, a scathing report on the capital city's dangerous pollution and its residents' poor health, to its lead role in mass demonstrations during the Velvet Revolution, the green movement took environmentalism to its zenith as symbol and surrogate in socialist Slovakia.

Moving into the post-socialist period, chapter 4 examines the disintegration of Slovakia's ecology movement in spite of new freedoms to demonstrate and new ecological problems that begged for protest. Focusing in particular on the cases of the Green Party's failure in elections and the Union's suicidal campaign against the Slovak government's Gabčíkovo Dam project, the chapter introduces the sudden and surprising clash between environmentalism and nationalism. Chapter 5 then explores how activists created new NGOs in an attempt to reclaim the public's attention through transnational issues such as nuclear energy and through spectacular direct-action protests. Chapter 6, however, assesses these efforts as marking the start of a post-ecological era, where symbolic representations of nature either clash with or are appropriated by ideologies of nationalism and free-market capitalism. In this era, global activism is perceived by citizens as a threat to Slovak culture, and landscape preservation, once a force of anticommunism, is commoditized by some activists to show their loyalty to nation over nature.

The conclusion connects the fundamental questions of the socialist period with those of the post-socialist transition by demonstrating how rumblings about ecology form a dialogue about ethnicity, place, and power. The web of culture within which environmentalism becomes entangled in a post-ecological era is not crafted—to paraphrase and depart from Geertz (1973)—from clear Weberian categories such as classes, movements, states, or laws. Rather, it is formed from disjunctures and contradictions born from uncertainty. Symbols of nature which at one time united people against imperial state power are themselves the site of conflict as competing representations of a past, present, and future nation. If the socialist regime was singled out as nature's antagonist, its absence highlights how culture, place, and nature are disparately defined and redefined by people experiencing change. By discussing other post-ecological conditions developing or occurring beyond East Europe, I also point out that shifts in environmentalities do not suggest an end to environmental politics. Rather, such shifts offer opportunities to consider new relationships of power between people, states, and institutions. The marginalization of environmentalism in Slovakia after the collapse of communism may be only a delay in the reformulation of a message with which the world will be changed again.

1 *Communist Environmentality*

IN THE PROCESS OF BUILDING SOCIALISM, NATURE WAS regarded as a passive entity and, with trademark Marxist rationality, designated with the simple status of material resource. Nature was not a political subject, such as literature, or a trade union, or religion. It was, rather, in the state-socialist imagination, a concern of the scientist and the engineer. This basic orientation to the environment was a foundational aspect of communist environmentality, which, through the configuration of nature as passive, appeared to place a decisive boundary between the realms of nature and culture. In fact, the communist regimes of the Soviet Union and East Europe considered their primary battle to be not with nature but, rather, with culture.[1] To build socialism in the Soviet Union not only required the conversion of peasants and petit bourgeoisie through repression and economic transformation, but also demanded the domination and reshaping of a wide range of traditional lifeways, from those of Central Asian pastoralists to those of Siberian foragers (Siegelbaum and Sokolov 2000). This was a mammoth project involving, on the one hand, intensive industrialization and the collectivization of agriculture, and, on the other hand, the reconfiguration of social institutions, the eradication of histories, and the implementation of massive layers of bureaucracy. The building of socialism after the communist takeovers in Eastern Europe between 1945 and 1948 involved many of the same strategies. This process extracted and consumed natural resources and reshaped and built over landscapes, all the while featuring the use of newer and better technologies for the glorification of socialism. Compared to the massive scope and cultural diversity of Russia and Central Asia, the smaller, more industrialized states of Eastern Europe perhaps posed less of a challenge. Many had sizable homegrown communist movements at the end of World War II. Others, such as Czechoslovakia, had had brief experiences with democracy. All of them were submitted to the same general patterns of cultural transformation through centralized economic development, education, and political repression.

If communist environmentality dictated that nature was to be used in the service of cultural and economic transformation, this materialist imperative treated humans in much the same way. Therefore, alongside the repression and surveillance employed to control culture, communism fostered a set of unique and often contradictory relationships between people and their environments. On the one hand, personal orientations to public spaces approached a condition of emotional detachment and, in some cases, complete disregard. On the other hand, individuals venerated nature as much for its spiritual and private value as they did for its recreational utility. At the same time, the state created bureaucratic departments whose purpose was to monitor and protect nature, alongside institutions designed to improve knowledge and develop technologies to exploit it. Yet significant and dangerous pollution problems, which naturally accompanied the engineering of a future utopia, were nevertheless generally concealed by the state or characterized as inconveniences or minor hardships to be endured as the price of progress.

Czechoslovakia provides a model example of communist environmentality, or what Agrawal (2005) conceptualizes as the historically situated power relationships between knowledge systems, institutions, and practices involved in the making of environmental subjectivities. These elements of environmental subject making emerged within Czechoslovak communism, beginning in 1948 and continuing until just after the hardline crackdown on political reform which followed the Prague Spring of 1968. Coinciding with the beginning of Czechoslovakia's period of renewed repression in 1969, termed *normalization* by the Husák regime, the state established both laws and institutions to protect nature and monitor pollution. These laws, however, were largely ignored, the institutions merely cosmetic. In addition to describing how landscapes and people were transformed and controlled in this system, I examine the contradictory relationships between society and nature that were both a product of and a contribution to communist environmentality. Emerging from these contradictions within both society and the state, volunteer nature protection became a sphere of activity in Slovakia that, surprisingly, the regime seemed to overlook, despite an increase in policies and technologies to control public life. This sphere of volunteerism, manifested in the Slovak Union of Nature and Landscape Protectors, was allowed to develop outside of the Communist Party bureaucracy as a "private" endeavor, and as such, slowly and unassumingly, began to draw nature as a subject into the realm of culture.

SLOVAKIA'S SOCIALIST LANDSCAPE

In the Slovak language, *príroda* (nature) refers to wild places in which humans do not live but into which they may certainly go. In common usage the term is frequently linked with recreation away from urban centers, or appears as the setting or subject of romantic fairytales and stories of folk heroes. In one Slovak fable about the changing seasons, *príroda* is personified as a family of brothers, who represent nature as well as control its power (Sturges and Vojtech 1996). *Životné prostredie*, meaning the environment, is a technical Slovak term not much used in everyday conversation. It refers specifically to an ecosystem, a scientific concept that includes human coexistence with other organisms and with natural but inanimate elements.

In building socialism, the communist party-states of East Europe shaped both nature and the environment to serve ideology. In doing so they created physical and symbolic landscapes to meet their needs, an endeavor James Scott (1998) refers to as projects of *legibility*. In other words, through comprehensive planning, administration, and ideological control, Scott argues, states make the line between the industrial and pre-industrial world, between the past and the present, dramatically readable. In the process of carving out its identity as a communist state, the Czechoslovak regime began to construct what Dean Ruggs terms the *socialist landscape* (Ruggs 1985:255).[2]

Beginning with the state-led industrialization and collectivization program, the Czechoslovak regime sought to increase production output and make agriculture more efficient. As part of this process, Slovakia's largely bucolic environment, consisting of extensive peasant farming, was vigorously collectivized between 1949 and 1960, bringing 95 percent of arable land under state ownership. Along with collectivization, an intensive program of heavy industrial development was implemented that mimicked Soviet practices of building massive manufacturing centers. These transformations also affected people at the level of social organization, interaction, and identity. Most people had little choice in this process, because the state became the major supplier of new jobs after 1948. Both industrial and agricultural programs accelerated an urbanization process that shifted rural populations of small family farms to rapidly industrializing towns and cities, or simply consolidated tiny villages into larger administrative units. If socialism lifted many people out of the ditches of peasant life on small farms and into factories or collective agricultural complexes, it also removed individuals from many of the responsibilities involved in sustaining their own resources and livelihood. The regime became the main owner and user of natural resources and gained hold of Slovakia's rural environment by effectively emptying it of residents. The result was a landscape of physical control and appropriation (Scott 1998:218).

At the same time, the state symbolically appropriated landscapes through the transformation of architecture. Through education and state-run media, people were encouraged to view industrial complexes that sprang up at the edges of cities as monuments of the progress of socialism. Out in the countryside, giant grain elevators and huge tractor houses defined the new profiles of agricultural life. Slovakia's urban spaces also assumed the unique pattern of socialist legality.[3] Within the city's inner sections, old structures decayed as the regime used existing funds to build new cultural centers, hotels, and stores. The state's manipulation of settlement patterns, which tripled the size of many cities, also required the construction of sprawling residential complexes. Outside of Bratislava, across the Danube River, an enormous housing development made up of hundreds of identical ten-story buildings, rose up around the single-family dwellings of the small village of Petržalka. By the end of the 1980s, 150,000 people, over one-third of the population of Slovakia's capital city, resided in this labyrinth of concrete-slab apartment blocks (*paneláky*), which covered only a few square kilometers (see figure 1.1). The names of Petržalka's pre-fab developments, such as Lúky (meadow), ironically referenced elements of nature that were no longer there. Because of their monotonous design, it is said, these buildings confused young children, who needed help finding their way home after school. Residents would place special marks on the front entrance of their complex to guide their child to their flat. Petržalka remained mostly residential and isolated, connected to Bratislava's Staré Mesto (Old Town) by only a single bridge. New buildings were also erected in regional towns to make space for an increasingly large industrial labor force and to provide offices for local

FIG. 1.1 Urban socialism in Petržalka. One-third of Bratislava's residents live in this section of the city, only a few square kilometers in area.

bureaucracies. These buildings, however, only mirrored in their blandness the gray, functionalist profiles of the residential *paneláky*.

Of course, new socialist construction projects often meant the destruction of older architecture and traditional communities. In fact, the damage inflicted on urban historical monuments and traditional architecture in Slovakia under state socialism was greater even than the devastation resulting from the final battles between the Nazis and the Red Army in Bratislava during the Second World War. For example, Bratislava's Jewish Quarter was completely demolished to build the eastern foundation and on-ramps for the massive Bridge of the Slovak National Uprising, which spanned the Danube River to open up access to the crowded neighborhoods of Petržalka. New socialist monuments displaying themes of conformity and progress replaced crumbling statues in villages and towns. Towering above the capital city stood the enormous obelisk of Slavín Monument, which commemorated the deaths of thousands of Soviet soldiers who had liberated Slovaks from fascism.

Although socialist projects dramatically changed the physical appearance of towns, basic municipal infrastructure tended to lag behind the cosmetic alterations required by the regime's legibility strategy, which relied so much on surface presentation. For example, sufficient funds for sewage plant construction, which began in 1958, were not included in the budgets of most new housing facilities. As a result, pre-communist wastewater treatment facilities could not adequately process increasingly high levels of heavy metals in local water supplies. These kinds of gaps in development were also the product of communist centralized planning, which failed to provide adequate state resources to local authorities who were directly responsible for services in municipalities. Underneath the official blueprint of the planned economy, informal patronage networks and direct barter exchange systems proliferated (Verdery 1996; Lampland 1991).

The progress of socialism targeted ethnicity in different ways. For example, ethnic Hungarians in Czechoslovakia, who mainly resided in Slovak territory, were encouraged to embrace *Czechoslovakism* as an expression of communist brotherhood. Traditional culture, however, viewed as essentially backward, needed special attention. Communist authorities thus confiscated or destroyed Gypsy wagons, which moved communities from town to town, and built new housing projects for Roma families. The state hoped to provide these traditionally nomadic communities with formal education and steady opportunities for labor, with mixed results.[4] Gypsy clan life often remained isolated from other parts of town life. In some cases, Roma communities altered the intended use of the modern *paneláky* housing to fit their extended family social structure and extensive economy. For example, a building's first floor might become stables for chickens, goats, and other animals, the second be dedicated to social events, and upper floors serve as family sleeping quarters.

The heavy-handedness of the state's management of people and places, however, was also accompanied by a significant degree of stability and security. Under the care of the socialist state, people received a range of benefits in the areas of employment, basic health care, social and economic services, and education (Lovenduski and Woodall 1987:373–80). A public health system was available to everyone in Czechoslovakia. State-owned businesses, if not the government itself, covered the cost of clinics, hospitals, and physicians (who were, in turn, only moderately paid).[5] In addition to medicine, childcare was provided (and paid for) by the state. All education, from grade school through university, was free, and accessible to both men and women. The universal state curriculum, of course, had to correspond with the ideological framework of Marxism. With an increase in the availability of education, however, Czechs and Slovaks enjoyed, along with most other East European societies, relatively high literacy rates. Some type of employment was guaranteed for all able-bodied persons and supported with a comprehensive social security system which included welfare services and modest pensions. Most people were eligible for retirement by the age of 60.

The benefits of socialism also came in the form of widespread public safety and spatial mobility. The rate of violent crime was low, and streets were safe. Public transportation was relatively cheap and widely available, at least in urban areas. The larger Slovak cities of Bratislava, Košice, and Banska Bystrica had extensive streetcar and bus networks, and were connected with one another and with hundreds of smaller towns through low-priced rail lines. Although most Slovak territory was mountainous, with low but lengthy and forested ranges, intrastate highways were well constructed and well maintained—with the aim, of course, to accommodate heavy military vehicles and industrial truck transport. Travel outside of the Eastern Bloc, however, was not allowed, except under special circumstances and usually under the watchful eye of state authorities. Serving as something of a counterbalance to this glaring restriction of human mobility, the state did not seem to mind that people routinely took six weeks of vacation from their work each year.

THE ENVIRONMENTALITY OF NORMALIZATION

When he became the Communist Party Chairman in January 1968, Alexander Dubček initiated a series of reforms in Czechoslovakia which included a relaxation of political repression, a rehabilitation of previously discredited public figures, limited private enterprise, and a nascent political pluralism in the area of local governance. These reforms were characterized by Dubček as "socialism with a human face" and became known as the Prague Spring.[6] This period of free expression and diversity of viewpoints was, however, short-lived. In August of 1968, Soviet and Warsaw Pact troops invaded Czechoslovakia, and Dubček was replaced by Gustav Husák. Husák was a hard-line communist who could be trusted by Moscow to strengthen relations with the Soviet Union—in "a spirit of ideological brotherhood"—and bring the country back onto the path of socialist development. This path was euphemistically termed *normalization*. Normalization was a set of economic and social policies that put

Czechoslovakia in lockstep with Moscow and which included serious political repression and ideological control over almost every aspect of public life. Husák quickly purged reform communists, including Dubček, from the Party, and imprisoned intellectuals who during the Prague Spring had criticized socialism's Stalinist past. Normalization meant full and explicit compliance with ideology. Any deviation from official discourse would be met with the loss of professional opportunities and, in some cases, imprisonment. It also came with some "rewards" for society, in the form of better availability of consumer goods, which the regime borrowed heavily to provide. Normalization also meant getting back to the business of economic centralization, which in turn meant an increase in industrial production, tied, of course, to the larger mission of improving Soviet security in Europe.

Thus, after Soviet tanks rolled into Bratislava and Prague, Slovaks started to build them as well. After 1968, the state escalated raw material extraction and basic industrial production. As the poorer and still more rural partner in the Czech and Slovak socialist partnership, Slovakia became a center for weapons manufacturing, including tanks, firearms, and the plastic explosive Semtex. Near the village of Dubníca in western Slovakia, a tank works was built. In Žiar nad Hronom, an aluminum factory served as a model of "normalized" industrial success. Heavy machinery facilities dotted the landscape. Yet over half of this industrialization involved the use of dangerous chemicals, the production of large amounts of metallurgic waste, and the emission of high levels of particle contaminants. Many factories and homes throughout the country (both in Slovakia and in Bohemia) released environmentally damaging by-products of low-grade, high-sulfur brown coal on a daily basis. On the outskirts of Bratislava, the Slovnaft chemical refinery pumped out fumes and particulates that would hover over the capital city, along the southern slopes of the Little Carpathian Mountains, during temperature inversions. Not fifty kilometers away churned the atomic-powered turbines of the Jaslovksé Bohuníce Chernobyl-type nuclear reactors (see figure 1.2). The plant's employees wore their contaminated work clothes home to their village during lunch hour, and several undocumented accidents were rumored to have occurred at the plant (Pollak 1991). To augment the energy output of Jaslovské Bohuníce, a massive hydroelectric power plant on the Danube River near the small town of Gabčíkovo was slated for construction, in cooperation with a sister project on Hungarian soil further downstream. The completion of the Gabčíkovo Dam and power

FIG. 1.2 Jaslovské Bohuníce. This complex of Soviet-style reactors is located about 50 km from Slovakia's capital city. Photographer unknown.

plant would mean the inevitable destruction of unique wetlands. Normalization, therefore, also meant an escalation in the amount and severity of ecological hazards and environmental damage.

The pollution that accompanied all of this development, however, was not merely written off by the regime as the price of "normalized" progress. Much of its danger was concealed from the public. Part of this concealment involved what Vaclav Havel so aptly called, in *The Power of the Powerless*, "a formalized language deprived of semantic contact with reality" (Havel 1978:47). Along with other forms of doublespeak and discursive obfuscation, the regime actually had in place a set of environmental laws. In addition to the Air Purity Law of 1967, the government passed the Water Act (1973), the Agricultural Land Protection Act (1976), and the Revision to the Forestry Act (1977). The 1968 Czechoslovak constitution, which was updated during Dubček's Prague Spring, also contained provisions for preventing environmental degradation, and formal principles of environmental responsibility. If normalization was, as Havel put it, the triumph of appearances over substance (Havel 1978:47), new environmental laws were no exception. Under these statutes, different ministries were charged with various aspects of environmental stewardship, a division of labor that was based ultimately on economic relevance. For example, all river systems fell under the jurisdiction of the Ministry of Forestry and Water Management. Large factories and mines, however, which relied on water sources for their operation, were the responsibility of the Economic Ministry. To coordinate these separate spheres, the official approach to environmental management was set up as a "guarantee system" through which administrative bodies oversaw the effectiveness of particular environmental standards. The official guarantee system contained a battery of fees and fines to be levied on polluters and was proudly characterized by the regime as a network of "collective responsibility." But the network really only functioned as an accounting adjustment between ministry budgets, because

> most of these paper policies were rarely enforced: the Party-State was both
> owner and regulator, both polluter and enforcer, both enterprise and banker,
> and had none of the checks and balances between these functions (Andrews
> 1993:14).

In some cases, a law actually replaced old problems with newer ones. For example, the Air Purity Law was referred to as "the 'chimney law,' because by regulating only local ambient concentrations it created an incentive to build taller smokestacks, worsening air pollution and forest damage downwind" (Andrews 1993:14). In practice, the guarantee system was a buck-passing operation which only reinforced industrial pollution. The overall result was that no agency could nor wanted to assume total responsibility for enforcing environmental standards.

In the case of nature protection, legislation did exist, but had no corresponding institution to enforce it. In 1955, Czechoslovakia passed the State Nature Protection Act, mandating a system of penalties and sanctions for the extraction of raw materials in designated protected areas. However, the agency that was supposed to issue these penalties and collect fines was not created until 1980. Even after it was established, the Slovak Institute for the Care of Historical Monuments and Nature Conservation (CHMNC) rarely imposed penalties for violating rules governing protected zones. By 1983, 24 plant and animal species had been wiped out and 373 species were critically endangered (SZOPK 1990). Slovakia's largest "protected space," the Tatra Mountains National Park, was controlled by the Ministry of Forestry and Water Management, which, like other branches of the state-run economic system, was responsive to centralized five-year plans and not to piecemeal complaints from a minor regulatory body such as the CHMNC. As for other national parks in Slovakia, most of these were under the care of the Ministry of Culture, against which the conservation institute had absolutely no power.

The regime also prevented scientists and researchers from raising issues or informing the public about environmental conditions. Even though the government carried out environmental impact analyses and air and water monitoring throughout the 1970s, the Party leadership considered this information to be "state secrets" and kept findings hidden both from the public and from separate research departments. In 1983, the Czechoslovak Academy of Sciences completed a rare and comprehensive report on environmental pollution that painted a very grim picture of the damage that industrialization had inflicted on the country's flora and fauna. The report identified a significant increase in the number of species threatened by acid rain, and a serious decline in water purity throughout the country. Not surprisingly, the regime withheld the report from the public, and citizens were never made aware that such research had been done.[7]

The environmentality of normalization comprised not only a set of empty laws and disconnected and inappropriately designated state institutions. It was also a system of government that accepted serious and often dangerous levels of pollution as the unavoidable price of progress. On top of this, it involved the deception of the public, which was prevented from receiving either a comprehensive or an accurate picture of the scope and condition of environmental problems. These relationships of environmental subjectivity, however, were not just unidirectional. They received substantial reinforcement from a population which understood that normalization was largely a system of appearances and which generally acquiesced to the paternalistic role of the state.

THE PUBLIC AND PRIVATE ENVIRONMENT

Alongside the contradictions in official and de facto discourses of Czechoslovak normalization regarding nature and the environment, Slovak society maintained equally contradictory relationships with *príroda* and *životné prostredie*. The first was based on the notion of socialist property and communal urban spaces owned and managed by the state. The second relationship was nurtured in private, represented by the conservation of household resources and by the *domček* (cottage) and garden plot that most urban residents were allowed to own and work by themselves. The former was shaped by state paternalism and collective management, the latter inspired by a pre-socialist Slovak peasant culture, a life of self-reliance and, from the regime's perspective, cultural "backwardness." Both relationships contributed to normalization as much as they reacted against it.

Throughout normalization, public spaces in Slovakia fell into disrepair, a process to which citizens contributed without apparent concern. People casually dumped dirty washing water from windows several stories up onto the sidewalks below. Although violent crime was rare, theft was a growing problem, especially of items that were in short supply. For example, car owners routinely removed their windshield wipers after parking their cars, out of fear that they might be stolen, as replacement parts were hard to find. State property was a primary target of petty theft. On one rail line in eastern Slovakia, over a six month period passengers made off with "12,788 pairs of curtains, 4,208 mirrors, and 633 light fixtures" (Time-Life 1987:112). Citizens of socialism mistreated common urban spaces under the premise that state authorities were responsible for maintaining them. This philosophy of disregard for public space was still very evident after the collapse of communism. Even in more prosperous post-socialist neighborhoods, one could still see the traces of socialist apathy toward the environment. Dlhé Diely, a new neighborhood built in the early 1990s outside of Bratislava and located high on a slope overlooking the Austrian border, is just one example. On the grounds of groups of tall and pristine *paneláky* lay piles of garbage and trash. Beside rows of parked BMWs and Mercedes, symbols of the new economic success stories of the post-1989 transition, grew unruly grasses and weeds, dotted with bits of paper thoughtlessly tossed away by passersby. Men urinated wherever they found a partially secluded wall, some relieving themselves in full view of major pedestrian walkways. Vandalism was rampant. Kids blew up fireworks in, or set fire to, public trash receptacles, leaving their contents scattered among pieces of melted plastic. All of these things were par for the course around housing complexes, on city streets, and around the public square.

If the city's public spaces during normalization were beyond the realm of personal obligation, so too were public and professional relationships. Corruption and bribery flourished. People paid off officials for favors, better jobs, and luxury goods, which were uniformly scarce and terribly expensive. Customers even bribed shop clerks to get ahead in long lines or to get an item in particularly short supply. Suspicion about the motives of others, and an increasing paranoia about public discourses, drove people inward. Like public spaces, many social and professional relationships were viewed as materialist and blandly rational. Like city landscapes, they were there to utilize, routinely pollute, and leave behind at day's end for private time with family and close friends.

In contrast to their neglectful behavior in urban public spaces, people kept the interiors of their very small apartments, which were the center of family and personal life, immaculate, ordered, and brightly decorated. For urbanites, "living within" was not only a political practice, as Havel (1987) so keenly interpreted it, but an everyday effort of personal conservation. In her collection of essays, *How We Survived Communism and Even Laughed*, Slavenka Drakulić, the Croatian writer and cultural critic, recalls how socialism produced an "ecology of poverty." During the regime, Drakulić vividly remembers, nothing was wasted. One washed the floor with a mop made out of worn suit pants. Old magazines and newspapers were hung on a nail next to the toilet. People drove their cars until they literally fell apart (Drakulić 1993:182).[8] Communism's centralized planned economy created a pre-consumer society of shortages and recyclables throughout the Eastern Bloc, where people tried to reuse practically everything they owned. In this ecology of shortages, environmental care and concern largely meant maintaining what were clearly demarcated as private places and personal things.

In addition to their small apartments, and to supplement their frugal lifestyles, most Slovak urbanites had small patches of land, usually located on the fringes of the city. On these tiny garden plots, which were often within sight of a factory or along railroad tracks, they grew a variety of vegetables, fruits, and herbs. On some plots, people also raised chickens or rabbits. Most gardens included small *domčeky* or *chaty* (cabins) that were built by the owners. One *domček* that I visited in 1994 had been under construction for the past eight years. It had been assembled gradually by a father and his son every fair-weather Saturday. Their small brick house was surrounded by cultivated plots of vegetable vines and berry bushes, and had an underground cinderblock cellar for storing beer, wine, and *slivovica* (plum brandy). The father-and-son team had only recently put in glass windows and completed the basic wiring for a couple of electrical outlets. Not all *domčeky* were this sophisticated, of course, and many were little more than one-room wooden shacks with no electricity or plumbing. Gardens, on the other hand, were often quite elaborate, with trestles supporting grape vines, or rows of slender fruit trees so skillfully pruned that their curling branches formed a virtual wall along the footpath. If a family did not own a garden plot themselves, they had access to one through relatives. Whether elaborate or bare bones, these private spaces were visited frequently, to tend to vegetables, have a family cookout, or throw a small evening party. The garden was a sanctuary, if only for a few days, that provided relief from the city and from the system. According to Paulina Bren (2002:127), this *chata* culture "thrived on the fantasy of the weekend getaway as a private retreat where one was left to one's own devices." At the same time, the pursuit of this rewarding personal experience was part of what drove widespread disregard for state property, as "employees would pilfer building materials from the workplace and steal time from working hours to build their cottages" (Dowling 2002:129).

Tempering these contradictory relationships to urban environments was a third space. Beyond the polluted city and town, the well-kept flats and personal gardens, Slovaks venerated and used nature through recreation and ritual. Aesthetically, much of Slovakia's landscape outside of urban areas and beyond state factories and farms appeared unscathed by socialism's rapid development. In late summer, Bratislava nearly empties out as its residents travel by train, bus, or car to the countryside for vacations. Some head to nearby villages to visit elderly relatives, others to state parks and mountains to go camping, trekking, or swimming. Slovakia's national park system, particularly in the Tatra Mountains, offered most of the country's citizens a reprieve from the dullness of the planned city and provided the beauty and solitude of wilderness. While gardens gave Slovaks weekend relaxation, private outdoor family time, and a few extra dishes to put on the table, national parks offered the opportunity for sustained exercise and rigorous excursions into the natural world. Along with mastering the fundamentals of Marxist economics as presented in the required school curricula, learning how to ski and going on one's first hike were basic rites of passage for Slovak children. Small rural villages also kept urbanites connected with the experience of a peasant life, a life engaged directly with the elements of *príroda*. Pig slaughters and wedding marches, each invoking and integrating elements of wildness and wilderness, were important traditional rituals even among urban families. Many city dwellers accessed these experiences during visits to extended family, some of whom still lived in the relatively remote isolation of a mountain village or farming town. Less common, but perhaps more controversial from the perspective of socialism, was the practice of tramping—packing a small rucksack and walking out into the countryside. Tramping was a makeshift vacation, structured only by the weather and the wandering paths of rural landscapes. This type of informal and rugged recreation grew in popularity after 1968, and maintained the idea that the "countryside was 'elsewhere' . . . beyond the reach of state control" (Bren 2002:128). Together, parks and villages, and small groups of trampers, comprised outdoor performances that countered socialism's monotonous blueprint of a modern, ordered, controlled and productive society—a society in which nature was mostly defined and experienced on a personal and private level.

THE INDEPENDENCE OF PERSONAL CONSERVATION

At a time when the regime in Czechoslovakia exercised such a significant degree of control over its citizens, it somewhat paradoxically permitted the emergence and growth of individual efforts to protect nature. In fact, volunteer conservation groups in both the Czech and Slovak parts of the federation began to formally organize at the height of state crackdowns on non-Party associations, writers, musicians, and artists. Beginning in 1969, when the Slovak Union of Nature and Landscape Protectors was formed, and about a decade after a similar Czech group was created, the party-state bureaucracy afforded nature enthusiasts a remarkable degree of freedom in developing conservation organizations built on the idea of voluntary participation and personal interest.[9] Even more interesting was the fact that Slovakia's volunteer conservation initiative remained completely outside of the Party framework, an independent status that its Czech counterpart failed to maintain. Yet, part of the explanation for this freedom afforded by state power to amateur ecologists and nature lovers involves contextualizing the emergence of this form of activism as a component of communist environmentality.

In the 1950s, volunteer nature conservation in Czechoslovakia first emerged as a makeshift endeavor. It was a pursuit initiated by urban scholars and teachers who worked at research academies or universities. Along with trampers and campers, volunteer conservationists went into nature to spend time, have a look around, and simply get closer to *příroda*. Petr Jehlicka and Joe Smith (n.d.) credit the inspiration for this form of nature recreation to the Western scouting movement of the 1920s and 1930s. Even in the Soviet system, outdoor engagement through camping and hiking, while imbued with state ideology, was a popular form of "time off" from labor (Siegelbaum and Sokolov 2000).

At the end of the decade, one group of recreational nature enthusiasts from Prague, under the leadership of Czech zoologist Otakar Leisky, began to organize what was essentially an informal association of colleagues and friends. In 1958, Leisky established the Association of Nature Protection, an official interest group within the Scientific Association of the National Museum in Prague. The Association's activities, which were at first closely linked to the scientific work of its academic participants, such as the identification of rare fauna or the study of bird migrations, also included weekend community brigades along the model of Czechoslovakia's once-popular tramping movement (Jehlicka and Smith n.d.). The Association organized brigades to clean up polluted rivers and streams, or observe wildlife *in situ*, and to enjoy the fresh air in the process. In 1969, "the Association broke away from the Museum Society and registered with the Ministry of the Interior . . . under the name Yew Tree— The Union for the Protection of Nature and Landscape," or Tis (Yew) (Jehlicka and Smith n.d.:10).

In Slovakia, a similar network of so-called volunteer nature protectors formed around the same time, in the early 1950s. But the Slovak enthusiasts had no formal organization for almost two decades. Like their Czech counterparts, Slovak volunteer conservationists were professors and researchers from universities and technical institutes who began to spend their leisure time in the realm of *príroda*, far away from their small urban offices. They also devoted their efforts to cleaning up trash along riverbanks or locating rare fauna in local forests. They would occasionally meet socially to share their personal interests. With the new Czech Union in Prague as an example, this loose network of mostly Bratislavans assembled in the capital city in 1969 and established the Slovak Union of Nature Protection (SZOP). In all, over 160 people attended the gathering, where, like at most official, socialist meetings at the time, they agreed on the modest administrative objective to better plan and organize what were a set of widely diverse interest groups. The Central Council of SZOP, which was also created at this initial meeting, actually began to deliver on the plan. Over the next several meetings, the Council crafted an ambitious republic-wide structure, which would include people interested in all facets of volunteer nature protection.

TABLE 1.1 Sections and Commissions of the Central Committee of SZOP (1971)

Special Sections	Special Commissions
Knowledge and Protection of Nature	Organizational-Legal Commission
Protection of Vegetation	Intraorganizational and International Relations
Friends and Protectors of Animals	Commission for Schools and Youth
Protection of Inorganic Nature	Information and Media Commission

Source: Randik 1989

In a spirit of good socialism, the Council renamed itself the Central Committee, with the aim to "unite individuals, organizations and institutions of the Slovak Socialist Republic in the interest of creating effective forces to support the protection of nature and creatures of the natural environment" (Randik 1989:2). The Central Committee created four sections, each specializing in one aspect of conservation, and four commissions which would serve as liaisons with the state and the public (table 1.1). Three years later, in 1972, the group changed its name to the Slovak Union of Nature and Landscape Protectors (SZOPK) so as to more accurately reflect the comprehensive scope of interests of its growing membership, who referred to themselves as *ochranári* (protectors). The *ochranári* of SZOPK considered their organization to be "the first fundamental success and historical landmark in the movement of volunteer workers and lovers of nature" (Randik 1989:2).

The most unique feature of these fledgling conservation unions with respect to the rest of Czech and Slovak society was their complete independence from the bureaucratic system of the Czechoslovak Communist Party. Not only did neither group have any formal party affiliation, they were not required to place their organizations within the framework of what was called the National Front. The National Front was the catchall communist term for all pre-1948 political parties and civic organizations which had not been outright abolished or outlawed by the regime. Although it lent groups who belonged to it, such as stamp collectors' associations or other hobby groups, an appearance of independence, the National Front was completely controlled by the Communist Party (table

TABLE 1.2 Structure of SZOPK with Respect to the Communist Party

	The Communist Party (KSS)
Slovak Union of Nature and Landscape Protectors (SZOPK)	Socialist Union of Youth (SZM)
	National Front (traditional political parties and NGOs)

1.2). One member of the Union explained that SZOPK escaped this fate because

> this sphere [conservation] did not exist before the 1948 period. What is even more interesting is that when SZOPK was created, it was still in the spirit of Dubček, and, since it was not a traditional party or organization that the communists had previously defined as a political threat, they [the *ochranári*] were not forced to join.

While many of the independent groups that had formed during Dubček's short tenure were being shut down, or tossed into the National Front, nature conservationists dodged the scrutiny of normalization's push to control all potentially political activities. While theaters closed, musicians were locked up, and intellectuals and writers were banished from their typewriters and sentenced to window washing, street sweeping, and other menial labors, Husák's regime appeared satisfied to leave nature volunteers alone on the argument that volunteer conservation was not even remotely political.

Any concerns among Party operatives about the Slovak organization's politics were perhaps assuaged by SZOPK's use of ideologically appropriate discourse when describing its mission. In state-run media, the Union described its "commitment" to socialism as a mission to acquaint the "widest layer of citizens with nature and her laws, with important questions concerning nature's conservation, and to educate citizens in the cultivation of a relationship with nature and with this, the cultivation of self-conscious, socialist patriotism" (Randik 1989:2). The Union's Central Committee also explicitly supported Czechoslovakia's socialist institutions for nature protection, regardless of whether people in the organization believed these institutions to be effective or at all serious about their official mandate. SZOPK even structurally mimicked the regime's style in its plan to develop the volunteer organization from the center outward and from the top down. According to one szopk member's recollection, Party bureaucrats interpreted the Union's primary purpose as fitting "very well with socialist ideology. The authorities told us, 'Go collect garbage in the woods, around the town. It is dirty everywhere. Go on a brigade on Saturdays or Sundays. People should be active in the name of socialism.'" As long as the group refrained from open criticism of the regime, it discovered that, as the years went on, no one in the Party seemed to care what its status was. Another *ochranár* active during the group's formation emphasized that "of course, we couldn't criticize Husák. That wasn't volunteer conservation. At least not at the time."

When the Union formed it remained a small organization of about two hundred people. Despite all of its comprehensive planning, about which its members did not hesitate to keep the state press informed, the Union lacked both the people and the resources to carry out its ambitious objectives.[10] Over the next two years, its membership concentrated on filling out the organization's structure. By 1974 the Union created nineteen new district branches in mid-sized towns throughout Slovakia, and separate city branches in Bratislava and in Košice.

In the Czech half of the country, however, Tis, the Czech conservation union, was not to be so politically fortunate. Early on, its members came under scrutiny by the Husák regime. Unlike the Slovak Union, in its bylaws Tis made not even *pro forma* mention of the leading role of the Communist Party. As its membership grew, which it did through the addition of several local branches around the Czech Lands, the Party eventually stepped in to "refashion" the organization into a more centralized and subordinate entity (Kilburn and Vanek 2004). Other developments in Prague during this period perhaps contributed to the regime's concerns about Tis. In 1977, Vaclav Havel, a Czech playwright, along with some two hundred other Czechs, signed a petition protesting the regime's poor human rights record. The document was known as Charter 77 and came to represent the core and spirit of Czech resistance to normalization, a topic which I take up in more detail in the following chapter.

In 1979, the same year that Havel and other Chartists were imprisoned, Tis was forced to disband completely. Its leading members were heartlessly invited to join a "new" conservation organization that had been created by government officials, called the Czech Union for Nature Conservation (csop). Tis leaders refused to become a part of it. However, many members of local branches throughout Bohemia and Moravia, "to whom CSOP was . . . presented as Tis's successor, joined the new Union" (Jehlicka and Smith n.d.:11). The local branch members in regional towns did not care whether their weekend excursion was part of the Party apparatus or not. From that point on, volunteer nature conservation in the Czech Lands would be one of the many arms of normalization.

Other volunteer initiatives also formed during this time but were focused solely on youth education and nature activism for young people. These highly popular groups, however, were not only attached to the Party system, they were started by it. In 1974, inspired by the Stockholm Conference on the Environment in Europe held the year before, a group of young Czech scientists from the Institute for Landscape Ecology started a one-year campaign for environmental education. The scientists promoted their project through the appropriate Czech Committee of the Socialist Union of Youth (SZM) and the magazine *Young World* (*Mladý Svet*). They chose a brontosaurus as the symbol for the campaign. "The Brontosaurus did not survive because he outgrew his possibilities" became the group's slogan. That summer, hundreds of young people organized a set of work camps, which were so successful that the planners decided to continue the volunteer program the following year. Interest in such summer activity continued to grow far beyond the duration of the project, and a large network of young Czechs, sponsored by the SZM, organized annually under the name Brontosaurus. Every summer Brontosaurus ran nature camps and brigades aimed at cleaning up and preserving forests, streams, and parks.

A few years after Brontosaurus was formed, the Slovak branch of the SZM organized a similar youth conservation "movement" in Slovakia. In the summer of 1979, the Slovak SZM held several youth camps designed as a competition to plan and implement various conservation projects. The campaign was called Strom Života (Tree of Life), and the young participants "concentrated on cleaning up nature and taking care of historical monuments" (Strom Života 1994). Although the regime was concerned that a few of the camps that were held had not been granted the proper official approvals from the central administrative body of the SZM, the event was repeated the following year. After a series of meetings among SZM leadership, Tree of Life was legally established in 1983 as a communist-approved youth environmental group (Strom Života 1994).

The pragmatic character of these energetic youth nature groups drew significant numbers of young Czechs and Slovaks to their ranks. Both groups' official designation as "movements" reinforced their volunteer, practical, and recreational character. Their literature remained nonpolitical. Strom Života brochures advertised the group as an opportunity to "live healthy lives, improve the environment, and most of all have fun doing it" (Strom Života 1994:1). The implicit purpose of Strom Života was to offer young Slovaks a more structured alternative to tramping or trekking, which had grown significantly during this period (Bren 2002). Strom Života camps were planned while students were still attending classes, and then took place during the summer when children and teenagers were out of school. In fact, many local clubs within the movement formed. Throughout the 1980s, both Brontosaurus and Tree of Life grew in popularity, drawing more and more participants each year.

Membership in all of these volunteer conservation groups, including SZOPK and the Czech Union, was more or less ethnically homogeneous. Slovaks joined SZOPK and Strom Života. Czechs attended Brontosaurus camps or were members of CSOP. In Slovakia, with its large Hungarian minority, Hungarian Slovaks also took part in both the Union and the youth movement. There were a few Slovaks who joined Brontosaurus, even though they lived in Bratislava and had to travel to Bohemia to take part in camps. In the case of SZOPK, a handful of Czechs became members in the 1980s, but were residing in Slovakia at the time.[11] But this ethnic division among volunteer conservationists was also a reflection of what the federation looked like in terms of Czech and Slovak population demographics, which were largely concentrated in their respective parts of the country. After 1968, the only lasting reform from Dubček's rule was a revision to the Czechoslovak Constitution which granted Slovakia slightly more autonomy, as a "republic" within a Socialist Federation. Each republic had its own national administration, and many former functions of the central government were placed under the jurisdiction of the new republic-level governments.

This constitutional change occurred at the same time that nature conservation groups started to organize themselves. Thus it is important to point out that "the Party" or "the regime" responsible for monitoring, approving, or controlling these organizations was in fact two different entities. Ideological divisions within the Communist Party itself became irrelevant after Husák took power, as he followed the will of the hardliners in the Party and never veered from loyalty to Soviet power. But at the level of everyday repression and concern for political deviation, the Prague wing of the party and its operatives in the secret police were particularly severe. In Slovakia, communist authorities continued to view SZOPK as ideologically in line with socialism and trusted the Union's leadership organ, the Central Committee, to oversee the Union's local branches. In fact, informal nature groups in areas far beyond Bratislava, that had formed before the Union was created, willingly joined the national organization. For example, a group of volunteers in Považská Bystrica that focused on environmental education for children and the conservation of the Stražovke Mountains joined the Union and became the district coordinating committee (OV) of SZOPK for their *okres* (district).

Beneath its district branches was yet another level of the Union's structure, the basic organization (*základná organizácia*, ZO). Basic organizations were groups of local volunteers who were, in theory, under the supervision of the district or city committees. As one activist explains, it was at the level of the ZO that any actual work was carried out.

> The concept of the basic organization was really what the Union was all about. It depended on whether or not people were interested in doing something. A new organization was formed at the local level. SZOPK was really created from below, and all of those other organizations were created from above.

It was also at the level of the ZO that the Union proved to grow not only in numbers but in diversity of interests and activities. For example, in 1981 Bratislava's town committee (MV) had a combined membership of 850, dispersed among 13 basic organizations (ZOS). Each ZO concentrated on a different area of nature, which in the case of the Bratislava groups ranged widely: the protection of local bat populations, mushroom collecting, nature trekking, bird watching, or, in one case, ground erosion in a city park. The largest district committee in Slovakia, in Liptovský Mikuláš, a town in the central part of the republic, had 22 basic organizations. The Liptovský branch of SZOPK claimed over 1500 members in 1982 (SZOPK 1982). That year, SZOPK national membership was an impressive 12,241, with two city branches and 36 district committees together overseeing a total of 194 basic organizations.

THE LIMITS OF FREEDOM

SZOPK's independent status was truly an anomaly during normalization. Party monitoring of the group concentrated on its Central Committee, what it did and what it said publicly. This was a strategy of control that perhaps also contributed to the organization's continuing autonomy.

Throughout the 1970s and early 1980s, the Central Committee leadership never diverged from what were considered to be appropriate areas of *ochranárstvo* (conservation). These acceptable areas included the study of the ethology, biology, or species diversity of flora and fauna within Slovakia's borders, essentially issues that celebrated the richness of the natural world. A brief sampling of articles and research reports published during the 1980s in *Poznaj a Chráň* (Know and Protect), the Union's national magazine, suggests rather tame and nonthreatening approaches within the endeavor of personal, volunteer conservation. In 1983, the January issue contained six articles devoted to children and nature education, three articles on frogs and reptiles, and five reports describing local conservation efforts in several of the Union's district branches. Only two articles covered topics addressing more human-oriented environmental subjects, one on the environment and human health, the other on the UN's 1982 World Charter for nature conservation. Neither of these pieces directly linked these topics to Slovakia's socialist society or government (SZOPK 1984). The 1984 February issue of *Poznaj a Chráň* offered similar fare: an article featuring amphibians, another two on endangered species, and reports describing a variety of local *ochranárstvo* brigades. In 1986, several articles on international environmental problems appeared, but were prefaced by the magazine's editors as issues that should be tackled by applying socialist ideology. The articles closed by suggesting that any solution to ecological problems could be solved through the efforts of rational science, a goal, one author noted, that was "presently one of the main tasks in the construction of a socialist society" (Chorváth 1986:1).

Even after the 1986 accident at Chernobyl in Ukraine, Union leadership stuck to safe environmental topics, and let the problem of nuclear energy remain a topic to be discussed behind closed doors. The state considered nuclear energy to be an industrial problem and therefore a matter for physicists and experts in atomic energy. After the Chernobyl crisis the Czechoslovak government did not even provide detailed information to its citizens, many of whom lived quite near the Ukraine border (Charter 77 1986:52). Similarly, the ecological effects of hydroelectric power stations on local environments were not considered to be suitable concerns for the Union's agenda. Rather, dams and reservoirs were conceived as the responsibility of technocrats in the sphere of state water management. In effect, the regime considered anything connected to industrial production or the energy sector to be closed to public debate and thus off-limits to the sphere of volunteer conservationists. The leadership of SZOPK, at least in the pages of *Poznaj a Chráň*, dutifully complied.

Despite its independence, SZOPK maintained a discursive loyalty to normalization into the 1980s. One of the impacts of the existence of such a comprehensive, national volunteer conservation organization was that it essentially ruled out the possibility of other volunteer groups taking on their own identities. Perhaps this was part of the logic behind the regime's generosity in allowing such an organization to escape its control. By encouraging and facilitating state-wide youth volunteer "movements," the Communist Party hoped to channel younger citizens, who would otherwise be trekking out on their own, into "organized" activities. For adult enthusiasts of *príroda*, to create anything beyond private nature hikes or bird-watching now required the "permission" of the Slovak conservation union's town or district committee, which, at least in theory, and as far as the Communist Party knew, required some type of registration and approval process. But basic organizations were, in reality, often informally created, and just as often casually disbanded, according to group interests and the activity level of participants.

Within this "honor system" of volunteer nature activism, only one case of explicit transgression occurred outside of Bratislava with any serious implications for its members. In 1980, several students at a medical university in Banská Bystrica started a group called Ekotrend. They registered with the district office of SZOPK as one of its basic organizations. Ekotrend was not much more than a bunch of friends who wanted to have a student "ecology club." Their aim was to hold discussion groups and to organize lectures about international environmental problems which, in their view, were relevant to Slovakia. Ekotrend began to publish a newsletter that, at first, contained only reprinted materials from Czechoslovak state press sources. Later, however, they began to write their own articles explicitly including information from Western environmental organizations, on topics such as acid rain and nuclear safety, particularly Three Mile Island, which they argued "also affected the situation . . . in Czechoslovakia" (Mesík 1995). One member of the group also included a couple of his own cartoons that alluded to pollution in Czechoslovakia.

In 1985, the Slovak secret police (Štatné Bezpečnosť, ŠtB) contacted the members of Ekotrend and demanded that they submit their material to Party censors before publishing it, or disband. Each member met with the agents in private. The president of Ekotrend, Juraj Mesík, was called last. One of the agents offered him an opportunity to travel to West Germany to study medicine if he dissolved the organization. Mesík refused. Following this encounter, the regional committee (OV) of SZOPK tossed Ekotrend out of the organization, explaining that the group was taking on the character of a "political party." Mesík had no choice but to close the "club" down. Without the SZOPK identity, Ekotrend would be explicitly illegal in the eyes of state authorities. Mesík later learned that a few personal connections through his school's administration had saved him from suffering more serious punishment.

> The administrator at my school, although he was a Communist Party member, took a liking to me. He was sort of a father figure. He knew that we had to break up the group, but he told the ŠtB that we were "kids who did not know better . . . they do things like this when they are young." He protected us from being kicked out of medical school. But we had to disband. We really had no choice in the matter.

The case of Ekotrend certainly suggested that although volunteer nature conservationism was granted a substantial degree of freedom from the Party, the limits to this freedom were clear: deviation from the discourse of normalization meant consequences. The socialist state thus not only viewed the environment as a resource, but also attempted to manage its human subjects within this discourse according to Party ideology. As a totalitarian system it could, and did, choose to ignore policies that were themselves the products of the state. The regime could also disregard the knowledge of its own experts who provided it with information documenting serious ecological problems. Moreover, it concealed this information from the public as part of its strategy of human management and political control.

Nevertheless, within the environmentality of state socialism was a space which the regime left to the initiative of ordinary citizens. Volunteer conservationism was a sphere in which private lives became social experiences through independent activities. Despite the Union's centralized appearance in terms of its organizational structure, this sphere was largely self-monitored and decentralized in practice. And like so many other areas of society, the regime conceptualized this organization of volunteers as a resource.

Here we find the paradox of communist environmentality. During a period of intensive cultural control, communist environmentality began to give up some of its claim over the subjects of *príroda* and environment. In a sense, SZOPK was viewed by the state as a way of protecting a part of itself from itself. Yet this particular realm of civic life was, in the end, neither something the state felt that it needed to own nor that it wanted to devote resources to control completely. At least this was the case in Slovakia. Thus, the party-state gave up a small part of its totalitarian self. It seemed at the time to be a very small part, since, after all, the state's mission had always been the domination of culture, which it viewed as residing elsewhere—in religion, or novels, or private enterprise. It was within this very small part of life under socialism that a group of Bratislava residents found in the Union an opportunity to repair and preserve dilapidated and neglected peasant dwellings of the past and, in the process, begin to integrate culture into the realm of nature.

2 *Hatchets versus the Hammer and Sickle*

AGAINST THE EFFORTS OF THE SOCIALIST REGIMES IN THE Eastern Bloc and the Soviet Union to subdue and control culture emerged the dissident. Dissidents were people who did not necessarily reject socialism but who were dissatisfied with the status quo, did not agree with the methods or the manner of the regime's power, and, in many cases, believed in the possibility that things could change.[1] Dissidents emerged from many walks of life, including the arts, education, religious organizations, and even the Communist Party itself. The most common expression of dissent was s*amizdat*, or self-produced writing, which emerged as a counter to state-controlled media. *Samizdat* literature circulated among the public and occasionally reached even wider audiences in the West (Komaromi 2004).[2] Other dissidents performed what was considered to be subversive music or art. Still others subscribed to and displayed specific religious beliefs which were contrary to Marxist orthodox atheism. All sorts of acts, from independent writing to worshipping in secret, were characterized by the state as deviant and therefore dangerous (Ramet 1995). The secret police did not hesitate to intimidate, interrogate, and, in some cases, imprison writers, worshippers, and musicians, regardless of the degree to which their beef with the regime was direct or explicit (Adelman 1984).[3] After all, from the regime's point of view, these were people who appeared to threaten socialism with what it considered to be the cultural weapons of subversion.

In post-1968 Czechoslovakia, the state's exceptionally severe response to criticism produced many dissident writers, performers, and essayists, including Vaclav Havel, who was by far the best known both within the country and in the West. After signing Charter 77, Havel, along with a few other Chartists, was harassed, hounded, and, on several occasions, detained and imprisoned by the authorities.[4] Slovakia, however, had only a handful of writers and artists who gained notoriety for their dissident views. Instead, the regime was most concerned about Catholic subversion, which existed in the form of the Secret Church.

According to socialist ideology, explicit religious believers were by definition deviants, and their continuing presence in society was decidedly subversive. But the plan to eradicate spiritual belief would require a long-term process of enculturation through formal education. In the meantime, the regime sought to keep religious communities in check by rewarding atheism and keeping a close watch on the official clergy, which was left to practice so long as it did not try to challenge the power apparatus. Members of the Secret Church, however, were citizens who followed traditional Catholic practices outside the framework of the official church. They recognized the authority of Rome and held private prayer groups in their homes (Doellinger 2002). Such behavior, fundamentally opposed to Marxist ideology, was by its very nature considered to be illegal by the regime.[5] But it was also largely invisible to the state—performed behind closed doors and within an insular community of faith which sought personal devotion, not proselytizing. Sabrina Ramet (1995:130) points out that the Secret Church was a defensive community which sought only to maintain itself in its most traditional form.

Volunteer conservation, however, consisted of public practices. But unlike music, art, and religion, nature enthusiasts did not seem a significant threat to the regime's power. Within professional scientific institutions, the state even allowed for limited innovations in materialist models of ecology. This was the case with natural scientists in Soviet Russia, who, as Douglas Weiner (2002) notes, were able to shape, if not explicitly deviant environmental messages, then at least new approaches to the science of ecology that challenged Marxist models. But this Russian revolution in eco-science remained largely inaccessible to public consumption or debate. In Slovakia, however, grassroots environmentalism grew in a public but overlooked space, led by the Union's volunteer conservationism of civic works and brigades.

The endeavors of one particular group of SZOPK members from Bratislava began to change this overlooked discursive space. These activists were primarily interested in protecting cultural monuments, but not the kind that the state had designated as such. The monuments with which these conservationists were concerned were not crumbling ancient

castles, of which Slovakia had an abundant supply, or more contemporary urban statues, such as the enormous Slavín Monument commemorating the deaths of thousands of Soviet soldiers in the battle to liberate
Bratislava from the Nazis. The objects of devotion and preservation within
this small group of *ochranári* were, instead, humble wooden cabins, called
drevenice. *Drevenice* were scattered throughout Slovakia's countryside,
the traditional and often isolated dwellings of nameless peasants and shepherds of a past world long gone. As such, they were of little consequence
to communist campaigns to reshape the land (Obrebski 1976; Dunn and
Dunn 1967).[6] Thus, almost without notice, alongside weekend bird watch-
ers, mushroom pickers, and nature trekkers, the Bratislava *ochranári* began
to quietly shift the meaning of *príroda* to include vestigial aspects of Slovak culture. Below I examine how, quite unlike dissidents who challenged
communism head-on with cultural critique, this particular group of SZOPK
conservationists stretched the legitimate discursive boundaries of *životné
prostredie* as it had been configured within communist environmentality.
Their concern for *drevenice* moved almost seamlessly into a wider contestatory space regarding the state's lack of protection of the broader environment and its contemporary population. In the process, the *ochranári*
were beginning to represent a part of civil society under socialism that I
call *anti-elites*. As anti-elites, the *ochranári* moved beyond brigades and
into the streets and parks of the socialist city. This subtle process of drawing culture into the sphere of nature protection unfolded gradually, beginning years before the Velvet Revolution, along the banks of an unassuming
mountain river far from Czechoslovakia's urban centers of state power.

FROM PRESERVING "NATURE"
TO PRESERVING "CULTURE"

The secluded valley of Kvačianská dolina cuts north to south through the
foothills of the High Tatras in Central Slovakia for roughly seven kilometers. Forming a deep, narrow fissure, the valley is flanked by steep lime-
stone cliffs, with two sleepy farming settlements nestled at each end. During
the Dual Monarchy, local villagers built two mills in the center of the valley. The mills exploited the swift flow of the Kvačianská River, which then
levels off beyond the valley and begins to slow down and widen about
ten kilometers further downstream at the town of Liptovský Mikuláš. In
1978, Liptovský town officials declared the upper mill a cultural monument and placed it in the care of the state. The lower mill remained in pri-

vate hands but was essentially abandoned by the owner's descendants, who had long since moved away. By the end of the 1970s, both of these late nineteenth century structures were on the verge of collapse.

In 1980, a group of SZOPK members from Bratislava purchased the privately owned mill and began to restore it. They also convinced the Liptovský District Office of State Nature Conservation to allow them to save the other one. Their careful renovations took place during summer months, when the conservationists from Bratislava could take enough time away from their regular professions to complete specific tasks. The band of volunteers from the capital city made their repairs with *sekerky*, small hand axes traditionally used by Slovak peasants for woodcutting, or, when the need arose, as weapons to defend their modest livelihoods. Over the next two years, in addition to putting on new roof shingles, the group filled in gaping cracks between the buildings' timber walls, refurbished the vital central support beams, remounted the mill's grinding wheels, and replaced their rotting wooden parts. During subsequent summer excursions the SZOPK volunteers fixed the interior cast-iron stove and repaired dams across the river, adding a footbridge that spanned the resulting reservoir. When the mills attained a state of habitability, the renovators organized year-round service shifts in order to maintain the buildings as a public museum open to hikers and trekkers, who frequently visited the isolated valley. Despite the backbreaking work that the project often demanded, one volunteer wistfully recalled his experience repairing the mills as a time of personal renewal.

> I remember the sound of ringing hatchets as we pounded nails into fresh wood.[7] I also remember lots of laughter and lighthearted conversation. We brought our families, our tools, and enough food to last a few days. At night we slept in sleeping bags under the stars . . . The work was certainly intense, but you know, it was really a vacation.[8]

The mission to save Slovakia's neglected *drevenice* and incorporate such work into the realm of nature conservation was the brainchild of Mikuláš Huba, a geographer in his early twenties from the Slovak Academy of Sciences in Bratislava. At the time, most SZOPK members were natural scientists or wildlife enthusiasts who went on brigades to collect specimens of wild plants outside the city or to photograph animals in the forests and hills along the Danube River. As a geographer, Huba had professional interests in both the natural environment and social history and looked to the Union to start a local organization that might address both of these areas. The Union's Bratislava branch gave its blessing and assigned his new group the number 6, or ZO 6 (*základná organizácia 6*). The Union never assigned formal names to its basic organizations, but simply assigned arbitrary numbers, which meant nothing in particular about the people or the group that acquired them. In the Union's bureaucratic record scheme, number 6 had belonged to an inactive group at the time. If such official recognition lent the organization an air of socialist formality, it also helped to keep its explicit purpose somewhat obscure.

SZOPK ZO 6 was founded in 1977, the same year that dissidents in Prague were drafting Charter 77. At first, the group was quite small, made up of Huba; his brother Marko, who was an art teacher; their parents; and a few of their friends and colleagues, including Peter Kresánek, an expert on historical monuments. Huba characterized the creation of his group as growing from the confluence of personal interest and social and professional circumstances.

> We were friends with a common interest. And Marko, my brother, was skilled in woodworking. We decided to form a group within SZOPK devoted to this aspect of conservation. Our family had often gone to Šip, in the Veľká Fatra mountains, for vacation and we knew that many of these places needed to be saved, or they would completely fall to ruin (Huba 1995).

They started out by traveling on weekends and during the summer to Šip, where they began to fix up a cluster of peasant cabins at Podšíp, a small clearing nestled just below the pine ridges of Central Slovakia (figure 2.1). As the group's work progressed they planned other projects. They began by organizing brigades to hunt for old buildings tucked away in villages or hidden in the countryside that were falling apart. As Milan Hladky, another member of ZO 6, recalled,

> Podšíp was the first action. We would meet there and work in that settlement. Then Huba suggested that we also work on other buildings. Although at that time it wasn't such a structured program. We would often go into the village and just have fun . . . meet with people there and walk around the village (Hladky 1995).

Folk architecture could be found throughout the Slovak countryside. A few *drevenice* still functioned as the homes of villagers living in the iso-

FIG. 2.1 Subversive volunteers. Members of the Slovak Union of Nature and Landscape Protectors (SZOPK) ZO 6 renovating folk architecture in Central Slovakia, summer 1986. During such brigades, Union members planned their research and writing on environmental problems plaguing society. From the SZOPK Archives.

lated quiet of rural poverty and old age. Many of these structures, however, had been long abandoned, which essentially placed them under the care of local branches of the state's Office of Monument Protection. The government may have designated a number of these structures as "protected" at one time or another in the past, but few, if any, had been consistently cared for. Many fell to ruin after a couple of decades of neglect.

Huba and his fellow *ochranári*,[9] however, avoided a direct critique of these ineffective and certainly underfunded state offices. Instead, they simply sought to perform, through volunteerism, what was actually the state's official responsibility. In an article devoted to the new group's work, Huba described the goal of his section as one of civic helpfulness and, in a way, a sort of grassroots model of what an ideal socialist state should be like.

> I should say that . . . it is not our aim to act as a substitute for the activities of professional institutions. We want to be more a model and supporter of citizens in this sphere—which continues to expand—and we want to help

these institutions, but'also to will them and inspire them, so that they act with greater enthusiasm in their activities (*SZOPK* 1986:27).

Because their brigades were in fact useful, and fit rather snugly into a Marxist rhetoric of productivity so often repeated in workers' slogans, Party apparatchiks did not challenge the work of Huba's group. This is not to say that petty bureaucrats never complicated matters or that they always provided their official approval. One zo 6 member recalled how, when her group informed the state office of monument protection about its intentions to rebuild a local cottage left to rot on the edge of town,

> [local bureaucrats] operated with the point of view that something had to be gained from the endeavor. And they were often quite confused about us, that they could not believe that we would spend so much effort doing something of a volunteer nature . . . for no real gain.

If the state allocated inadequate funding for the preservation of larger public monuments, it had even less interest in saving run-down peasant houses. Another member of zo 6 remembered that when the group

> asked the local *primátor* (mayor) whether it was possible to get surplus wood and nails for the Kvačianka project, he said "No." He then added how curious it was to him that we would spend our vacation and our own resources on rebuilding such outdated and dilapidated structures—symbols of poverty and backward traditional life (Igor 1994).

szopk's Central Committee (uv) was not much help either. All of the government funding that the union's administrative organ received was earmarked for the publication of *Poznaj a Chráň* and to pay for an office staff. In order to do their work effectively, the members of zo 6 would have to find materials on their own. The *ochranári* pooled their own personal resources and asked friends and colleagues for modest donations, mainly for wood and to buy new tools. In a sense, the group's financial independence allowed them greater freedom to set their own agenda, a situation that was very different from that of organizations belonging to the Party or to the National Front, which, although wealthier, were constantly monitored through governmental budgetary oversight.

In addition to being on their own in terms of resources, basic organizations in szopk were also essentially unsupervised. Although the uv office was in the capital city, it was the City Committee (Mestský Výbor, MV) of Bratislava that was officially responsible for overseeing basic organizations that it registered. As with the UV, most of the people holding leadership positions in the MV were Communist Party members. But the City Committee, with over twenty basic organizations under its supervision—each conducting its own volunteer brigades—did not try to control what any one of its groups actually did. In fact, members of the MV considered the work of ZO 6 to be a rather harmless pursuit, and even welcomed the effort to preserve the anachronistic elements of Slovak identity and history. Its projects, like the ones at Kvačian or at Podšíp, were featured in the MV's periodical *Ochranca Prírody*, and thus were discursively incorporated into the Union's definition of *príroda* (nature) and *krajina* (landscape). In his articles for the magazine, Huba described the early work of ZO 6 as a practice that tried to temper "the destruction of the genuine manifestation of one culture, the culture of our predecessors" (Huba 1987:24). He argued that it was Slovakia's "historical obligation to preserve and uncover its message" (Huba 1987:24). The message of folk architecture *in situ* was as much a part of nature conservation as any other more conventional sphere of ecology. For, according to his group's view, these "anonymous architects of our national culture, the peasants and shepherds, woodcutters or miners" had lived a life of harmony with the natural world (Huba 1987:21).

This new form of conservationism emerged in quiet opposition to the regime's philosophy of planned, progressive development—a philosophy advocating the restructuring of the rural landscape with a focus on the control and collectivization of both resources and people. The volunteers from ZO 6 frequently encountered this socialist worldview in their brigade work. One member recalled,

There was a woman, a communist and a member of the women's organization in a small town. Her group thought the older buildings were ugly and wanted them destroyed. They asked the regional office to tear them down before the celebration for the Slovak National Uprising Anniversary, despite the fact that they were officially listed as historical monuments. And sure enough, they started to tear them down. Peter Tatár and Huba tried to stop them by asking the local officials if they were going to enforce the law governing the protection of monuments. They argued that this law should apply to these buildings. But there was nothing they could do. No one in that town cared about this law or about these *drevenice*.

The members of ZO 6, however, saw in these tiny buildings a larger historical message about the future of society and recognized in their decay the symbolic degradation of Slovak cultural identity. As one *ochranár* put it:

> Folk architecture was really a symbol of the past that needed to be refused by society. After 1948, the state encouraged the refusal of everything older. With these arguments, neither the state organs of monument protection nor local governments took care of them. They did look after some things, like symbols of states, for example castles, towers, or fortresses. But to go below this, essentially to the smaller dwelling of the ordinary person, well, no one really cared about these (Hladký 1995).

Over the next two years, ZO 6 grew to number some forty members who met religiously, gathering once a month throughout the year at five o'clock, the time of their very first meeting. By the mid-1980s the organization had carried out numerous weekend and summer brigades, eventually preserving or restoring over 200 buildings.

Despite the Czechoslovak regime's reputation for aggressively controlling practices that were considered to be antiprogressive, Party officials viewed the Union and its basic organizations as mainly a form of recreation, a sentiment that the members of ZO 6 themselves shared. Huba explained:

> It really was our vacation time. We took the children on the train to Rohač, and a bottle or two of wine, and spent a couple of weeks with friends around the campfire. In the day we worked, and worked. In fact, none of these projects are ever "finished." There will always be more to do there. But it was fun to us . . . not something that was necessarily pressing. It was "recreational conservation."

This form of activist recreation appealed to people on a deeply personal level. It was an opportunity to trade the gray concrete *paneláky* apartments of the socialist city for a log near the fire under a starry sky. Many urbanites during state socialism relied on visits to kin members in villages to escape the confines of cities and find private solace in their private *chaty* (Dowling 2002). But renovation work was socially and discursively different from Czechoslovakia's country *chata* phenomenon, whereby urbanites visited extended family in villages or gardened on the outskirts of the socialist city (Salzmann and Scheuffler 1974; Simic 1973; Verdery 1983). While a few ZO 6 projects were in places where members had relatives nearby, most were in remote places far from kin networks. Nevertheless, the social experience of brigades was also clearly important. *Ochranári* routinely brought their families along, including children, who played in nearby forests or rivers while the adults pounded nails and chopped shingles. Brigade participants gathered in the evenings for supper and singing by an open fire, talking late into the night over a bottle of homemade *slivovica*.

On another level, the brigade experience encouraged increasingly broad and critical reflections among *ochranári* on issues beyond landscape preservation, issues such as ecosystems and urban lifestyles, personal health and political philosophy. ZO 6 members often described SZOPK brigades as approaching what they considered to be an experience of ecological harmony. Participants followed a more or less traditional lifestyle, with no access to electricity, indoor plumbing, or telephones. To practice ecology, if only for a few weeks a year, was certainly an opportunity to weigh in on the existential pressures of urban socialism—its noise, pollution, and everyday oppression.

On still another level, brigades were a way to connect with Slovakia's rural population and their way of life. One member stressed that the *ochranári*

> were not like a bunch of kids from the city going to party in the country. We were genuinely interested in how things were made, how older people [people in the past] did things. We talked to villagers and we would play music with them. Folk music, you know. I played the *gajda*. We really became involved in village life when we went on brigades.[10]

At first, local residents did not understand the group's veneration of these broken-down buildings. The old hovels that SZOPK chose to repair were considered to be especially shameful, eyesores, by many local residents. Some villagers were also suspicious of the altruistic character of the group.

> People around Podšíp would see us on the road. Once an old man asked us what we were doing, and when we told him he was completely shocked. "It is not possible," he said. "Did you steal something?" They could not understand that people would come with their own things, even buy wood for shingles (Juraj 1994).

Another *ochranár* recalled that "people thought that there must have been something that we were gaining from our renovation projects. Or that we were being paid by somebody for our work. They just couldn't believe it" (Podoba 1994).

Implicit in this "ecological" practice of traditional living, repairing old buildings, and mingling with the rural poor was a private protest against totalitarianism and the repression and monotony of normalized society. This theme had been raised a decade earlier by Dušan Hanák, a Slovak documentary filmmaker. In his 1972 film, *Pictures of the Old World* (*Obrazy starého sveta*), Hanák vividly recorded the lives of elderly rural Slovaks. Although they lived in abject poverty, their narratives expressed a deep sense of independence and endurance in the face of history's callous changes. A particular concern of Hanák's lens was the elements of traditional life: tools, songs, art, and architecture. The film was criticized by the regime for its "aesthetics of ugliness" and banned by the Communist Party. Indeed, it was not until after the Velvet Revolution that it was shown publicly in Slovakia. Hanák's villagers were identical to the elderly residents who lived near SZOPK's projects. Like these elderly citizens who seemed to have been at best forgotten and at worst purposefully ignored by normalization, the recreational activism of SZOPK was both physically and symbolically engaged in the past.

For citizens seeking an escape from socialist urbanism, the *sekerka*, or hatchet, became a symbol of a resistant, even rebellious lifestyle, one that included increasingly open and critical thought and action about the environment and about Slovak society and culture. The hatchet represented the preservation of a way of life that not only had been discouraged by socialist ideology but was also the target of state destruction and the victim of public neglect. Though the *sekerka* suggested self-reliance and rural culture, its message transcended these values. Self-reliance and rural independence were themes that were buried beneath socialist imagery, and relegated to folklore under the regime. According to the *ochranári*, the *sekerka* was a tool that celebrated history. It was anachronistic technology that, if pulled from the context of folk dances or museum displays of pre-revolutionary culture, could be wielded as a grassroots weapon of defiance. One did not need requisition forms from the Party bureaucracy to wield the hatchet, to make shingles, or to mend walls. As they chopped wood and patched the cracks between cabin beams, SZOPK members cultivated a spirit of openness and freedom. People gathered after the day's work to discuss social problems and to debate issues that went far beyond architecture and preservation, like health care, philosophy, and pollution.

BEYOND BRIGADES

Preservation brigades were at first the only activities of ZO 6. By the early 1980s, however, the group's unmonitored status and the secluded locations in which they carried out their work encouraged some of its members to discuss other contemporary ecological issues in greater depth. One of their first forays into environmental problems linked to socialism concerned a Czechoslovak-Hungarian plan to build a series of dams along the Danube River. In 1977, in a spirit of socialist cooperation, these neighboring states had signed a treaty which stipulated joint ownership of the Gabčíkovo-Nagymáros dam system. It was a huge water project, which included the construction of a weir just south of Bratislava and two massive hydroelectric plants at the towns of Gabčíkovo, in Slovakia, and Nagymáros, in Hungary.[11]

Three SZOPK members from ZO 6, a Czech hydrophysicist and two Slovak professors from the Natural Science Faculty at Comenius University, began to gather research on the long-term effects that the project would have on the Danube River Basin. Pavel Šremer, the Czech *ochranár*, had signed Charter 77 when he was living in Prague and had been forced to move to Bratislava, where his wife's family had an apartment. Šremer had also been barred from professional research positions and university teaching, and instead found a modest job as a floor operator at the Slovnaft chemical factory on the edge of Bratislava. Along with his more fortunate Slovak colleagues, Šremer quietly began to collect information on the Gabčíkovo project's impact on the large underground water table beneath the capital city. In 1981, the trio wrote up their findings on the Gabčíkovo scheme in *Ochranca Prírody* (Nature Conservation), the Bratislava City Committee's monthly periodical. Their article was unprecedented, expressing openly a concern that the dam would have long-term consequences both for the Danube's ecosystem and for the surrounding watershed's natural environment. In the late 1970s, Charter 77 had been vigorously attacked by the regime for disseminating a similarly critical report on serious levels of pollution near the coal-processing centers of Bohemia's so-called Black Triangle. Slovak authorities at first appeared to follow the usual course of regime reaction to airing the state's ecological dirty laundry. The Bratislava City Committee was asked by the

Central Committee of SZOPK to shut down *Ochranca Prírody* for six months. Although never arrested, Šremer and his colleagues were put under surveillance. But after a few months, the City Committee resumed publication of its magazine and pressure on SZOPK appeared to ease. The group's transgression seemed to have earned them a mere slap on the wrist.

Although Šremer and his partners refrained from publishing anything further on the dam issue over the next several years, other ZO 6 members continued to use the pages of *Ochranca Prírody* to extend the scope of the group's environmental activism. For example, in the mid-1980s, a group of ZO 6 activists, together with their colleagues in another local section, ZO 7, openly challenged local city officials' plans to cut down two trees in Bratislava's castle district. This exclusive district was home to many party bigwigs and powerful bureaucrats. One tree was slated for removal "because it was in the way of a party official's planned garden and summer house" (Filková 1995). In an effort to stop the city, members of ZO 6 appealed to public opinion by contacting newspapers and other media in protest. They also appealed to city residents' Catholic sentiments in a makeshift symbolic demonstration, which ultimately won their case.

> We encouraged residents to try and stop them from cutting down the tree. We even organized a group of students to place crosses around the tree as a symbol of public protest. I could not believe it when we finally convinced the man to build on another site (Filková 1995).

Emboldened by this first success, the *ochranári* followed with a second confrontation with municipal authorities. In the same elite district, a hundred-year-old oak had been marked for removal by the city, which claimed that it was diseased and needed to be destroyed. Two ZO 6 members raised the issue at a monthly meeting, and the group voted to form a special committee to stop the city from cutting it down. As Maria Filková, the head of the new committee, recalled,

> Several members wrote letters directly to the city, arguing that the tree should be protected. It should be a city monument. We kept telling people about the [local government's] poor record of monument protection as well as Bratislava's crumbling historic district and paucity of civic greenery. We

started a petition through the city committee and circulated it among the organization and the public (Filková 1995).

Unable to convince the city, the *ochranári* lost the battle. After the tree was cut down but before the stump was pulled out of the ground by a bulldozer, several ZO 6 members cut a *koláč* (cross-section) off the remaining trunk during the night. They preserved the piece with lacquer, as evidence that the tree had been perfectly healthy, contrary to the claims of city officials. They kept the *koláč* in Bratislava's Horský Park, where visitors could see (and actually touch) an explicit symbol of the government's irresponsibility toward the environment.

Still other ZO 6 members broadened the targets of the group's growing criticism by incorporating other social issues, such as religion, into its notion of civic environmentalism. In 1981, Ján Budaj, who had joined SZOPK some time earlier, initiated a campaign to protest the state's removal of crosses from Bratislava's Ondrejský Cemetery. Bratislava's local government argued that "the crosses did not serve [the city] because it was a socialist capital." Budaj boldly accused the mayor's office of "stealing the stones and selling them in Austria for money" (Budaj 1995). Budaj, who was tall and mild mannered, with a deep voice and a quiet gaze, had a reputation as a dissident. He had been barred from attending university by the secret police because of his political involvement with cultural and artistic groups in his high school years. Like Šremer, Budaj could not find a job beyond menial labor, and worked as a coal stoker. As a member of ZO 6, Budaj published *Cintorínske príbehy* (Cemetery Stories), a *samizdat* piece about the environment. In his essay he criticized city officials for destroying an important Slovak cultural landscape. His article, to which he openly signed his name, circulated among the city's small intellectual community. Over the next few months, however, Budaj stopped attending ZO 6 meetings. He feared that he had compromised the organization. Other members believed that he was being watched by the police, yet the regime made no moves to shut down ZO 6.

In addition to these urban projects, the Bratislava *ochranári* increased the number and range of their renovation efforts throughout the entire country during the 1980s: an eighty-year-old stone church outside of Stupava, near the capital city; a whitewashed, thatch-roofed stable in Borský Peter (three hundred years old); an abandoned shepherd's shelter in Kokávka (two hundred years old); and a Habsburg-era town house in the heart of Bratislava's official, but dilapidated, historical district. Unlike other SZOPK sections or branches in districts beyond Bratislava, that limited their projects to the towns or regions where they were founded, ZO 6 members seemed to be working everywhere by the middle of the decade. Their preservation projects were diverse in both style and location, ranging from isolated cabins tucked away in Central Slovakia's green valleys to inhabited homes in the low foothills that brushed the Ukraine border. The *ochranári* used a few *drevenice* as vacation *chaty*, but the rest were essentially civic museums open to anybody to see and experience. Minutes of a ZO 6 meeting in May of 1984 indicate not only the group's wide geographic range but also its increasingly broad scope of interest, from brigades far beyond Bratislava to municipal initiatives promoting environmental education (figure 2.2).

MINUTES

—Brigade to Kvačian Mill, May 12–14

—Action to protect Bratislava's Lužný Forest

—Proposal to announce and carry out an action to protect Bratislava's State Nature Preserves

—Brigades to Bratislava's parks, May 19

—Other work with youth: Pioneers Natural Science Expedition

—Reconstruction of Čiernobálog wooded railway

—Archeological research and protection of archeological monuments

—Excursion to the construction site of the Danube River dam

—Closest excursions: Lamač, Zahorska Bystrica, Horna

—Completion and distribution of information materials

(*Source:* Mikuláš Huba, personal archive)

FIG. 2.2 Minutes to SZOPK ZO 6 Meeting, May 3, 1984.

This growing spectrum of action, in turn, introduced the organization to local people in villages near renovation projects and put them in touch with other groups of conservationists throughout Slovakia. By 1984, with around 100 members, ZO 6 was also becoming one of the fastest growing organizations within the Union. What had started as an informal group of friends with a practical interest in doing something both ecological and recreational grew into an active and diverse group, the largest in the

Union's twenty-year history. By 1986, ZO 6 had over 400 members (see table 2.1).

The Union itself had been growing as well (table 2.2), and this growth suggested that volunteerism was an increasingly attractive endeavor for many Slovak citizens living under socialism. Through the Union people could find local groups with similar public and civic-minded interests in the realm of nature protection. In a way, the Union's steady increase in membership and popularity masked the more rapid growth in specific basic organizations such as ZO 6. Moreover, the ballooning membership of ZO 6 led to several of its most active members being voted onto the Union's City Committee, including Huba, who was elected chairman of the MV. Maria Filková, who had led the group's semi-successful protest against tree removal in the city's old quarter, was voted on as MV secretary. Since the organization's inception, there had been a sort of balance of committee members on the MV. Roughly half the committee were Communist Party members, or at least exhibited explicit loyalty to the Party, and the rest were independent or nonaffiliated members. When Huba became chairman, this balance began to shift slightly in favor of non-Party representation.

Another shift occurring at about the same time was the creation of more basic organizations in SZOPK's Bratislava branch. For example, at the beginning of 1987, thirteen members of ZO 6 who had joined the group as university students studying in Bratislava formed their own basic organization, ZO 13. They had known each other as children from excur-

TABLE 2.1 Membership in SZOPK Basic Organization 6 (ZO 6)

Year	Number
1977	10
1979	40
1980	60
1984	100
1985	250
1986	400

Source: SZOPK ZO 6 Meeting Minutes, 1977–86

TABLE 2.2 National Membership in SZOPK, 1970–85

Year	Number
1970	500
1975	1,700
1980	10,300
1985	13,000

Source: Poznaj a Chráň, Ekopanorama

sions and camps as members of the Socialist Union of Youth's Tree of Life movement. They wanted to concentrate their work on the capital city. Together, ZO 6 and ZO 13 began to dominate SZOPK in Bratislava. Most of my informants told me that by the late 1980s, the City Committee and ZO 6 were practically one and the same organization. In the view of one *ochranár* from ZO 13,

> Basically, ZO 6 and 13 were the largest and most active groups, not only in the city, but also in the entire country. When Huba became the chairman of the City Committee, SZOPK MV literally became ZO 6 in spirit. Most of the positions were held by active members of ZO 6, and they encouraged more radical people in other Bratislava basic organizations. We were feeling pretty confident in those days (Juraj 1994).

The City Committee, for the most part, served an entirely bureaucratic and administrative function, overseeing the registration of new basic organizations. It was also supposed to be the unofficial watchdog unit for the national organization. The committee was expected to monitor its basic groups. Although officially it had no power to prevent a group from doing something, the committee could officially disapprove of a group's actions with a majority vote of the committee's members.[12] The committee's real power was in its direct control over what was being published in its bimonthly magazine, *Ochranca Prírody*. Like other publications of SZPOK, such as *Poznaj a Chráň*, this periodical was intended only for an internal readership. As MV representatives, ZO 6 activists now had a significant say over the magazine's editorial staff. With its clear majority on the City Committee, ZO 6 now managed the direction and content of the magazine, and neutralized any resistance from older, more conservative committee members. At the end of 1987, the Bratislava *ochranári* found themselves, partly through design and partly by circumstance, leaders of a growing grassroots environmental movement.

ANTI-ELITES

Most types of dissent in Czechoslovakia and elsewhere in the Eastern Bloc did not take the form of consistent and sustained collective action (Ramet 1995). To reduce the risk of being shut down, many dissidents lived quite isolated from one another, carrying out individual acts of resistance or defiance through the written word. Occasionally, their work found a wider audience throughout the Eastern Bloc by re-entering the region after translation and broadcast by Western media. But dissidents, in an effort to maintain control of their message and to evade persecution by the state, rarely met together. In fact the "members" of Charter 77 never considered themselves to be a group or political organization. Rather, they identified themselves as a loose network of individual citizens concerned with human rights. The Chartists produced documents and proclamations, continuously rotating the main representatives of the "network" and always trying to avoid explicit pretension to an opposition identity. Regardless of this tactic, the state considered Chartists subversive and was quite effective in responding to individuals who had signed the petition with a range of sanctions and punishments. Likewise, exile literature and dissident theater could be easily undermined by Party rhetoric, which characterized them as fantasies of bourgeois corruption, an interpretation supported by the prizes and awards bestowed on them by the opulent and evil capitalist West. The Slovak Writers' Union, which began producing, if not openly anti-regime literature, then veiled critiques of the regime using symbols of Slovak identity, was an exclusive group, and their works were not widely circulated among the public (Liehm 1973). Beyond the handful of dissident writers and poets unconnected to Charter 77, the only other deviants by which the regime was preoccupied were the Secret Church. Although these religious activists frequently met as a group, the meetings of this secret organization were just that, secret—an understandable strategy in light of the explicit (and implicit) discouragement of traditional religion on the part of the Husák regime. Like Chartists, Secret Church members were subject to a barrage of threats, harassment, limited opportunities for their children in education and employment, and, in some cases, imprisonment.

These traditional totalitarian methods of castigation, however, although readily available, were rarely visited upon members of Slovakia's environmental community. Volunteer environmentalists were allowed to exist as an officially independent group, and the Party acknowledged the legitimacy of the structure to which activists belonged. The regime interpreted volunteer environmentalism as both the pursuit of personal interest and a productive social practice. According to Ján Budaj, this perhaps naïve conceit was the Union's basic protection against more direct Party control.

Essentially the communists underestimated the dangerousness of the greens. "They will gather paper and mushrooms in the woods," they thought. The

Union wasn't in the National Front. I cannot stress the political importance of this fact more. The regime kept watch over political organizations. Are stamp collectors political organizations? The communists thought so. Sportsmen, everybody. But the *ochranári*? "They will gather mushrooms, perhaps" (Budaj 1995).

These mushroom gatherers and trekkers, however, straddled formality and informality. The Union's centralized bureaucratic structure obscured an emerging politicization among members at the local level. In zo 6, *ochranári* were beginning to experiment with the multivocality of ecological discourse. Through their unique integration of culture and nature into the subject of conservation, the *ochranári* discovered a *liminal* space, a status between legitimacy and dissidence (Turner 1967). This space was not only symbolic or semantic, but quite functional and practical. They held an official status in the social and political roster of the regime, yet did not fall under the direct channels of control and co-optation of which other associations and groups became victims. Their open and explicit concern for the past encouraged and inspired others to think about the future. If the Bratislava activists were not considered to be dissidents, they nevertheless espoused and advertised an alternative to the rationalized but increasingly ineffective Party bureaucracy and *nomenklatura* system.

In one sense they formed a nascent social movement, existing separately from "other collective actors such as political parties or pressure groups" and certainly with a "concern to defend or change society" (Scott 1990:6). But unlike a social movement, which traditionally poses "at least the threat of mass mobilization" (Scott 1990:6), the burgeoning activists performed a more traditional intellectual function in socialist society. They were not really *anti-politicians*, according to the framework of scholars of socialism, although they did eschew direct questions of socialist theory or Marxist doctrine, a hallmark of anti-politics (Konrad 1984; Milosz 2001). In and around Bratislava the members of zo 6 were gaining a sort of elite status among the various countercurrents of socialist society. Sabrina Ramet (1995) has called these currents of criticism throughout East Europe the *great transformation*, a process in which people from a wide range of social backgrounds and experiences looked for alternative spaces within the framework of regime repression. But unlike many intellectuals in the more or less acquiescent academies of sciences and research institutes, the activists in szopk were blatantly informal and unpretentious in their approach to civic leadership (Konrad and Szelenyi 1979; Bozoki 1999; Snajdr 1999). The members of zo 6 were also quite different from the anti-politicians represented by dissidents who had signed Charter 77, who worked mostly through writing and never acted as an organization except on paper. The *ochranári* were, instead, quite public and explicitly a collective, and, most of all, informal and egalitarian. In effect, they were becoming anti-elites of socialist culture.

Abner Cohen characterizes cultural elites in open, democratic systems as "sharing the same basic culture of the society in which they [live], but achieving distinctiveness in terms of their special style of life" (1974:101). Elites define themselves through "their patterns of interaction, cooperation, and coordination of corporate activities through communal relationships," rather than by a set of criteria shared by individuals "such as income, academic qualifications, possessions, the hierarchical level of administrative positions they occupy, and so on" (Cohen 1981:232). Elites operate in a "continuing dialectic with changing economic and political interests and alignments," cultivating their status through performed activities, their relationships with each other, and, more importantly, how these are manifested in the larger society (Cohen 1981:216). Cohen argues that elites mystify their power in order to ensure their collective survival. This mystification is accomplished as a series of *dramaturgical* strategies, or what Taylor (1994) has recently called *performances*, where elites "have to 1) informally close . . . boundaries within a formally open system; 2) develop a network of moral relationships in order to fulfill utilitarian ends; 3) practice sponsored recruitment under the principle of equality of opportunity; 4) evolve small-scale, face to face, communal relationships in order to [sustain] a large-scale organization; and 5) articulate a rational ideology in a non-rational cultural formation" (Cohen 1981:220). These performances mask the composition of an elite group, making it difficult for outsiders to explicitly connect the elements that make up its identity. Through these symbolic dramas their status is obscured.

In the closed systems of state socialism, elites did not require such a mystification process to claim power. In fact, all of the communist regimes in the USSR and East Europe were founded on the notion of an explicit elite, a vanguard with the mandate to lead society on a developmental path toward true communism. In some socialist states, most notably Hungary, intellectuals enjoyed prominent reformist roles in the revision of Party doctrine (Konrad and Szelenyi 1979). In normalized Czechoslovakia, organizations and individuals perceived to be elite were either completely co-opted and consistently controlled, as were political parties and writer's unions, or summarily outlawed, as were the Boy Scouts (Olivo 2001; Priban 2004).

But Slovak nature protection, unlike its Czech counterpart, escaped the heavy hand of regime repression. In the closed system of state social-ism this uniquely liminal group followed a different performative logic, and its members became what I will term *anti-elites*. Applying Cohen's analysis to a closed system, anti-elites during socialism gained power not by resolving relationships, but rather by leaving them open and unre-solved. The members of ZO 6 became anti-elites through a process of mystification that was essentially an *inversion* of the pattern of elite for-mation common to open systems. They achieved this first by opening up boundaries in a totalitarian system with formally rigid social and pro-fessional categories. Membership in SZOPK ZO 6 was literally open to anyone and was acquired by simply getting involved. All one had to do was show up at a meeting, express one's interest, pay some small dues, and membership was granted, complete with an ID card. Although the secretary kept rosters of meeting attendees and their addresses, the group was, in all other respects, quite informal. People who were not interested in working on brigades could contribute to the organization in a num-ber of other ways. For example, some *ochranári* chose to work on the group's annual calendar, which included a wide array of educational events related to nature conservation. A young female student who had a pas-sion for photography began to document the proliferation of the group's renovation work. Other members helped organize more purely social activities, for instance, seasonal celebrations with environmental themes. Being an *ochranár* began to mean the freedom to create one's own style of volunteerism. As Huba recalled,

> The various aspects of these activities created an atmosphere among us that we were really offering an alternative. An atmosphere where a person could say what he liked or didn't like, express opinions openly. In this sense, we really weren't afraid, we didn't care if anyone "heard" us, it didn't matter if the ŠtB [secret police] was around, because we felt that we didn't need to do what we were doing in secret (Huba 1995).[13]

Ochranári who concentrated mainly on renovation work not only tol-erated the group's diversity and lack of boundaries, but were gradually drawn into its other activities.

I never wrote anything. I only worked on *drevenice*. I mean, it did not matter that I only went on brigades. People expected me to come. I had good tools. I really enjoyed the brigades. As for political actions. Writing and such. There were many who were much better at it and I didn't really want to write. I did some office work. I made copies of some things (Halama 1994).

One student joined in 1985 because of his interest in Slovak history. After working on the group's Kvačianska mill project, he began to link ecology with his historical studies. He told his friends about SZOPK, and they joined that same year. One woman, who had just arrived in Bratislava for a new job, heard about the group through a friend. She had been searching for a social network because her entire family still lived in a small village in eastern Slovakia. At her first meeting she was overjoyed to find "people who were interested in society in such a positive way" (Šimončičova 1994). Through their openness, the Bratislava *ochranári* attracted a diverse range of individuals, who in turn helped to increase the group's level of energy and resources. As one *ochranár* describes, diversity was a positive thing in the eyes of the group's informal leadership, because it reflected an ever-broadening notion of environmentalism.

If you wanted to work on *drevenice*, you could. If you wanted to help with brigades around Bratislava, fine. If you wanted to focus on other issues, like something controversial, such as water dams or nuclear energy, there were people in ZO 6 who were interested in this as well. In fact, there weren't enough things that we could have been working on (Hladký 1994).

SZOPK further developed their anti-elitist character by encouraging a network of utilitarian relationships to fulfill moral ends. The group's principle of recreational conservation contained two dimensions of utilitarianism: care for the self through healthy, constructive use of one's free time, and care for the environment through conservation. Both dimensions contained inherently moral values. Individuals devoted their time outside of professional life not simply to preserve elements of a disappearing culture or landscape but also for personal satisfaction.

One ZO 6 member joined after finding out about the organization while skiing with a friend at Čertovica, a popular winter vacation resort.

I was telling her about my family's old *maštal* (stables), which we were trying to convert to a *chata* for visiting in the summer. I still wasn't finished with the roof, and wondered if I could get some advice. She told me to come to the SZOPK meeting back in Bratislava . . . that there was a group who worked on these things and somebody would surely know what I should do to finish the house. All I had to do was show up (Halama 1994).

When Igor showed up, not only was he surprised to find a large gathering of people from all walks of life engaged in open discussions about society and nature, he was impressed with the group's record of practical work. After going on a couple of summer brigades, he told his schoolmates about ZO 6 and convinced them to join as well.

Elites in an open system distinguish themselves through cultural performances that mark them as a collective working toward certain ends (Cohen 1974). These ends are both universalistic and particularistic, but usually fall on a continuum that privileges one or the other function. The conservationists in ZO 6 set as their explicit mandate the general goal to repair traditional landscapes and, in so doing, enrich Slovak society by preserving its past. This universal objective complemented the array of particularistic aims that individuals could realize as members of the group.

> Before the revolution, we could only quite simply define values and ideas. But to realize them or act on them in your profession was out of the question. There were people among the *ochranári* who treated it as their professional careers, and of course many who only did it to express these values. It was a place to do more than what the regime offered at the time (Budaj 1995).

As its membership grew in diversity, the group's credo, "*Poznaj a chráň* [to know and protect]" came to mean more than the protection of nature. It began to signify an altruistic attitude toward other people, and suggested as a larger goal the protection of the human condition.

SZOPK activists also turned Cohen's third elite strategy, sponsored recruitment under the guise of equality, on its head. Although the group went through the motions of granting formal membership, issuing cards and creating rosters, anyone who was interested, whether old or young, male or female, was welcome to join its ranks. Most of its members were intellectuals or professionals, but this did not prevent those without advanced education from becoming part of the organization. Nor was there a requirement that a person have any prior experience in nature conservation or formal training in environmental science in order to join the group.

Finally, in place of articulating a rational ideology, ZO 6 championed a nonrational, even romantic, ideology, within a socialist society that promoted what Stokes (1993) calls a hyper-rational cultural formation.[14] Life in normalized Czechoslovakia was indeed hyper-rational, organized from the top down in the service of Marxist-Leninist ideology. Everything required a purpose, and everything had a function that led to the overall goal of building socialism. Even the notion of volunteer conservation had initially been rationalized by the founders of SZOPK, who had planned out the entire structure of the Union before it even got off the ground. Devoting precious private time to public conservation, however, was considered by some Slovaks to be completely irrational. Villagers were often puzzled as to why the organization preferred to mend old structures rather than build new ones. "It is a symbol of poverty, you know? Peasants: Drudgery and a hard life of backbreaking work," commented one woman who was watching the group repair a stable one hundred years old. But while their work seemed like irrational deviance to some observers, one could not characterize it as destructive behavior. In fact, their projects were also exercises in revitalizing the self by romanticizing the culture of the past. An *ochranári* brigade was a life without electricity and indoor plumbing, a way for city dwellers to experience Slovakia's bucolic pre-communist heritage.

Like their anachronistic work, the *ochranári's* notion of leadership also suggested a romance with irrationality. While authority within the group was structured on the surface according to formal leadership positions, it was the group's policy that anyone who spoke up could have a say in the decisions and actions of the organization. While it was the case that Mikuláš Huba held the elected position of ZO 6 president throughout the 1980s, more bureaucratic positions, such as chair and vice chairs, were constantly rotated among rank and file members. In addition to Huba, two other activists, Ján Budaj and Peter Tatár, led the group's move toward increasing diversity and its confrontational direction. They promoted tolerance of different viewpoints, a phrase which became the group's slogan. As Budaj explained, whatever one did in the context of ZO 6, it was accepted by everyone else as a form of *ochranárstvo*.

In my opinion, this new *ochranárstvo* meant a renewal of values. A respect for life and a respect for values, like the *drevenice* or public greenery—basic values. The communists wanted respect for Leninism, for Marx, for the working class. But these were values that no one believed in. People were hungry. They were hungry for values. Some looked for it in Christianity. But many people looked for it in these *ochranári* (Budaj 1995).

Through these discursive strategies the members of ZO 6 generated a distinct identity as anti-elites who directed an array of individuals, both professionals and nonprofessionals, into an ever-widening field of social action based on volunteerism and, through this, the opportunity for self-realization. The organization's inclusiveness, accommodating people with a variety of interests, not surprisingly led to debates among its membership about Slovakia's ecological problems. But different viewpoints only encouraged more openness. The groups held refereed discussion sessions after lectures by guest speakers. In this casual atmosphere, people were emboldened to express rather critical opinions about the environment and about society. The numerous factions that inevitably began to form within the group only increased energy and excitement. Despite its plethora of interests, the group's leaders were able to maintain unity in the organization by keeping discussion civil, and, above all, focused on practical questions.

> I know there were many viewpoints, and there were several sides to every issue. But to be able to air opinions openly within a forum, and that was what ZO 6 meetings became, a forum, was really exciting. I looked forward to coming to *ochranári* meetings because I knew something real was going to be discussed (Juraj 1995).

The group's growing membership roster included a wide spectrum of people, from artists and intellectuals to housewives and laborers. According to one new member who joined in the late 1980s,

> I felt as if I had walked into a free space where one did not have to worry about watching what was said or who was saying it. Literally, I was shocked to find such a group of people. They were not interested in my political position, my status, or my education level. They wanted to know what I wanted to do, what I was interested in. It was like an island in the grey world of normalization.

By 1986, this atmosphere of openness began to attract members of Slovakia's relatively small dissident writers' community.

Most of Bratislava's popular dissidents were members of SZOPK, even if they were only passive members. In ZO 6 were people like Langoš, Snopko, and Gál. These writers came because the *ochranári* were some of the only people in Bratislava actively doing something, actively discussing things. It could be anything (Luboš 1995).

As anti-elites, the members of ZO 6 were as explicit as they were mystifying, moving ecological activism in Slovakia along a unique road. It was a path quite different from those traversed by environmental movements in the West. In Western Europe and North America, nongovernmental organizations grew out of a liberal, largely middle-class culture, concerned with civil rights, grassroots activism, and a growing critique of consumerism.[15] In these societies, the open strategies that challenged elite centers of power, such as petitions, private fundraising, and public demonstrations, were not only possible, but easily achievable during the 1980s. Being "green" in these participatory democracies meant lobbying for and organizing around specific ecological issues.[16]

By contrast, Slovak environmentalism under socialism began as a form of "green recreation," a harmless, nonpolitical practice. This recreation, however, became more than a vacation in which to pursue anachronistic hobbies. As we will see, Slovak environmentalism was transforming into a social and discursive space in which people not only wanted to save nature, but also preserve symbols of Slovak identity in the face of socialist oppression and imperialism. Conservation provided the frame within which new environmental and social ethics were nurtured and promoted, and into which a growing movement eager to talk about citizens' rights and public advocacy was born. The conservationist's *sekerka*, a humble tool used to preserve and repair Slovakia's cultural and historical landscapes, became a symbol of everyday resistance to totalitarianism, representing the regime's disregard for its people and their environment. This neglected back door into the world of public environmental activism attracted a range of intellectuals, community leaders, and dissidents who, in addition to changing the political character and function of the Union, would also take the helm of Slovakia's opposition community as the regime collapsed.

3 *"Bratislava Aloud"*

NO ONE GAZING ON THE LANDSCAPE OF EAST EUROPE IN 1987 would have predicted—and no one in the West did predict—that communism's total demise would occur only two years later. Hindsight now affords us the ability to tease out the clues—some glaring, some not so obvious—that suggested what was about to happen. Throughout Eastern Europe and the Soviet Union, signs of change were all around. In 1985, Gorbachev assumed leadership of the Soviet Union, introducing a series of internal social and economic reforms. In East Germany, peace activists were attracting not only students but church leaders. Pope John Paul II, the only Polish pope in Catholic history, was making visits to the region, revealing the extent and depth of spiritual life that survived behind the closed doors of many apartments. An initial papal visit was scheduled for Velehrad, Moravia in 1985. When it was cancelled, 100,000 Czechs and Slovaks showed up anyway (Stokes 1993:152). In Hungary, not only was there talk about the possibility of multi-party elections, but the Party began to distance itself from its own history (Bozoki 1999).

Just as these developments indicated something different on the horizon, however, other details confirmed the continuation of communism's control. Although a fledgling ecology movement called the Polish Ecology Club had started in Poland in 1980, by 1987, with martial law still in place and Solidarity outlawed, it remained small (Hicks 1996). In Kazakhstan, far to the east and deep within the Soviet Union, a 1986 student uprising was brutally suppressed by state security forces and local law enforcement. In Romania, Ceauşescu's rule permeated all facets of private and public life: all typewriters were registered with the secret police, and young children were brainwashed in communist youth associations to spy on their parents. Czechoslovakia, in particular, seemed completely immune to change elsewhere. The harassment and imprisonment of dissidents continued. Gorbachev's more open regime appeared only to encourage the Husák government to tighten its grip on society. But only two years later, the regime was gone, and Czechoslovakia joined the rest of East Europe in its transition from communism.

The *ochranári* became central characters in the Velvet Revolution, and their environmental organization served as the foundation for Public Against Violence, the civic movement that, along with Civic Forum in the Czech Lands, wrested power from the regime. This revolution actually started when the members of SZOPK boldly decided to take their growing volunteer forum on ecology public. In 1987, at the height of repression, the *ochranári* published *Bratislava/nahlas*, an open report on the state of the environment in and around the capital city. In *Bratislava/nahlas*, the members of SZOPK vividly defined ecology as a problem for all Slovaks, clearly exposing the regime's exploitation of people not only as resources to be used but as victims that had been abused. This singular act transformed volunteer conservationists from anti-elites of a nascent civil society into popular discursive representatives of broader Slovak society. With this new status, the *ochranári* began to devise new initiatives and social reforms under the rubric of environmentalism, more than a year before the fall of one of the Eastern Bloc's most rigid regimes. In the moment of communism's collapse, the *ochranári*'s ability to use nature as a metaphor for society brought them to center stage. Each cold November night during the Velvet Revolution, as masses of Slovaks gathered in Bratislava's public square, people turned their ears to listen patiently and hopefully to the voice of ecology.

MEETING "MINUTES"

Throughout the period of normalization, the Czechoslovak regime successfully repressed criticism of the state through relentless censorship of the press and other media. The official periodicals of SZOPK were, in theory, subject to this same control. Even though the Union's monthly magazines were intended solely for distribution among its members, the publication still required review by government and Party censors in the Ministry of Culture. Upon passing this process, the periodical staff was given an official number, indicating state approval of the issue's content.

On top of this overt censorship, circulation was limited to the organization's official membership roster. For example, in 1987, *Poznaj a Chráň*, the monthly periodical of the Union's Central Committee, which was available to all SZOPK members throughout the country, had a publication cap of 20,000. Similarly, *Ochranca Prírody*, the magazine produced by the Union's Bratislava City Committee, had a press limit of 1000 in 1986.

The members of ZO 6, buoyed by its earlier forays into public activism, decided to challenge these repressive publishing restrictions. The group's membership roster included a number of people who were competent writers and who used this craft in their everyday professions in science, education, media, or the arts. More than half of the *ochranári* held advanced degrees, and several held posts in the Slovak Academy of Sciences or with the Bratislava Office of Monument Care and Nature Protection. Still others worked as journalists. One was a medical doctor. The *ochranári*'s increasingly well-attended meetings not only took on the character of an intellectual forum, they were turning into ad hoc public resource centers.

Recognizing the potential of the group to serve as an expert forum, Ján Budaj, one of the few among the *ochranári* that the government had actually labeled a dissident, proposed in 1986 that ZO 6 issue a report on the condition of Slovakia's environment. That same year, Budaj had been inspired by Gorbachev's visit to Prague to promote his policies of *glasnost* and *perestroika*, which were now in full bloom in the Soviet Union. The Husák government, however, had given no indication that it would introduce similar reforms in Czechoslovakia. Nevertheless, a few Slovak intellectuals who remembered the days of Dubček's Prague Spring saw in Gorbachev a renewed hope that there might one day be change, and these writers and artists found in SZOPK meetings a place to talk about these developments. Budaj submitted that the time had arrived for SZOPK to make more open demands regarding the country's environmental problems. Budaj later explained that, to him,

> It was obvious that ecological and political problems were becoming one and the same. It really did not help us, in my opinion, to repair one house, or fix one roof for free, when the communists were destroying an entire quarter of the city, or pulling apart the cemetery (Budaj 1995).

In arguing his case to the group, he proposed that they present a report based on sound research, collected by scientists and other experts. It should cover in detail the various ecological problems clearly evident in the capital city. Budaj also suggested that, more than simply recounting a list of cold data, the report should include recommendations for each of the problems that it revealed. This all sounded reasonable to the rest of the group. But Budaj's concluding suggestion was his boldest by far: rather than submit this document to the state, the group would make the report available to the public.

Over the next twelve months, the *ochranári* carried out their research in secret. In addition to drawing on their own expertise, members discreetly asked other scholars and scientists at universities, at hospitals, and at technical institutes for help. They chose people whom they knew, either through personal or professional connections, and hoped that no one would expose their plan. In October of 1987, the *ochranári* released their report to the public. The document, like other *samizdat* literature of the time, was manually typed and printed on rough paper. The title of the report, *Bratislava/nahlas*, alluded to Gorbachev's recent Soviet reforms. *Nahlas*, the Slovak adverb "loudly," invoked the Soviet leader's specific policy of increasing openness or *glasnost* (voicing). In keeping with the theme of openness, the report's 23 authors identified themselves on the inside cover and also listed the names of some 40 professionals that they had consulted. The group had cleverly published the report in the guise of an appendix to the group's meeting minutes.[1] With 16 chapters totaling 62 pages, the publication was the longest that the group had ever produced.[2]

The text of *Bratislava/nahlas* opened quite modestly. Its collective authors stated in the preface their hope to "articulate the interests of the citizens of Bratislava," and "renew the relationship of the residents with their city" (Budaj 1987:i). What followed, however, electrified the public. In language that moved easily from technical concepts to vivid ethnography, specifying well-known streets and neighborhoods and openly naming industries and factories, each chapter of *Bratislava/nahlas* focused relentlessly on the ecological problems plaguing Slovakia's capital city. Together these chapters unveiled a comprehensive portrait of a city and its people caught up in an unfolding environmental crisis.

The report began with an alarming account of the city's air pollution and its likely sources. It alerted readers to the case of several employees of the Georgi Dimitrov Chemical Factory who had been hospitalized for brain damage due to inhalation of hydrogen monosulfide. The city's chemical industries combined with exhaust from its motor traffic resulted in a concentration of particle pollution in the town center that was 13 times permitted levels. In the sphere of water quality, the report described how the Slovnaft Oil and Chemical Works dumped 15 tons of petroleum waste per day into the Danube River. Overall city water quality was disturbingly poor, with only 48 percent of all industrial waste plus household sewage undergoing any form of purification. Not only were surface waters seriously contaminated, but the large underground lake beneath Bratislava was critically threatened by waste seepage from Slovnaft and other industries. The report also described how local hospitals routinely discarded low-level nuclear waste directly into the public sewage system, after an ineffective dilution process. The soil in and around Bratislava was heavily polluted by chemical ash and dust. Most of the surrounding landscape suffered from erosion due to deep mechanical plowing. The report warned readers about a planned nuclear power plant in the Bratislava suburb of Mlynska Dolina, where 70,000 people would be living within a two-kilometer radius of the reactors.

In addition to these nightmares regarding the city's natural resources, the report detailed the extremely unhealthy condition of the city's social environment. Noise pollution was heavy practically everywhere in the city. Living conditions in highly concentrated apartment blocks were unsafe, and services were woefully inadequate. Healthcare was of low quality, and there were not enough hospital beds or medications for patients who needed them. If these problems were not alarming enough, the report also revealed that Bratislava had the highest number of tumor-related deaths in Slovakia. Incidence of cardiovascular diseases, infant mortality, and miscarriages had all increased dramatically over the previous two decades. In 1986, the report claimed, roughly a third of all children in the city had had cases of infectious pneumonia.

The *ochranári* shrewdly avoided directly implicating the regime as responsible for the maladies that they presented. Rather, the members of zo 6 simply described reality. Yet in doing so, the *ochranári* crossed a line with the regime, breaking an official silence about pollution and other ecological problems in Slovakia. At the same time, although it was construed by the regime as a political act, the publication of *Bratislava/nahlas* was a move that the state had not expected and was certainly not prepared for. One of the coauthors recalled that "it was not possible to say anything about the *nomenklatura*, but [it was] difficult [for the regime] to prevent us from a discussion of forests, water, and the health of the people" (Pauliniova 1990:46). *Bratislava/nahlas* quite simply turned the socialist world upside down, exposing it to be not an orderly or purposeful society with the promise of equality or progress, but a social and environmental disaster that was not only disorderly, but downright dangerous to human life.

Indeed, the government was unable to counter, with any honesty, a single argument presented in the report. Instead, and not surprisingly, state authorities tried to undermine the *ochranári* through the usual tactics of totalitarian repression. First, the secret police tried unsuccessfully to confiscate all copies of the damning text. But the *ochranári* had made over 3000 copies—more than twice the number they were officially allowed for internal material. They had distributed stacks of the document all over the city, leaving them near newsstands or beside café doorways.[3] Moreover, people who first got their hands on the text read it and then lent it to others, who then clandestinely duplicated it and passed it on to still others. A copy soon found its way into the hands of Voice of America in Munich, where it was translated into English, then published in Voice of America's *Research Report* series.[4] The narrative of *Bratislava/ nahlas* was then rebroadcast as oral text, back into Slovakia.

The secret police next attempted, also unsuccessfully, to arrest and detain the key authors of the report. One *ochranár* described how, when she was picked up for questioning, the police "wanted to know who wrote which chapters. I told them at the interrogation that 'everybody wrote everything.' We decided that this is what we would say if they came for us" (Filková 1995).

Interrogators were immediately frustrated by the group's collective writing strategy, which made it difficult to link specific authors with particular pieces of text. The authors who were detained also stuck by their position that the report was an internal appendix, some notes to meeting minutes, and thus technically not required to be reviewed by state censors. As minutes, the *ochranári* argued, the text did not even need to be submitted to the Union's editorial committee. Nor did it require, the detainees pointed out, an official publication approval number.

In the face of mounting public pressure, the regime was reluctant to hold members of the Union for long. In cafés or on street corners, people said "*Držím Vám palce* [I'm crossing my fingers for you]!" to individuals whom they recognized as activists in SZOPK. Many of the people who authored chapters held respectable professional positions and were well known to local residents. Rather than make additional arrests, the Communist Party fell back on a strategy of discrediting the report's contents.

It first attempted to debunk ZO 6 through the Union's official magazine, *Poznaj a Chráň*. But the SZOPK Central Committee's official response was mild. In a brief statement, buried on page four and blandly titled "Position of the Central Committee of SZOPK," the committee vaguely complained that the *ochranári* in ZO 6 had used "unreliable information sources" and "poor methods of research." It then methodically criticized the Bratislava organization for abusing its publication protocol, dryly pointing out that the number of actual copies far exceeded its official membership (SZOPK, *Poznaj a Chráň* 2 1988:4). The statement evasively concluded that, since the report covered the city's social and economic situation, its arguments were technically beyond the expertise and concern of the Union. It did not even mention the report's provocative title, in what amounted to a half-hearted editorial hand slap.

A more public challenge came from the Communist Party in the form of a newspaper article. In *Pravda*, the Party's official newspaper, in a piece entitled "*Nič nového pod slnkom*" (Nothing new under the sun), the *ochranári* were accused of manipulating data and misrepresenting information so that the group could subvert the regime (Piškorova 1988). Such an argument is the equivalent of what Mateosian refers to as complaints about complaints, where the second complainer "lifts the relevance of a reply to a topic and slips in a response to flaws concerning the actions, motives or character of the [first] complainant. The device changes topics, shifts blame and responsibility, formulates the topic or action, switches defensive to offensive positions and expands the sequence" (Mateosian 1993:44–45). And indeed, the *Pravda* article did not directly address any of the specific claims in the report. The *ochranári* responded to these allegations by demanding to meet the article's author. They quickly discovered that the piece had been written under a pseudonym. *Pani* (Ms.) Piškorova, the purported author, turned out to be a seventy-two-year-old woman caring for her eighty-year-old invalid husband. Upon meeting members of SZOPK, Piškorova not only told them that she did not write the article, but also that she admired their work, and she joined SZOPK that same day.

The regime finally resorted to simply accusing the *ochranári* of being enemies of socialism. Immediately following the *Pravda* piece, government officials began to refer to ZO 6 and ZO 13 as "anticommunist," even "anti-Czechoslovak" organizations, and characterized them as dissidents and "enemies of socialist society" (SZOPK, *Ochranca Prírody* 1–2 1988). But by this time, no one seemed to be listening to the regime. Instead, the residents of Bratislava were flocking to SZOPK meetings and asking doctors about their own well-being. And rather than allowing the regime to fall silent, members of ZO 6 responded to charges of dissidence and criminality by writing more articles about the city's ecological problems. The *ochranári*, as a discursive community, had at least elicited a response to their call for a public forum. That this response was one of denial that such problems existed only served to support the case of ZO 6 in the eyes of the public, who could see quite clearly from their own experience that *Bratislava/nahlas* told the truth. Throughout 1988 and 1989, members as well as guest authors wrote highly critical articles in *Ochranca Prírody* on a myriad of topics and issues, openly signing their names to their work. The magazine's circulation more than doubled, and the periodical became a popular venue for a growing discourse about social, ecological, and political issues. Younger Slovaks, especially university and high school students, joined the organization in record numbers. *Bratislava/nahlas* marked the beginning of an open challenge to the communist regime. The *ochranár*, the environmentalist, assumed a new status under socialism: perceived by the state as an enemy of society and by the people as a champion of their well-being.

A GREEN ISLAND IN A GRAY WORLD

The publication of *Bratislava/nahlas* was an unprecedented and courageous act, given the regime's successful record of controlling dissent and opposition in Slovakia. The report mustered a beleaguered population to become, if not directly defiant toward the state, then more openly critical of its shortcomings and failures. Emboldened by the popularity of *Bratislava/nahlas*, Martin Butora, a sociologist at the Slovak Academy of Sciences and a ZO 6 member himself, described the organization, in a 1988 sociological essay for the Academy, as a group of "positive deviants." For Butora, positive deviants were people who were interested in social change but who had remained isolated from each other during the silence and repression of Czechoslovakia's period of normalization. The members of SZOPK, Butora wrote, were "deviant" in their avoidance of the official channels of communist culture, but "positive" because their volunteer work served a practical and valuable function within society. The *ochranári* offered to literally anyone who was interested a place for solidarity, for communication, and for collective action. They offered people what Butora termed an "island of positive deviance"(Butora 1988:4).

These positive deviants had started a conversation about the environment that came in the form of a discourse about everyday reality for Slovaks living in the urban claustrophobia and pollution of late socialism. These problems about which the *ochranári* so vividly wrote were the grim realities from which communist elites also suffered. Party operatives also had to endure poor infrastructure and decay, even in the more desirable neighborhoods of the city. Poor air, polluted water, and long-term illnesses did not discriminate between *nomenklatura* and common citizens. The message of *Bratislava/nahlas* was, as one *ochranár* put it, a poignant discourse on truth.

> So here we were, a small part of this conservation organization, and we wrote something that was not censored. *Bratislava/nahlas* electrified people. It electrified them because in that material that we compiled and presented was the truth. They knew it. Everybody knew it. We were speaking about reality.

In articulating this reality, the *ochranári* became public celebrities. Even as such, however, they tried to continue performing their anti-elite status, one that had kept them, until this point, above politics. As one member recalled,

> We were a legal organization. Our priority was not to create a political organization, but to look for alternatives, especially in the sphere of the environment . . . We had a wider conceptualization of the environment, which included cultural aspects and social problems. This was what we outlined in *Bratislava/nahlas*.

Despite the fact that they had often encountered puzzled faces wondering about their devotion to *drevenice*, the vestiges of the past, their volunteer pursuits began to acquire a positive moral character in the eyes of Slovak society. This moral status was not lost on the organization's growing membership. As one *ochranár* recalled,

> The *ochranári* simply began to live more freely. And they created an atmosphere in this community of solidarity with each other. A community where being an *ochranár* wasn't a career. I mean, there was completely no money for it. It was in this community where the personalities grew. This was the big gift of green politics before the revolution. It was about freedom. And

it was here where specialists, intellectuals, even lay persons, could speak about not only the condition of nature but the condition of culture and society.

By 1988, the tone of *Ochranca Prírody,* the City Committee's conservation magazine, began to highlight the new moral leadership roles that environmental activists were assuming. The Union's Bratislava branch also began to attract well-known intellectuals to its ranks, including several members of the Slovak Writers' Union. People who had been prevented from pursuing formal education because they had refused to join the Communist Party or had engaged in what the regime considered to be dissident activities found a welcoming home within ZO 6. The group became a network where dissidents, reformers, and even a few more hard-line Party members gathered to discuss environmental and social problems.

Through this network, the *ochranári* expanded its social activism in order to address the specific problems outlined in *Bratislava/nahlas* and to speak for the subaltern voices of socialist society. Within SZOPK's Bratislava branch, new initiatives were created to address a range of urban policies. For example, several *ochranári* formed Komisia Bratislava (the Bratislava Commission), to champion a range of social concerns, including healthcare and residential life. Other members started Bratislava Bez Barier (Bratislava Without Barriers), a civic campaign to alter or remove the countless urban obstacles that people with physical disabilities faced daily throughout the city. Still others created Bicyba, a grassroots association that promoted the use of bicycles as an alternative mode of transportation for commuters, who otherwise had to endure crowded electric tram cars or heavy automobile traffic. Other SZOPK initiatives included an anti-cigarette campaign, Stop Nicotin! to discourage the nearly ubiquitous use of tobacco by calling attention to its numerous environmental and personal health hazards, and Archa, a public relations collective which aimed to educate citizens about pollution and quality-of-life issues through art and media.

SZOPK's Bratislava branch also began to sponsor public events for the residents of the capital city. In March 1989, ZO 6 held an event called Zelenú Zeleni (Greens Greening) in Bratislava's old quarter. In this public demonstration, ZO 6 members took to the streets with banners, wore buttons identifying them as *ochranári,* and began to clean up local civic parks. Joining them on this action was the elderly Piškorova, the woman whose name the regime had borrowed to discredit *Bratislava/nahlas.* Later in the year, the MV SZOPK sponsored an event they called Day of Joy

(Deň Radosti), in reference to a 1972 Dušan Hanák film of the same name which documented the "happenings" of the late 1960s socialist thaw under Dubček. The SZOPK event was a public celebration that blended cultural events such as music and drama with environmental education. The regime, however, attempted to censor the gathering even before it began.

> Twenty-four hours before the official start of Day of Joy, the telephone rang at the City Committee office. It was the Bratislava Department of Culture. They would only approve the event on the conditions that, one, the newly voted member of the MV, Ján Budaj, who had been scheduled to speak about the activities of the *ochranári*, did not participate in the program; and, two, we were under no circumstances to invite invalids up to the podium (Gindl 1989:3).

Budaj, of course, had been followed everywhere by the secret police. He was specifically targeted for his prominent role as *Bratislav/nahlas*' publisher, and authorities were concerned about his skyrocketing popularity. The government's attempt to prevent people with disabilities from prominent public appearances only lent additional legitimacy to and support for SZOPK's new initiative Bratislava Bez Barier.

Events such as Deň Radosti also spotlighted the *ochranári*'s newest recruits among the city's cultural and artistic community. Milan Knažko, a well-known film actor, joined the organization in 1987 and spoke publicly about the need to make more information about environmental problems available to citizens (SZOPK, *Ochranca Prírody* 3–4 1989:43). In January of 1988, a popular writer from *Literarný Týždenník*, Luboš Jurík, also joined SZOPK ZO 6. His weekly column reopened a debate about the events of 1968 and the repression that followed. Even members of the clergy began to align themselves with the Union. For example, Ján Sokol, the beleaguered Bishop of the Catholic Church in Slovakia, which had been tightly controlled by the regime, gave a full-page interview in *Ochranca Prírody* firmly supporting the activities of the *ochranári*. "[We] are all in one boat," the bishop observed. "One of the spheres that this rule has begun to carry over into praxis is the sphere of environmental protection. I believe that it is the beginning of a process that can lead to improving dialogue, cooperation and action in the entire society" (SZOPK, *Ochranca Prírody* 1–2 1989a:40).

Complementing the *ochranári*'s civic actions in Bratislava, *Ochranca Prírody* became a broad forum for surprisingly open discussions about social transformation. Each issue throughout 1988 and 1989 included more pages and had a more critical tone than the previous one. In various articles the *ochranári* demanded specific changes to public spaces and civic life. For example, they insisted on the public resurrection of Milan Štefánik, the Slovak general who had helped create Czechoslovakia as a new country after World War I. They asked that Štefánik's name be returned to the Bratislava street that had borne it before 1948. The *ochranári* also proposed to reorganize the city's service infrastructure in order to increase resources for the isolated residents of Petržalka, who comprised almost a third of Bratislava's population. They boldly declared the capital an "open city" and demanded that *prestavba*, the Slovak translation of Gorbachev's *perestroika* (economic restructuring), be fully implemented by the government.

In addition to motivating the country's tiny dissident community, the *ochranári* inspired greater participation in the regime's environmental youth movements, Brontosaurus and Tree of Life, as well as increasing activism among SZOPK basic organizations throughout Slovakia. The number of summer camps operated by Strom Života ballooned, with over 400 taking place in 1988. As if to distance itself from the Party, the Slovak Socialist Union of Youth began to stress Strom Života's nonpolitical status. In the Czech Lands, a Brontosaurus pamphlet noted that the group was "a movement rather than an organization . . . it has no members, no membership fee, and nobody knows how many people are working [in it]" (1989:4). Like Brontosaurus, Strom Života boasted in its literature that it was "not an organization or political party, but a program . . . open to anybody who is not careless about the state of our environment" (Strom Života 1989:1). Growing membership in other local branches of SZOPK throughout the country further suggested the *ochranári*'s impact on Slovak civil society. The year before *Bratislava/nahlas* was published, ZO 6 alone counted nearly 250 members. In 1988, its membership jumped to 600. By 1989, people stopped recording the names of those who attended events and meetings, as hundreds more joined. Similar increases were recorded in the Union's ranks outside of Bratislava, as membership leaped from 13,000 in 1985 to 28,000 in 1988. *Bratislava/nahlas* had clearly propelled ZO 6 to national notoriety, and there was now talk among some members of SZOPK about forming, even if only symbolically, a green party. By the end of the 1980s, whether or not they had intended to do so, the *ochranári* had become civic leaders in Slovakia's capital city.

But the *ochranári*'s influence in the Union did not stop with Bratislava.

In 1989, the year of the Velvet Revolution, practically 80 percent of the leadership on the City Committee was comprised of ZO 6 members. One activist told me that even by 1988 "the Bratislava MV *was* ZO 6." As part of its accelerating wave of civic activism, the MV hosted a conference on April 22, 1989, in honor of Earth Day, at which they proclaimed a bold new vision for environmental policy and activism in Slovakia. Peter Zajac, a prominent Slovak writer who had attended the conference, wrote in *Ochranca Prírody* that the event "signal[ed] the potential birth of a new cultural communication." Zajac concluded that the *ochranári*, "with rucksacks, tennis shoes, [and] practical clothes," characterized a fresh spirit of civic awareness in Slovakia, a "portability . . . something that somehow says: 'there, where we are, is also culture'" (SZOPK, *Ochranca Prírody* 3–4 1989b:51). At the Earth Day meeting, the Bratislava *ochranári* proposed a list of changes, subsequently published in *Ochranca Prírody*, that would significantly transform the entire Union and which it planned to present at the sixth congress of SZOPK, slated for November (SZOPK, *Ochranca Prírody* 3–4 1989). The MV first demanded that the Union perform an investigation into the fate of Ekotrend, the rogue environmental group in Banská Bystrica that had been shut down with the help of the ŠtB. Juraj Mesík, Ekotrend's founder, had now joined ZO 6 in Bratislava, where he was attending medical school. Second, it requested that secret ballots be used in the upcoming elections for national officers at the fall congress. Andrej Fedorko, the Union's current chairman and a member of the Communist Party, had held this position for the past fifteen years. The MV hoped that by holding elections by hidden ballot, the national membership would be emboldened to institute change at the top levels of the Union. Finally, the MV put forth a plan to create more contact between regional committees and between basic groups throughout the country. The City Committee sought to reshape the entire Union on the model of ZO 6.

The sixth national SZOPK congress was held during the first week of November in Bratislava's Hotel Carleton, a huge building just a block from the banks of the Danube River. Unlike past Union congresses, this event drew hundreds of people. Activists described the mood as intense; people were clearly excited in anticipation of change. Although Bratislava activists expected significant resistance from older and more conservative Union members, particularly from regional organizations around the country, their proposal to vote by secret ballot was quickly adopted. The Central Committee would be comprised of the 45 people who received the most votes from the general membership. Mikuláš Huba won a clear victory with the most votes, and was proclaimed chairman, becoming the first person not a Party member to hold the position.[5] But this remarkable mini-revolution within the Union was to be suddenly and surprisingly eclipsed. One week after Huba's election to SZOPK's national chairmanship, the mass demonstrations that marked the opening of the Velvet Revolution began. The *ochranári* would be at the very center of the overthrow of communism in Slovakia.

THE VELVET REVOLUTION

By the fall of 1989, the political and social landscape of Eastern Europe certainly showed signs of change. Solidarity in Poland resurfaced with the open and eager support of the Catholic Church. Mass demonstrations were taking place throughout cities in East Germany. Hungary's communist regime was not only contemplating major reforms but allowing multi-party elections for the first time in over 40 years. In many Eastern Bloc cities, social currents of resistance, critique, and open protest were becoming much more frequent, including street theater, musical performances, youth art, and demonstrations (Ramet 1995). The performative aspects to these anti-authoritarian movements visibly highlighted the regimes' weakening grip on public discourse (Kenney 2003). But no one gazing on this broader discursive terrain could predict the massive upheaval of political power about to occur in Czechoslovakia. Amid all of these developments, Czechoslovakia remained relatively silent.

In Slovakia, there were few stirrings of serious oppositional activity beyond the efforts of the Bratislava *ochranári* and the *samizdat* texts of underground writers during the two years prior to the Velvet Revolution.[6] On a cold March evening in 1988, members of the Secret Church, the clandestine network of Bratislava's Catholic worshipers, held a candlelight prayer meeting in front of the Slovak National Theatre. The police used water cannons and cars to break up a growing crowd of a few thousand. Many of these so-called "demonstrators" were merely curious bystanders. Although the public was infuriated, nothing came of what appeared to be a rather ad hoc event. More than a year later, in May 1989, Alexander Dubček, the famous Slovak reformer from the Prague Spring, unexpectedly appeared at the funeral of Dominik Tatarka, one of Slovakia's few dissident authors. At the ceremony, however, even though several thousand mourners were in attendance to honor Tatarka, Dubček made no public speech. Again, nothing indicated anything out of the ordinary was about to occur. The only other notable public event in Slovakia was environmental in character. On November 16, 1989, a group of 500 students gathered in Bratislava on the eve of the International Day of Students to voice concern over a nuclear reactor that was planned for construction in Mlynska Dolina, a Bratislava suburb. This reactor was to be a teaching facility for Comenius University, and it had received critical coverage in *Ochranca Prírody* (SZOPK, 3–4 1988c:12–13). Many of the student demonstrators were younger members of SZOPK. But like the Secret Church's public prayer session or Dubček's sudden reappearance after years of public absence, nothing came of the Bratislava protest.

The following day, everything changed. On November 17, well over 50,000 students gathered in Prague's Wenceslas Square to commemorate the deaths of students killed by the Nazis during the Second World War. The demonstration was violently put down by security forces. This brutal police response led to several days of mass protests and strikes around Czechoslovakia. These demonstrations began to coalesce into makeshift civic movements within a couple of days after the police violence in Prague. In the Czech Republic, this public coalition formed around Vaclav Havel and other Chartists and was called the Civic Forum. In Prague, Havel addressed gathering crowds nearing half a million strong. In Slovakia, the civic movement was named Public Against Violence (Verenosť Proti Nasiliu, VPN), and was literally created in the offices of SZOPK's City Committee in Bratislava. Several *ochranári*, among them Ján Budaj, Maria Filková, Peter Tatár, Eugen Gindl, and Juro Flamík, formed VPN's coordinating committee. Joining them were Martin Butora, the sociologist; the writer Fedor Gál; and the actor Milan Knažko. On November 20, Ján Budaj, the dissident-conservationist, and Milan Knažko, the popular actor who had also joined SZOPK, spoke to several hundreds of thousands gathered in Bratislava's Slovak National Uprising Square (figure 3.1). They announced the formation of Public Against Violence and asked the crowds to join in this broad movement to demand investigations into the violence against the student demonstrators in Prague. The address Budaj gave the crowd for VPN's headquarters was the office of the City Committee of SZOPK. From this office, statements were issued and demands were drawn up for roundtable meetings with the regime in Prague.

Around the country other *ochranári* assumed administrative and leadership roles during these tense and exhilarating days.[7] The experience of

FIG. 3.1 Greens at their zenith. Ján Budaj, member of SZOPK ZO 6 and founding editor of *Bratislava/nahlas*, addresses a mass demonstration during the Velvet Revolution in Bratislava, November 1989. On his coat, Budaj wears a pin bearing the symbol of SZOPK. He was elected chair of Public Against Violence (VPN), the civic coalition that assumed power in Slovakia as the Czechoslovak regime collapsed. Photograph by Pavol Mikulášek.

Juraj Mesík, the medical student who had founded Ekotrend and later joined ZO 6, is representative of the way members of SZOPK, along with students and activists from the Secret Church, helped to connect the rest of Slovakia as the regime began to collapse.

> I was [in Hungary], but I came back to Bratislava at night and met with Jano Budaj. He told me what was happening and how the day before they had had the first meeting, and that Public Against Violence had been formed. Later that evening I went to another meeting of VPN, where the first declaration of VPN was read. I took a bunch of copies of the declaration and took the night bus to Banská Bystrica. The next day I went to Martin to speak with students there. But the students there were already mobilized by students who came from Prague. I read the declaration and I helped them to formulate some of their own declarations. Later that evening they had a big meeting with the dean and professors of the school. The students felt that they must do something but they were afraid, that there was nobody to speak there because they were subordinate to the professors, so they asked me to speak on behalf of them. I spoke. That night I went back to Banská Bystrica and I stayed there.

Having moved from town to town, Mesík unwittingly became a voice of the Revolution and a source of information for those who were far from the massive demonstrations in Prague and in Bratislava and who were following the astounding events on television.

I felt it was much more important to stay [in Banská Bystrica], and it was. One interesting thing that was quite typical happened that Tuesday. I left a bunch of declarations with my wife, and she went to the hospital and gave it to friends and colleagues and they started to pass it around there. And in the afternoon she went to the square and there were many people standing around just waiting for something to happen. But there wasn't anybody there who was prepared to do something. Everybody was afraid to take initiative. But she was there with a stroller with our son, and she had the copies of the declaration in the stroller. She looked around and saw many faces she knew, people from church, from town, just waiting to see what would happen. She started passing around the papers and then people came to her seeing that there was somebody. "Read it!" they said to her. "Read it so other people can hear. There aren't enough copies for everybody!" She was the first speaker in the square that day.

On November 28, Vaclav Havel, backed by representatives of the Czech Civic Forum and Slovakia's VPN, met with Vladimir Adamec, prime minister of the Czech and Slovak Socialist Federative Republics, to begin negotiations for what would essentially result in the handover of power from the Communist Party.[8] By the end of December, Havel was elected the president of Czechoslovakia, and free elections for the first time in 40 years were slated for June.[9]

GREEN SLOVAKIA

Within just a few weeks, the unthinkable had happened. Czechs and Slovaks now faced the prospect of building a new democratic system. This was, understandably, a period of tremendous public euphoria and great expectations throughout society. The *ochranári*, of course, hoped that the transition from socialism would be a markedly ecological one. These hopes were based on what appeared at the time to be overwhelming evidence. Nearly two-thirds of SZOPK's Bratislava City Committee had been among the direct architects of Public Against Violence (now headed by Ján Budaj, the editor of *Bratislava/nahlas*) or had been key supporters of the new civic movement. Other prominent members of SZOPK ZO 6 enjoyed high status as potential leaders in the new government. Butora, the sociologist and green sympathizer, was appointed as personal advisor to the newly elected President Havel. Eugen Gindl, a coauthor of *Bratislava/nahlas*, became the publisher of VPN's official newspaper, *Verejnosť* (The Public).

Peter Kresánek, a longtime member of zo 6, ran successfully for mayor of Bratislava. Mikuláš Huba already headed the Union of Nature and Landscape Protectors, an organization that by the close of 1989 numbered in the tens of thousands. Other szopk members served as organizational and operational volunteers for vpn, often working 18–hour days.[10] In no other case of the fall of communism had an environmental movement played such a central role. An American observer noted how Slovakia's ecology movement was not only "indistinguishable from the opposition [to the regime], but was in fact orchestrating it" (Endicott 1998:1).

One of the logical first steps to take, now that the Union found itself at center stage, was to form a new political party. In fact, plans for an ecology party had already been underway prior to the regime's collapse. Juraj Mesík, one of the party's founders, later explained that several *ochranári* had originally hatched the idea as a form of protest and confrontation, with little pretense that the organization would actually become a party. In the spirit of *Bratislava/nahlas*, these activists simply

> wanted to make the issues more prominent in society. An illegal party would serve such a purpose. The regime would have to explain why there was an illegal party, then the burden would be on the Communists to make sense of this action. That was the strategy (Mesík 1994).

Yet this quite daring plan, which could well have landed its organizers in prison, was foiled by the revolution itself. On November 18, just as demonstrations were forming in Prague and Bratislava, Mesík was in Hungary meeting with contacts there about the logistics of establishing an illegal green party. By the time he returned, other *ochranári* within the Union had already started to create an ecology party. On November 28, 1989, members of the Union announced the creation of the Green Party (Strana Zelených, sz), and a new term was now introduced into the Slovak vernacular: *zeleni* (the Greens).

Party activists characterized the Green Party as an "incorruptible political representative of the ideals of the nongovernmental organization szopk" (Pauliniova 1990). When the call for free elections was made a few days later, Green Party activists convened a federation-wide meeting in Počuvalda, a small village in central Slovakia, attended by delegates from Moravia and Bohemia.

The creation of an ecology party, however, raised some important questions for the rest of the *ochranári* in szopk. They wondered if other members of the Union would have to profess loyalty to the party. Others worried that the Green Party would siphon off SZOPK support from VPN. Still others wanted to know what, exactly, this new party meant to accomplish. The party's founders responded by pointing out that, since so many SZOPK activists took on leadership roles with VPN, their new party could only provide further support for what appeared to be turning into a hugely popular post-regime environmental movement. In the words of one new Green Party member,

> It only seemed natural to me to form the Green Party on the basis of the Bratislava *ochranári*. After all, we had experience under socialism with green issues. We knew what needed to be done. If there were to be a green party, it had to be on the basis of the movement. I began to draw up a platform based on the work I did as an *ochranár*. It was logical, right?

Their arguments were further supported by new public opinion polls, which showed that throughout the first half of 1990 ecology was at the top of a list of dozens of concerns among Slovaks (Center for Social Research 1990).

If these arguments were not enough, the need to create a Green Party became even more evident as concerns surfaced about VPN's ability to survive for the long term. VPN leaders saw as their immediate task to defeat the Communist Party, which was also allowed to participate in open elections slated for June. Although the regime had given up its power, the party was still intact, and people feared that the communists would find a way to win the elections. In order to secure victory at the polls, VPN tried to remain as comprehensive and inclusive as possible, titling its campaign A Chance for Slovakia. Many rank-and-file members of SZOPK supported VPN, with the understanding that beating the Communist Party in open battle was essential. One member of VPN reasoned that

> it was necessary to build a stable democracy before any real progress on the environment could be achieved. After the revolution we now had a chance to do this, to create a new system. This was a far greater project than anything I had imagined before 1989.

Thus, while VPN was explicit in its anticommunist position, it did not clearly state its position on other areas of social, economic, and political life.

In early 1990, a very clear justification for pushing forward with the new party came when the disclosure that Ján Budaj had collaborated with the secret police in the late 1970s raised doubts about the veracity of VPN leadership. With his prominent position in VPN, Budaj became one of the first victims of *lustrácia* (lustration), the process of locating people who had cooperated with security authorities under socialism whether for political, financial, or personal gain.[11] Such "collaborators" were immediately barred from holding public office for five years. Budaj, who had commanded such popularity before and during the Velvet Revolution, decided to step out of political life.[12]

Budaj's admission of past cooperation plunged Slovak society into a state of paranoia, and created internal tension among the *ochranári*. Other SZOPK members had also appeared on the ŠtB's list of informants and collaborators, particularly during the time of *Bratislava/nahlas*' publication. Although nothing could ever be proven, and it was likely that many of these names were listed as the result of fraud, rumors also began to surface that a Prague branch of the Green Party was being created by the secret police. Although no one could substantiate this allegation, people became suspicious. None of the Slovaks or Moravians who met in Počuvalda to found the party had personally known the people in the Prague delegation. Nor had any of the Prague activists been involved in conservationist circles in Bohemia. The fact that Prague party operatives had proposed regional party autonomy aroused further suspicions, particularly among Bratislava activists who saw environmentalism as a Czechoslovak movement. They wondered whether this was a move on the part of the secret police to divide the party's ranks. Fears of secret police infiltrators also surfaced among regional party activists when people with no prior experience with ecological issues began to aggressively seek leadership positions on local party committees. One informant explains,

> I was asked by many to help form the Green Party because they told me they were afraid that the secret police were starting one here in Slovakia. There were so many rumors about parties being created by the ŠtB, as a way to stay in power. I thought, why not? I felt that I could do a good job, and actually that I would be more qualified to help make a party, so I joined.

In light of what appeared to be regime conspirators seeking to divide and weaken the party, many SZOPK members felt that they should start to get personally involved. During the party's February congress in Brno, what was viewed as a bid by the Prague Greens to control the party was blocked by Slovak *ochranári*.

Whether motivated by political aspirations, green values, or communist conspiracies, most *ochranári* nevertheless considered their leadership roles to be temporary. Juraj Mesík, the party's first chairman, saw his role as that of an architect who would help build the organization and then move on.

> I did not want to be a politician. I did not want to be involved in politics all my life. The plan was to help create a green party and then go about my own business. The idea was to help create something, make it work, then let others do the actual business of politics. Perhaps it was rather naïve.

Like Mesík, other *ochranári* naïvely figured that as soon as the party was established, high-profile personalities from the Union, who had first joined VPN, would then take up leading roles in the Green Party. One *ochranár* recalled how

> no one who did the real work in forming the party became candidates. We had expected those leaders among the *ochranári* to come back from VPN and run under SZ. I certainly did not want to be a candidate. But I felt it was important to help form the party.

This spirit of reluctance was also evident among the candidates who actually decided to run on behalf of the party. For example, two of Strana Zelených's star candidates, Mikuláš Huba and Gabriela Kaliská, were both *Bratislava/nahlas* authors and prominent ZO 6 activists. Yet Kaliská, a professional ecologist, and Huba, the chairman of the Union's Central Committee, ultimately ran as independents on the Green Party list.

Like other new parties, the greens spent the first half of 1990 simultaneously building the party structure and campaigning. In their official announcement as a party on November 30, 1989, the Green Party defined post-socialist environmentalism in Slovakia as having two parts: "1) a political party (similar to those that existed in Western Europe) and 2) a nongovernmental organization that worked outside of politics (such as Friends of the Earth and Greenpeace)" (Pauliniova 1990:23). The party promised to operate as a formal political representative of the Union and to fight for the issues that it had established. By February 1990, one-third of SZOPK's membership had joined the Green Party. Going into the June elections, sz was relatively strong, boasting 50,000 members in Slovakia alone, far above the 10,000 needed to qualify as a party.

At the beginning of 1990, the Green Party polled well, receiving as high as 18 percent. It maintained an average of 10 percent right up to the early summer campaigns. In a mid-May poll, however, the party drew only 8 percent. On the eve of the elections, several polls predicted only 4 percent for the greens (Jehlicka and Kostelecky 1992:213). There were several reasons for this drop in support. First, even before the elections, Czechoslovakia's coalition government responded quickly to public concerns about pollution. Jozef Vavroušek, a Czech scientist and a szopk member, who had been a consultant for *Bratislava/nahlas*, was tapped by Marián Čalfa, Czechoslovakia's last Communist prime minister, to create and then head a new Federal Ministry of the Environment. By March 1990, separate environmental offices were established in each republic: a Czech Ministry of the Environment and a Slovak Commission for the Environment. The creation of these state organs signaled to the public early on that the government promised to do something about the country's severe environmental problems. Second, other political parties saw the value of including an environmental plank in their platform, a move foreshadowed by Jiři Dienstbier's response in the first days after the Revolution to a reporter's question as to whether there would be a green party. Dienstbier promptly replied, "This country needs all parties to be green" (Garton Ash 1990:109).

It turned out that to "be green" immediately after the Velvet Revolution was quite easy. Since no party except the communists had the burden of a prior political record, commitment to the environment could be demonstrated with mere campaign promises. Moreover, vpn could back up the environmental planks of its platform by simply referring to its origins in szopk. Many of its members also enjoyed widespread name recognition as conservationists. In fact, the real political battle quickly materialized over the challenge to produce a post-regime economic program. On this issue the Green Party had failed to take any specific stand. While it denounced the regime's over-industrialized planned economy, it also seemed to reject market reforms, which it described as rampant Western consumerism. Ultimately, vpn urged citizens not to cast ballots for any of the smaller parties in Slovakia, including the Greens, because, they argued, support for them would actually result in an indirect vote for the communists. Green Party activists saw this as a form of betrayal: "At first they [vpn] promised everything to us. Then they didn't want to form

TABLE 3.1 Results of the First Democratic Elections, Slovak Republic, June 1990

Political Party	Percentage	Seats (SNC)
Public Against Violence (VPN)	29.3	48
Christian Democratic Movement (KDH)	19.2	31
Slovak National Party (SNS)	14.0	22
Communist Party (KSS)	13.3	22
Hungarian Coalition	8.7	14
Democratic Party	4.4	7
Green Party (Strana Zelených)	3.5	6
Alliance of Agrarians	2.5	–
Social Democrats	1.8	–

Source: Štatistická ročenka CSFR 1991:630

some kind of coalition with us or a free collective. They wanted all the parties to join under the name of Public Against Violence."

Although relations between the two organizations began to cool during the campaign, most Green Party members continued to expect that their fellow *ochranári* in VPN would reach out to them to form a coalition after the elections were over.

Compared to election outcomes for the other new parties that formed after the Velvet Revolution, those for Slovakia's Green Party were less solid than expected but far from disappointing. In Slovakia, despite the overwhelming popularity of VPN, the Green Party received 3.5 percent of the vote (see table 3.1). In the Czech Lands it won a surprising 4.1 percent. In the end, neither outcome exceeded the 5 percent threshold needed to gain seats in the Federal Assembly or the Czech National Council. Due to the large number of parties registered in Slovakia, however, a minimum of only 3 percent had been set for the Slovak National Council. This resulted in six seats for the Slovak Greens, whose deputies now included the *ochranári* team from ZO 6 consisting of Mikuláš Huba and Gabriela Kaliská.[13] The Green Party had won a small but clear victory in the post-socialist political arena.

Communism's surprising and total collapse gave both Green Party activists and SZOPK members an intense hope for the future of the environmental movement. While Charter 77, under the charismatic and moral leadership of Vaclav Havel, was the heart and soul of the Czech Civic Forum, the *ochranári* had been the engine of Public Against Violence. After the Green Party gained a small foothold in the Slovak parliament, party activists and SZOPK members demonstrated their unity in the new free press by starting *Zelené Slovensko* (Green Slovakia), a weekly newspaper insert focused on ecology and on environmental politics.[14] Throughout 1990, week after week in the pages of *Zelené Slovensko* Slovaks could read about a wide spectrum of ideas and issues pertaining to the environment. From pollution to public policy, from politics to personal life, it was the antithesis of communist environmentality: open, altruistic, communal, and most of all candid. For the first time the public could read, without fear of the state finding them out, about the depth and scope of local and national ecological horror stories affecting their lives: a factory pouring chemical waste into nearby streams, the specific poisons in the city's drinking water, the details of brown coal consumption, and the sorry state of supposedly protected forests. But Slovaks also saw for the first time in the pages of *Zelené Slovensko* the internal and occasionally contentious debates within the movement itself.

In fact, *Zelené Slovensko* would prove to be the last public forum uniting the various members of Slovakia's ecology movement. The *ochranári* had seemingly won an immeasurable victory in the Velvet Revolution. With this victory, however, also came an important loss. The Slovak ecology movement's primary dialogical partner, the socialist state, was now gone. This fact did not mean that communist environmentality had disappeared along with it. Instead, the ideas and relationships against which Slovak environmentalism emerged—a narrow idea of nature, the exploitation of resources both material and cultural, the lack of diversity of views and opinions, and, not least, the construction of symbols to feed the power of the state—would simply become refashioned and realigned in the politics of post-socialism.

4 Nation over Nature

ON DECEMBER 10, 1989, SLOVAKS WERE ALLOWED TO LEAVE their country freely for the first time in over forty years. On that day, border officers cut through the barbed-wire fencing separating a corridor of overgrown grass along the perimeter of Petržalka from the manicured meadows and fields of Austria. Over 100,000 Slovaks walked through this small opening in the infamous Iron Curtain to the nearby Austrian village of Hainburg, a quiet community of only 6,000. This scene at the edge of Western Europe was later described by Juraj Podoba, a ZO 6 member, as utterly surreal. "A mass of people squeezed through the fence and just started walking. It was a weekend exodus. We went into the shops, and we were amazed at the products on the shelves, the abundance, the variety. Everyone was silent, just looking, just staring."

This incredible experience of being able to window-shop in the West, an experience that had been only a distant dream for so many, was but one of the many new freedoms resulting from the Velvet Revolution. For example, demonstrations were no longer illegal, and open expressions of opposition no longer state crimes. New publications and periodicals now decorated street kiosks. Many of these papers were offshoots of several *samizdat* publications that had been created in the final months of the regime, and a few, at least in the early days of the transition, looked to be of about the same home-produced quality. The biggest freedom, of course, was the opportunity to participate in politics. By January 1990, 68 new parties were formed.[1] Older, more traditional parties from Czechoslovakia's interwar state were dusted off, released from their confinement in the National Front, and resurrected as viable political entities.

It is now cliché to describe nongovernmental organizations after the collapse of communism in East Europe and the former Soviet Union as sprouting, popping up, or proliferating like "mushrooms after a spring rain" (Stokes 1993). Yet this worn-out simile is nevertheless a quite accurate depiction of the relatively rapid emergence of a new civil society throughout most of East Europe. In Slovakia, however, independent environmental NGOs actually took much more time to appear after the fall of communism than the other groups which made up Slovakia's post-socialist civil society. Among these were religious and charitable associations, media foundations, women's NGOs, and social and health service organizations. Two obvious reasons for this tardiness in the area of ecology were the tremendous popularity and the national scope of SZOPK during socialism. At the very beginning of the transition, SZOPK's overwhelming influence on environmental politics and policy appeared to be a foregone conclusion. Even with the creation of an ecology party by some of its former activists, and despite the fact that it was now possible to create new independent NGOs, most *ochranári* remained with the organization. This decision seemed logical in light of the social and political impact that the Union had made just prior to the regime's collapse. As further evidence, new national opinion polls placed ecology at or near the top of public concerns, above even unemployment and rising crime (Center for Social Research 1990).

But if the *ochranári* had managed to bring nature into the realm of culture, culture was also undergoing a significant transformation in the wake of communism's fall. This was not only the case in Czechoslovakia but throughout East Europe in 1990, and, two years later, in the former Soviet Republics. The immediate post-socialist atmosphere was framed not simply by the question of who would now run the country (which in some cases, like that of Nursultan Nazarbayev in Kazakhstan, would be the same person who ran it before) but also by differing ideas regarding what these new societies and their new economies would look like. Would they have completely free markets or large state-owned sectors? Would political power be centralized or dispersed? In Czechoslovakia, very different answers to these questions would appear along ethnic lines, sparking a resurgence of nationalism, most notably in the Slovak half of the federation. In fact, by October of 1990, the so-called "nationality problem" catapulted past all other public concerns and began to pull both culture and nature into a dialogue about place (Center for Social Research 1990; 1991).

Only three years after the Velvet Revolution, on January 1, 1993, Slovakia officially broke away from the Czech Republic, and each became an independent state.[2] The cause of the split was a confluence of several events, a mix of separate histories, perceived past wrongs, uneven development during state socialism, and present insecurities about the future. Not everyone had supported the breakup, either in Slovakia or in the Czech Lands. There had been much debate about how to resolve differences between the two societies, and little clear agreement on proposed compromises. But many Slovaks (and Czechs) appeared to approve of the change. In Slovakia, the occasion was celebrated by a larger-than-usual onslaught of the fireworks and parties that traditionally mark St. Sylvester's Day, the start of the new year.

Most of the *ochranári* from ZO 6 had been opposed to this so-called Velvet Divorce, not only because they had considered the environment to be a Czechoslovak issue, but also because the division of the country distracted society from what they viewed as more important problems facing Slovakia's future. These issues included the lack of effective environmental laws, the absence of a state body with power to enforce such laws, and the continuation of what they considered to be environmentally harmful state-owned projects, such as the Mochovce nuclear power plant, which was slated to be built with a Chernobyl-quality safety system.

The return of nationalism, which was a pervasive phenomenon early on in the transition, had a significant impact on the Slovak ecology movement. The ecology movement at first followed what appeared to be two complementary paths after the fall of the regime. While most *ochranári* remained in the Union, hoping to play a leading role in Slovakia's nascent civil society, a few entered politics through the Green Party. As the transition progressed, however, both paths became direct engagements with the politics of nationalism, with important implications for future activism. Many of the *ochranári* who remained in the Union actually stoked nationalist fires in the attempt to fight them. In the case of the Green Party, its supporters either directly promoted the politics of identity or saw no choice but to follow the crowd. If freedom had opened the way for Slovaks to experience a new social intimacy through national pride, this same freedom seemed at first to push the rest of the world, including the environment, to the sidelines of public discourse. Such an assessment, however, which several *ochranári* attempted to advance as events unfolded, was perhaps a naïve evaluation. Instead of pushing nature aside, nationalists reclaimed nature as their own, and in the process initiated the emergence of an ethnicized environmentality in post-socialist Slovakia.

THE RETURN OF SLOVAK NATIONALISM

The arrival of new political forms does not necessarily mean the appearance of new ideas. Old ideas may just as easily be reconfigured and repositioned into new political relationships. This was the case with the idea of an independent Slovak state, a very old idea in the historical and political experience of Slovak culture and society. For centuries, Slovaks had lived under Hungarian (Madar) rule in Europe and underwent, during the mid-nineteenth century, a process of acculturation described as madarization. Madarization primarily involved the restriction of formal education to the Hungarian language. Education was a requirement of the kinds of professions and livelihoods in the Habsburg Empire that allowed access to modern European society. The alternative was the life of the peasant, which the majority of Slovaks followed well into the early twentieth century. When the state of Czechoslovakia was created in 1918, under Wilsonian principles of self-determination, Slovaks, now free from Hungarian domination, ironically disappeared as a distinct identity. As junior partners in a democratic experiment, the Slovak half of the country served as an agricultural support system for an industrialization and modernization process in the Czech Lands. For many Slovaks, then, the opportunity to have their own state, on the eve of the Second World War, was an attractive one, despite the controversial conditions under which it would be possible. From 1939 to 1945, Slovakia became independent, but under the sponsorship of Nazi Germany. Slovaks still debate whether this state was built upon and led according to a fascist ideology of blood and soil. But its existence was short-lived anyway. Communism brought Czechs and Slovaks back together in 1948 and, as in other ethnic narratives throughout East Europe, united anachronistic "nations" in pursuit of a Marxist utopia.

This was the short version, and the short version was what many Slovaks who championed separating from the Czech Lands of Bohemia and Moravia often promoted. It was a narrative of oppression under shifting oppressors. The icons of autonomy and self-rule, such as Jozef Tiso, the Catholic priest who led Slovakia's wartime independent state, unfortunately indexed an ethnic chauvinism in the eyes of Western observers, and for many Slovaks and Czechs who did not support independence as well. There were other icons of Slovak nationalism, including Antonin Bernolak and Ludovit Štur, who codified the Slovak language by the mid-nineteenth century, and Matica slovenská, the Slovak cultural organization, formed in 1863, which had served over a century as a caretaker of ethnic national consciousness.[3] But it was Tiso and the very real example of the wartime state that provided supporters of Slovak autonomy with a recent enough precedent to make their arguments resonate.

Therefore, as winter 1990 gave way to spring, public gatherings concerning Slovakia's identity in the post-communist state of Czechoslovakia started to appear. Rallies by the new Slovak National Party (SNS) in March 1990, held on the very same site as the Velvet Revolution's mass meetings in Bratislava, called for greater rights for Slovakia in the federative partnership. Some in the crowds even demanded outright independence. The November cries of "Dubček, Dubček!" honoring the reformer of Czechoslovak socialism during the Prague Spring, were substituted with demonstrations displaying photographs of Father Tiso (Butora, Butorova, and Rosova 1991:436). Not surprisingly, these new demonstrations used some of the same symbols and slogans that were used in 1989. "The clinking of keys or spontaneous collecting of money at their meetings . . . tried to create the impression of a natural continuation of the Revolution" (ibid.:436). Renewed cries of "Slovaks, Stand Up!" however, did not refer to a resistance against totalitarianism, but were "transformed by supporters of the [SNS] into a shout demanding rights for those connected not only by the same blood, the same mother tongue, the common soil of their forefathers, but also their plebian origin from time immemorial" (ibid.:436). The focus of discontent at these public rallies was, surprisingly, Public Against Violence, which supported the notion of keeping Slovaks and Czechs within the same state. With shouts of "*Totalita VPN!*" supporters of the Slovak National Party accused VPN activists of despotism and corruption.

While members of the far right Slovak National Party were instrumental in sparking the flames of nationalism, the politician mainly responsible for fanning those flames and shaping them into a political discourse was Vladimir Mečiar. Mečiar did not start out as a nationalist. At one point, during a television interview, he berated the president of Matica slovenská, the revitalized Slovak cultural organization, for his nationalist stance (Kirschbaum 2005). Mečiar became Slovakia's prime minister in 1990 as a member of VPN, but broke away from the civic movement in 1991 to form the Movement for a Democratic Slovakia (HZDS). Mečiar and his HZDS supporters viewed VPN, which was led at the time by Fedor Gál, a former *ochranár* from ZO 6, as too closely oriented toward Prague politics. VPN retaliated by having Mečiar dismissed as prime minister. Ján Čarnogursky, a Catholic dissident who had led the Secret Church under communism and who led the Christian Democratic Party (KDH), temporarily replaced Mečiar. In mid-1992, HZDS won Czechoslovakia's second round of elections following the Velvet Revolution, and Mečiar again became prime minister, a post he would hold on to until 1998. Through HZDS, Mečiar began to capitalize on a growing nationalist sentiment in Slovakia and effectively used it to consolidate his power.

Slovakia's national revitalization, however, must also be understood in light of events elsewhere in Eastern Europe. In fact, the entire region witnessed a resurgence of ethnic and national movements among minority populations that had either been tightly controlled or gingerly tempered by the communist regimes. Ethnically homogeneous states, such as Hungary, began to express solidarity with their minority communities in other states. For instance, in 1990 Jozef Antall, the new president of Hungary, proclaimed that he was the leader of 15 million Hungarians, of whom only 60 percent actually lived in Hungary. The fact that 600,000 of Antall's Maďars lived in Slovakia only served to justify Slovak insecurities about their own identities vis-à-vis their Czech partners, and instilled significant concern about the potential for ethnic violence. Indeed, Slovak-Hungarian relations in the post–Cold War world started out rough, and intensified with Hungary's withdrawal from the joint Gabčíkovo-Nagymáros dam project at the beginning of 1990. As I will explain below, this Hungarian departure from the project was only the beginning of a wave of nationalist attention on the part of Slovaks centering on the Gabčíkovo Dam. Conversely, Hungarians, especially those living in Slovakia, became alarmed by growing public debates in Slovakia about setting language policies for minorities, which targeted mainly Hungarians and Gypsies. The specter of ethnic-based disputes leading to violence loomed large in the minds of people in both Hungary and Slovakia. Real-world examples were close to hand. In June 1991, for example, Slovenia and Croatia declared independence from Yugoslavia. War broke out that autumn in the Balkans, continuing in various manifestations of ethnic conflict until the Dayton Peace Accords put a stop to the war in Bosnia in 1995.

In addition to an ongoing dispute with ethnic Hungarians, Slovak nationalism was also fuelled by grievances with the Czech half of the federation over its strategy of economic reform. Expressed broadly as Prague-centrism, Slovaks' concerns included the pace of reform and the decision of Vaclav Klaus, the Czech prime minister, to back a rapid transition strategy, whereby privatization would occur quickly and comprehensively. By late 1991, Slovakia was suffering from an unemployment rate of 11 percent and in some places as high as 20 percent (FBIS 1991:8), evidence that a quick move to market capitalism would be much more painful for Slovaks than for the Czechs. Unemployment in the Czech Lands, by comparison, was low, holding steady at 5 percent. For many people in Slovakia struggling with rising prices of even the most basic foodstuffs, the Czech push for accelerated economic reform appeared as yet another example of Prague's lack of concern for the country's historically junior partner. A growing number of Slovaks interpreted this indifference as part of an ongoing relationship in which Czechs viewed Slovaks as the federation's "backward" second-class citizens.

The return of nationalism in the Czech Republic did not help matters either. Miroslav Sladek's Republican Party embraced the ideas of right-wing extremism, which focused on the Roma minority and on Vietnamese guest workers as threats to the well-being of Czechs in the post-socialist transition. Czech skinheads openly supported the Republicans at their increasingly frequent public rallies. Sladek's proposal to send the Gypsies "back to the south [meaning Slovakia] from whence they came" (Hockenos 1993) only confirmed for many Slovaks the need to counter such overt xenophobia and protect their own struggling society.

Slovak nationalism thus had pre-communist origins and post-communist influences. Once nationalist sentiments flared, under the deft political guidance of Mečiar they permeated almost every nook and cranny of political life. During the initial stages of this return to nationalism, two particular developments within Slovakia's environmental community pushed ecology directly into the arena of identity politics. The first involved SZOPK's public debut as a post-communist activist organization. In early 1990, the Union boldly decided to take on the Gabčíkovo Dam project and try to stop its completion. The second was a debate within the fledgling Green Party about its own identity. It was one of the only parties in either the Czech Republic or Slovakia to have been created as a federal party, and now the federation appeared to be falling apart at the seams. Below I examine how, in both of these cases, nationalism dominated and almost destroyed ecology before the transition from communism had even gained momentum.

CASE ONE: GABČÍKOVO AND THE ENEMIES OF SLOVAKIA

After the regime's demise, SZOPK decided for several reasons to step up its opposition to the Gabčíkovo Dam project . First, throughout its years serving as the voice of ecology under communism, the Union had always been against any version of the dam that had been under consideration by the Czechoslovak government. Although it had not made the dam a focal point of its challenge to the regime, the group had gathered a substantial amount of information about the project's negative impact on the Danube River ecosystem. Second, Hungarian opposition to the sister dam at Nagymáros, led by the Danube Circle, a Hungarian environmental group, had been a huge success. Activists in the Danube Circle marshaled tremendous public support in favor of shutting down the dam at Nagymáros, which at the time was about 20 percent completed. In August 1989, a reform-minded Hungarian parliament decided to stop their side of the project (Harper 2005). On the eve of the Velvet Revolution, the dam at Gabčíkovo was about 80 percent finished. But after witnessing how Hungary's environmental movement had practically built itself up on the dam issue alone, and in light of their own popularity among the public, Slovak activists saw in Gabčíkovo an opportunity to continue their momentum as a movement. Third, the Union thought that by opposing Gabčíkovo, it could link up with other East European environmentalists who were against the project and increase its stature at an international level. Fourth, the *ochranári* truly expected that the new Green Party would be successful in the first post-regime elections, in 1990. Last, and certainly not least, they assumed that Public Against Violence, whose primary leaders had been members of the Union, would support them politically in their fight to stop the dam.

At the end of 1989, several SZOPK members formed ZO Podunajsko, a special basic organization created specifically to research the environmental impact of the government's project.[4] Through this organization, the Union opened its 1990 campaign with a combination of public awareness initiatives, petitions, and lobbying efforts. ZO Podunajsko took an uncompromising position, refusing to accept any variation proposed by the state and cheekily proposing its own Variant H, which called for abandoning the project entirely, returning the river to its natural course, and creating a nature preserve.

But the Union's lobbying efforts in the new democracy proved disappointing, particularly when it became evident that several Green Party deputies refused to take a firm position on the dam project. One activist explained that "Huba would back us, I knew this. But the other [Green] deputies, they said that the dam wasn't good, but they only proposed alternatives. Our allies in the parliament were not really allies. They were concerned with their own political survival."

Despite the ambiguous position regarding the project among its allies in the parliament, the Union began a series of public demonstrations, which they organized in cooperation with newly contacted environmental groups in Austria and Hungary under the moniker Eurochain. Eurochain involved the creation of a human chain along the Danube River, stretching from Hainburg, Austria, passing through Slovakia at Gabčíkovo, and ending at Komárno, in Hungary. The first demonstration took place in February 1990, but with only a few Slovaks from SZOPK participating. Most of the 60,000 protestors were Austrian and Hungarian activists and citizens. A few months later, Eurochain planned an even bolder action. In July, several Slovaks, along with their Austrian partners, chained themselves to a pumping station at the dam construction site. The activists prevented the opening of the pump with which workers were to begin filling a canal that was part of the dam system. The protestors remained locked to the pump for a month, until they were physically removed by Slovak police and project guards. Activists' claims of police harassment and beatings were published along with photographs showing officers forcibly dragging demonstrators from the area.

The Eurochain protest could be characterized as the first "direct action" campaign in Slovakia, where individuals tried to physically prevent the operation of environmentally damaging technology. Despite the international attention that the demonstration attracted, a participant described the protest as a futile effort to effect change among the Slovak public.

We had the attention of the whole of Europe, even the international community. But we could not get the attention of the Slovak government. They would not listen to us. They just continued with the project as if there was nothing stopping them. We even made it a point not to have Hungarians from Hungary at the demonstrations. We wanted to show that the residents of Slovakia were also against the dam. That here, too, was also a voice against the project. This is why we did the blockade.

In response to the protest, Julius Binder, the project's chief engineer and the dam's major public relations figure, quickly redefined the project in cultural terms, circumventing ecological arguments with questions about the future of Slovakia's energy situation.[5] He argued that the fight for Gabčíkovo was "the political fight for the Slovak Republic, for the nation" (*Slovenská Republika*, April 29, 1993). "It is a case of what an entire generation has given as a tangible certificate of maturity and technical courage, not only for itself but for the whole nation as well" (ibid.). Binder craftily characterized the dam as a "place of national pilgrimage" where Slovaks gathered to celebrate their independence at the site of a work of "national honor and pride" (Binder 1993). In fact, by 1993, the dam was proudly featured in promotional brochures published by the Slovak government as a national monument and a must-see tourist attraction for visitors to Bratislava. On any given weekday, one could join hundreds of Slovak schoolchildren on a scenic boat ride down the Danube to the hydroelectric plant, to closely observe the massive system of locks in operation and to witness, firsthand, the irrefutable evidence that Slovakia had arrived on the European stage.

In a joint interview in *Mosty*, a Czecho-Slovak news weekly, Binder faced off with Mikuláš Huba, who was now serving as a Green Party deputy and one of the few in parliament who vociferously opposed the project. Huba sincerely presented a set of complex arguments, including a detailed account of the dam's threat to the biological diversity of the region's microenvironments. But his technical expertise, demonstrated with scientific terms that were likely unfamiliar to the broader public, was no match for Binder's simple and vivid remarks about the practical needs of a new society. Binder skillfully positioned the dam in a symbolic landscape of a Central Europe rife with aggressive and threatening neighbors. He argued that

[the Danube Circle's] aim was not (and is not) to search for the best environmental and economic solution but rather . . . to damage the Czechoslovak— and especially the Slovak—economy . . . In this unstable political and economic situation they could better pursue the policy of autonomy for Hungarian minorities and, later, the restoration of the Hungarian Empire (*Mosty*, May 1995).

The Union tried to respond to Binder's rhetoric of national identity with its own symbolic weapons. Activists frequently characterized the project as a "vestige of state socialism" and as a "monument of totalitarianism" (SZOPK 1993). The *ochranári* belligerently and sarcastically proposed their own variant, Variant H, which they promised would ensure the protection of the "natural value of the Central Danube Region" because it involved scrapping the entire project (Šibl 1993:1). Despite the fact that Jozef Vavroušek, a former SZOPK member who was now Czechoslovakia's first Minister of the Environment, saw the project as a check on the inefficient and polluting burning of brown coal, the Union continued to condemn the plan as totalitarian paternalism and state manipulation of the public mind.

The public, of course, responded to the side that placed the dam in a national context, imbuing it with cultural and social meaning beyond mere energy production. Binder's media campaign inspired intense emotion and public support for Gabčíkovo. He successfully repackaged the communist-era project as a Slovak dam that the people required as a fundamental coordinate of their new post-socialist identity. In the post-socialist world, Binder claimed, Slovakia needed a piece of the Danube. The Union's conservationist paradigm, which argued vaguely for Slovaks to respect the sovereignty of nature, was woefully ineffective against such a shrewdly packaged symbolic discourse of national sentiment. And as the dam became a central focus in what was becoming an international dispute between Hungary and Slovakia, the Union's continued attempts to challenge the project only became more futile. In a media environment that was increasingly saturated with nationalist representations of Gabčíkovo, any press coverage gained by SZOPK for its protests only served to harm the organization's reputation. Activists initially and naïvely assumed that, given their popularity after *Bratislava/nahlas*, people would listen to evidence and seriously consider their well-researched arguments, which had been proven in the past to represent the public's best interests. The *ochranári* figured that the state would respond to their concerns with challengeable technical inaccuracies or bogus environmental impact reports, which could be used to demonstrate to the public how little the authorities had changed concerning environmental matters. With this strategy in mind, the *ochranári* continued to vigorously and consistently characterize the dam as "a legacy of a state socialist megalomania" (Šibl 1993). But it was ultimately the dam's builders and the Ministry of Forestry and Water Management who successfully assumed the role of defenders of the public good. Binder and the Ministry couched the dam's narrative in terms of Slovak self-sufficiency in the sphere of energy production and Slovak technical proficiency in realizing such a goal. Ever the savvy politician, Prime Minister Mečiar cleverly inverted SZOPK's position that the dam was a totalitarian misstep by borrowing the *ochranári*'s old strategy of using nature as a culturally unifying antipolitical message. He resituated environmental discourse to frame Hungarian opposition to the actions of the Slovak state, boldly advocating, "On the Danube apply the laws of nature, not political solutions" (*Narodná Obroda* October 30, 1992). With this invocation of the power of *príroda* in support of national autonomy, Mečiar undermined Slovakia's domestic environmental movement, of which SZOPK was the lone representative.

The fight against Gabčíkovo was the public debut of Slovakia's environmental community after state socialism. Yet, unlike *Bratislava/nahlas*, where the regime was challenged to respond to ecological maladies that the public was aware of but was unable to discuss openly, the *ochranári*'s battle against Gabčíkovo was a fight in which environmentalists had the tremendous burden of proof. They needed to articulate their opposition to the project in a manner that all Slovaks could identify with. Their failure to meet this burden brought environmentalism under the scrutiny of a post-socialist public restless with identity politics and suspicious of outside assessments of Slovakia. The Gabčíkovo campaign only amplified the few but increasing links that activists were forging with international environmental organizations. Greenpeace International, the World Wildlife Fund, and Friends of the Earth all came out in support of the Hungarian, Austrian, and Slovak organizations that collectively challenged the dam project. Many Slovaks learned about these international environmental NGOs for the first time through local news stories covering SZOPK protests against the dam. Not surprisingly, they concluded from the pro-dam coverage that these international groups did not represent the interests of Slovak society.

As a symbol of Slovak sovereignty that was clearly helping alleviate transition anxieties among the public, Gabčíkovo also became a litmus test for the goals and loyalties of the Slovak Green Party. Five out of the six deputies in parliament ended up supporting the dam's completion, driving a wedge between SZOPK and its sister organization in the new parliament. Nevertheless, Slovak activists refused to abandon their opposition and continued to confront proponents of the project with the globalist arguments of an environmental discourse that offered a broad social critique, but no clear answers to the present problems Slovaks faced. The Eurochain campaign not only failed miserably, but irreversibly damaged the reputation of SZOPK, permanently straining its relationship with government authorities. Moreover, as the country moved further into the transition, SZOPK activists found it difficult to disassociate themselves from the controversy, even as they tried to pursue other ecological issues. The battle against Gabčíkovo would not be easily erased in continuing dialogues between environmentalists and the larger community. In 1993, Binder charged,

> Huba, Šibl, Mesík, Trubiniova . . . if these are so-called friends of Slovakia, then Slovakia does not need any enemies. They are very dangerous people. And various governmental organizations to which they have appointed themselves, who say they are ecological, in actuality they are not. They are organizations paid from outside. Paid so that they can destroy us (*Slovenská Republika*, April 29, 1993).

In a desperate move to return Slovakia's environmental movement to the revolutionary and inclusive spirit of 1989, Mikuláš Huba and his colleague, Peter Kresánek, who was now mayor of Bratislava, sent a letter to the Pope.

> Dear Holy Father, we turn to you because, as you know, 22 April, the day of your first visit to Slovakia, was at the same time announced as the day of the Earth . . . for the survival of the planet. We would be very grateful (thankful) if you would, in the spirit of your New Year's message, also address (for the people of Slovakia) the challenge to give more respect to their natural and cultural heritage (Huba 1990).

Other former members of the City Committee of SZOPK also published a plea against the rise of nationalism in the public arena.

> For many years now our City organization, whose membership includes members of Czech and Hungarian nationalities alongside its Slovak members, has attempted concrete activities, without pay and in our own free time, to save and propagate threatened natural and cultural values not only in Bratislava but all over Slovakia. Thus we understood and today understand patriotism—measured by our relationship to Slovakia, our homeland—to be actions and not empty slogans (*Narodná Obroda*, November 30, 1990:6).

Yet, along with challenging "each citizen . . . to celebrate understanding and tolerance" SZOPK activists cynically and condescendingly accused society of cowardice during socialism. "We ask, 'Where were you in the past, loud patriots of today's tribune? Who hindered you then to love Slovakia and to demonstrate this to her with actions?'" (ibid.:6). But the names attached to the statement were those of individuals who themselves had not been actively part of the organization. All of the members of the City Committee were now involved with other work, whether representing the Green Party, managing Public Against Violence, writing for a newly independent media, or advising the new federal government. The Velvet Revolution pulled away many of the charismatic and capable individuals who had made SZOPK the most active social movement in Slovakia. Those who had remained with the organization were now being labeled enemies of Slovakia, an identity they would carry into the rest of the decade.

CASE TWO: THE SLOVAK GREEN PARTY

When the Green Party was founded, most *ochranári* in SZOPK thought it was a logical expansion of the socialist-era environmental movement and would serve as an effective political mouthpiece for the movement and as an ecological watchdog in the Slovak National Council. As other scholars have noted, most of the founding members of SZ were veterans of Slovakia's environmental movement under state socialism, with no previous relationships with other parties or political traditions (Frankland 1995; Jehlicka and Kostelecky 1992; Waller 1989). Of all the new political personalities after the collapse of communism, Green Party activists seemed well suited to serve as a voice for ecology in the new parliament.[6]

By late 1990, however, the Green Party unexpectedly found itself confronting questions of cultural identity, including its own. For example, as the debate over the future relationship between Slovaks and Czechs—the so-called "hyphen battle"—took center stage, Green Party deputies were forced to put aside proposals for new environmental laws and weigh in on the increasingly popular debate about Slovak autonomy. The Slovak National Party submitted a bill crafted by Matica slovenská, the Slovak cultural organization, demanding the creation of a language law. The law would mandate Slovak as the official language of the republic. VPN supported a slightly less hegemonic version that limited requiring knowledge of Slovak to government offices. To the surprise of many *ochranári* who remained outside of formal politics, Gabriela Kaliská, a Green Party deputy, was one of the six members of parliament to propose passage of the Matica Act into law. The other five deputies were from the overtly nationalist SNS. Kaliská argued her case in the pages of none other than *Zelené Slovensko*. In an article entitled "My Slovak," she suggested that the Matica proposal would facilitate the integration of the Hungarian minority into Slovak society. She demanded that the "Slovak Republic must, according to the Matica proposal, secure for each citizen universal conditions for completely acquiring the Slovak language" (*Zelené Slovensko*, October 17, 1990). She rejected the more moderate VPN proposal on the grounds that it would increase the disintegration of Slovak society, asking "Is [Slovak] not needed elsewhere in life?" (ibid.).

Reaction to Kaliská's move from within the Green Party membership was mixed, and exposed a substantial degree of disunity on many issues beyond ecology. One member from Moldava nad Bodvou protested that "SZ must not put the interests of one group over another . . . the problems which led to the creation of Straná Zelenych are global problems and common to the whole world. Therefore, the policies of SZ must have a character that is beyond nationality and above ideologies" (SZ Moldava nad Bodovou 1990). The local party leadership from Čadca, however, supported Kaliská's position with the argument that "we have decided to [support the act] from bitter experiences in southern Slovakia where we cannot understand the Hungarian part of the population." They closed their anti-Hungarian statement, however, with the qualification that they did not "want to separate from the Czechs" (ibid.).

In fact, as discussion about various versions of the language law intensified within the party, Kaliská once again drew the Green Party into an internal debate about Slovak national identity. On September 23, 1991, less than a year after the language law proposal, she introduced a motion in parliament to resolve the question concerning Slovak sovereignty (*zvrchovanosť*).[7] Kaliská openly championed some form of greater Slovak autonomy from the Czechs. Four other Green Party deputies backed her proposal. This motion by a representative of a federal party shocked many *ochranári*, who had not only cooperated with Czechs before the revolution, but who had also considered it the role of the Green Party to place ecological problems, which were supposedly beyond identity politics, at the top of the party's list for parliamentary action. At the same time, Kaliská's move to assume a leadership role in the parliamentary debate over Slovak sovereignty inspired other Green Party members to propose that the party disassociate itself from the federal party structure and operate solely as a Slovak political party. In response to Kaliská's proposal, several of the Green Party's founders wrote a critical article in *Zelené Slovensko* accusing Kaliská and other deputies of abandoning the party's main role, to act as a political representative of the NGO environmental movement by prioritizing ecology in the National Council.

As the debate about the character and priorities of the party continued, most of the Green Party's founders quit the organization. This first split among party activists resembled the fissure that developed within the German Green Party in the mid-1980s. But unlike the fate of its West European neighbor, which divided over the issue of building a coalition with traditional left parties, resulting in a compromise of political practice (Bramwell 1994; Kitschelt 1989), the Green Party's first schism materialized around the issue of national identity, and thus became a compromise of cultural politics. The fault lines were broadly characterized in the press as a separation between "federalist" and "nationalist" greens (Fabian 1992). Other political parties in Slovakia did not have to face this problem. In fact, the Green Party was the only Slovak party that was established on a federal level, with affiliated organizations in both Bohemia and Moravia. But the split was more than just this simple division of geography, and was interpreted by members themselves in various ways. These varied interpretations grew out of important differences in environmental political philosophies, ethnic identities, and the experience of party members in the pre-transition environmental movement.

The "federalists" held firm to the position that the Green Party should prioritize the environment over all other political issues. For some, this meant maintaining a Czechoslovak identity so as to include all constituents in a dialogue about ecological degradation, something that did not confine itself within borders or to particular nations, and that affected not only Czechoslovakia but other countries in the region as well. Although the Slovak environmental movement had developed quite separately from its counterpart in the Czech Lands, there had been a degree of cooperation between the two. Now that the regime was gone, many *ochranári* hoped to significantly increase cooperation between Slovak and Czech activists. The continuation of this cooperation was viewed by the "federalists" as vital to solving environmental problems and ensuring that new ecological legislation would be effective. As Federal Minister of the Environment, Vavroušek had encouraged such collaboration based on his own personal involvement with the Slovak *ochranári* under socialism, and he remained a proponent of an integrated Czech and Slovak environmental movement, in both its political and its nongovernmental forms.

Although geography was not the sole determinant of the divide between federalists and nationalists, there were some identifiable trends. One local sz organization that backed the pro-federal wing was located in Čadca, a town on the Moravian-Slovak border. Its members argued, in a letter to party leaders, that having a federal party was essential. They noted that

> on the other side of the Morava River is the Czech Republic and the main coal power plant in Hodonin, which is the largest source of ecological destruction in our town. How would a nationally oriented sz stop the pollution from the Czech Republic that settles in our territory? (sz Čadca 1990).

For many Green Party organizations based in Slovakia's border towns, it was clear from their own experience that environmental degradation did not discriminate between nations. Moreover, these party members had closer ties with local Czech greens, and they considered the federal orientation of the party to be essential for effective cooperation on transborder issues. Not surprisingly, local Green Party organizations in southern Slovakia also supported a federal orientation, particularly on the grounds that ethnic identity should not dictate the spirit of the party. Since many parts of southern Slovakia had large Hungarian minorities, sz organizations in this region often included significant numbers of ethnic Hungarian members. This was the case despite the fact that several Hungarian parties, which formed specifically to represent this ethnic minority, dominated these border areas, a fact that caused great concern among Slovak nationalists in other parts of the country, to the consternation of local Slovaks who had lived side-by-side with Hungarians their entire lives. For example, the Green Party office in Komárno, on the Hungarian border, spelled out its view in a letter to the party leadership after the Piešťany Congress in February of 1991.

> In our ranks we also have colleagues of Hungarian nationality, to whom we must take as the truth that the "Slovak" Green Party has begun to elastically and distinctly submit to the general political mood of the Slovak political scene. It seems to us that many "patriotic" members of sz have already removed the word "ecology" from their dictionaries (sz Komárno 1991).

One SZ leader in Šahy, another Slovak-Hungarian border town, vehemently opposed the idea of a nationally oriented party with the statement that "although I am a Maďar, I am a Czechoslovak! The Green Party should be a green party, not a green-brown [fascist] party."

Other federalists hailed from the ranks of the Bratislava *ochranári*. Most of them had been active members of the pre-1989 movement and could take credit for founding the party during the Velvet Revolution. Taking the view that the Green Party should be an ecological party above all other political ideologies, these fundamentalists argued that the idea of federalism inherently supported an ecological worldview. They recalled that under state socialism the *ochranári* in SZOPK ZO 6 had prioritized openness, altruism, and collective action for the environment. Although these activists had focused most of their campaigns during socialism on ecological problems in Slovakia and not in Bohemia or Moravia, throughout the communist period they had desired to work more closely with Czechs and Hungarians and to develop relationships with international organizations. Federalists believed that a Czecho-Slovak Green Party would offer an alternative choice for people who believed it important to solve environmental problems, and for which such problems transcended republic-based politics and nationalist debates.

The nationalists in the Green Party, however, used a similar rationale in their fight against federalism. They argued that most voters in Slovakia would support a nationally oriented ecological party, and that the environment was better served if the country operated independently from the Czech Lands. As such, it would attract more voters who clearly wanted to support the environment but who felt strongly about the need for more basic rights for Slovaks vis-à-vis Prague or who were worried about Hungarian chauvinism. These nationalist arguments were essentially pragmatic, resembling the arguments of "realists" in the German Green Party as it forged a coalition with the Social Democrats (Bramwell 1994:93). Some nationalists explained Deputy Kaliská's support of the Matica Act as a pragmatic attempt to form a coalition with the Slovak National Party in order to increase the party's political capital and staying power in parliament.

When most of the Green Party deputies decided to support the Gabčíkovo Dam project, they argued that large hydropower projects were realistic solutions to the country's energy problems. If Slovakia existed outside of the influence of the Czechs, the institutions put in place for overseeing environmental legislation would operate more effectively. Slovak green politics needed to be defined in a Slovak political arena. The "realists" wanted first to define the boundaries within which environmentalism could operate. Furthermore, they argued, a national party could better integrate elements of the NGO movement if it represented greens in Slovakia alone.

Both federalists and nationalists accused the other side of not acting in the interest of the environment. To make matters worse, both camps were further divided internally. Among the "nationalists" were "autonomists" and "pragmatists." The autonomists held a local view of environmental politics, desiring not only "independence" from the Czechs as a party, but total decentralization of the party. These individuals saw the leadership of SZ as dominated by Bratislava activists. The pragmatists in the nationalist camp felt that seeking compromises on other, higher-profile political issues was necessary in order to make gains for the environment in the future. This pragmatism was represented by Peter Sabo, the party's second chairman and one of the six deputies in the Slovak National Council. Sabo, a conservationist from Piešťany, took a long-term approach, and supported the nationalists over the federalists in the hope of maintaining the party's political survival. As a compromiser, however, Sabo lost support from both factions and subsequently capitulated to the more vocal autonomist wing.

In the federalist bloc there were divisions as well. In one camp was Mikuláš Huba, a green fundamentalist and, at the time, one of the party's deputies in the Council. He refused to compromise on what he viewed as the party's ecological priorities and declined to participate in debates about Slovak autonomy. Huba constantly argued for a federal environmental platform that was transnational in scope. Representing yet another faction was Juraj Podoba, a party founder who wanted the organization to follow a Western European green party model. For Podoba, green politics were certainly based on sound environmental policy, but included other social and economic issues, which necessarily involved resolving questions of national identity within the federal structure of Czechoslovakia. In an article in *Zelené Slovensko,* Podoba asked,

> Where do greens belong? What do we want from our party? Will it be an ecological party in Slovakia which will be interested only in problems of the environment, and on remaining political questions be without conceptions, to be tossed about in the stormy sea of Slovak politics? Or will it be a Slovak national ecological party? In this case, it must also reckon with

the creation of analogous Hungarian, maybe even Czech or other national ecological parties, which would be not partners with the Slovak party, but its greatest enemy.

The third choice could be a political party that is not only interested in ecology and conservation, but also in protecting people . . . that is interested in social problems of people on the street, that engages in the values of national culture, a non-consumer lifestyle, and the values of saving the cultural heritage of the Slovak nation. A party without an inferiority complex that can join the European green movement as an equal partner (*Zelené Slovensko*, October 12, 1990).

Podoba's references to "protecting people" and "saving the cultural heritage of the Slovak nation" were reminders of the multifaceted volunteer work of the conservation movement under state socialism. As a member of ZO 6 he had not only helped to protect Slovakia's cultural heritage by participating in *drevenice* brigades in the countryside but also coauthored chapters in *Bratislava/nahlas*. Podoba's remarks were also a critical jab at those Green Party members who had not been active in the movement prior to 1989 but who had joined only after the threat and menace of the regime had disappeared. Podoba's questions highlighted the very fault lines threatening the party's survival and underscored the heart of the problem of green politics in the transition. In the absence of totalitarianism, greens could no longer rely on a dialogue consisting of a simple opposition against the state. As the *zeleni* became part of the state, and part of the political process of democracy, it was necessary to clearly and realistically define what and who the party would represent.

Podoba's article, which also appeared in *Kulturný Život*, a pro-federal literary weekly, was met with accusations of elitism from other party members. After 1991, Podoba was censored from publishing in *Zelené Slovensko* because, according to him, Sabo, the party chairman, considered him to be a divisive force.

But regardless of his hopes to play compromiser between the two factions of nationalists and federalists, Sabo decided to call for a special congress for June of 1991 to settle the matter once and for all. In his memorandum announcing the congress, he urged members to consider the fact that

The Federal Party really only exists on paper. And there is now a new Prague party that is allied with the [far right] Republican Party—this needs no commentary! We should have a new congress and resolve our differences. If not, as the functioning chairman I am prepared to step down anytime. Do not break the Party—we can find a solution. We are the fifth strongest party in Slovakia (Sabo April 20, 1990).

Podoba did not attend the Žilina congress and was subsequently the first to break away from the Green Party. Over the next year, most other founding Green Party members followed him.

By 1991 both federalists and nationalists accused the other faction of forsaking environmental issues. Nationalists viewed the first party schism as a case of *complementary schismogenesis,* where a small heretical sect breaks from the ranks of a parent group (Bateson 1958:176).[8] In this interpretation, supporters of federalism had been more concerned with party structure and were unable to compromise on this point. Sabo, the beleaguered chairman, later cynically concluded that "in reality, no one was 'green'; neither side would find a compromise." He accused both sides of being more concerned about the structure of the future state than about the health of the environment.

The solution agreed upon at the Žilina congress was discursively schizophrenic but politically clear. The membership voted to support Slovak autonomy and yet still remain within a federal arrangement with the Czech Republic. With this new resolution promoting autonomy, however, the party officially changed its name to Strana Zelených Slovensko (SZS, the Green Party of Slovakia) and registered as a new party, effectively declaring its independence from the old federal party. Those who stayed away from the congress in protest would have to re-register the federal party in Slovakia if they wanted to continue as a separate party. In a lame attempt to appease federalists, Sabo endorsed the establishment of a Green Union (Zeleni Unia) which would, in theory, connect the now-separate republic-level Czech and Slovak parties.

Despite its new name, the Green Party's vision remained quite unclear. On the one hand, it aspired to serve the goals and values of the old SZOPK. On the other hand, its deputies, whether out of a genuine commitment to the issues or out of a strategic effort to attract wider support for the party's future, pulled the party into other political battles. Moreover, its heterogeneous membership base also contributed to the party's poor sense of unity.

Strana Zelených manifested itself from a wide spectrum of people. Such an array, that there really was no conception of what exactly a green party is.

Nature lovers joined, but so did technocrats who only wanted to improve a limited sphere of the environment. Or nationalists joined who wanted to augment Slovakia, without realizing a wider connection with green philosophy. There was no time to crystallize the party. Everything was "in process" and from this a lot of improvisation flowed (Šremer 1995).

This spirit of improvisation was evident in the urgent requests for information made in the fall of 1991, prior to the June 1992 elections, by the Green Party secretary to the Green Party in Sweden. The secretary asked for any and all examples of "the principal laws about environmental problems—such as general ones, laws concerning specific issues, nuclear power, waste, water, eco-tax, etc. Also laws about the right or method of referendum in your country" (Trubiniova 1991). Despite the fact that the Slovak Green Party had won a legitimate place in the political arena, both its mission and its structure were significantly underdeveloped.

At the same time, the creation and evolution of the Slovak Green Party ultimately challenged *ochranári* to choose their loyalties as the political system opened up. It also distracted environmentalists from other goals, including supporting the creation of civic organizations and new NGOs, the crucial need to raise funds for this type of activism, and increasing networks with other environmental groups beyond Slovakia. Ultimately, the hyperdevelopment of the Green Party resulted in ambiguity that confused both the public and the *ochranári* about what in fact an ecological party was supposed to stand for. One voter described this problem.

> I didn't vote for the SZS because they were running in a coalition with the old communists (SDL). How could I vote for them? I didn't want to vote for the SZA because they were now with HZDS, completely unbelievable, eh? I mean, on the verge of fascism. I wanted to vote for an ecology party, but how do you choose between fascists and communists. I decided not to vote (Eva1995).

Ultimately, all the attempts at compromise, growing disillusionment among the party's founders, and, most of all, increasing confusion among supporters following the sequence of name changes sealed the political fate of the Green Party.

The Slovak Green Party actually survived the first five years of postsocialist politics and entered the period of independence with a somewhat consistent parliamentary record, falling generally to the left.

Whether its platform could be considered green remained a matter of opinion, but its voter base stayed relatively stable.[9] In 1994, the party split yet again, this time along fault lines more common to Western greens, concerning coalition partner choices. When the Green Party decided to enter into an election coalition with the Party of the Democratic Left (SDL)—the former Communist Party of Slovakia—several members splintered off as a new party and joined in coalition with Mečiar's HZDS. This new faction took the name Slovak Green Alternative (SZA).[10] Each "ecology" party managed to win a handful of parliamentary seats in 1994. The staunchly nationalist orientation of SZA became quite clear when its leadership announced that the party "wanted to urge the Slovak National Council for an independent language law for mixed territories in Slovakia" and to "secure a Slovak school in each community of the Republic" as well as to "secure the conduct of religious ceremonies in the Slovak language" (*Slovenská Republika*, May 22, 1995). Mentioned far beneath these cultural goals was the party's mission to "create material growth for society with the minimum ecological destruction of nature" (ibid.).[11]

THE EMERGENCE OF ETHNICIZED ENVIRONMENTALITIES

When Czechs and Slovaks separated in 1993, equally vibrant celebrations occurred in the Czech Lands and in Slovakia. Western observers and Czechs and Slovaks themselves all noted that in this ethnic split in the center of Europe, there was no violence. Unlike the breakup of Yugoslavia, which resulted in a series of devastating conflicts of secession, civil war, and ethnic cleansing, Czechoslovakia's separation was peaceful. Carol Skalnik Leff (1997) explains the nonviolent separation of the Czech Lands and Slovakia, referred to as the Velvet Divorce, as the outcome of several factors. These include the state's federal structure under communism, which prepared the way for an easy split, the fact that very few Czechs lived in Slovakia and vice versa, and the larger geopolitical situation of emerging economic opportunities (Leff 1997:138–39). But it is the children in a divorce, and not the parents, who often suffer. The splitting up of Czechoslovakia, which was claimed as a triumph by some Slovak nationalists, affected both the old conservation union and Green Party activists in different but equally disastrous ways.

The activists who remained in the Union, and who had enjoyed an almost celebrity status during the Velvet Revolution, were shocked by the sudden lack of public support for their group and surprised by what they saw as a spurious integration of ecology into nationalist causes. The public seemed to care little about their meetings or their agenda. Attendance at SZOPK events was weak—even regular members were "busy" with other things. On top of this, the Union now had the reputation of harboring national enemies. In the case of the Green Party, even political ecologists were surprised by its failure. For example, Frankland (1995) placed post-socialist green parties at the focal point of political and social change in the region, predicting that "[g]reen parties will be important actors in the maintenance of sound environmental policies, democratic participation and the ongoing transformation" and that they may "yet salvage the revolutionary ideals of 1989–90" (Frankland 1995:341–42).[12] Both Green Party members and SZOPK activists attempted to explain their failures by noting that they were quite unprepared for the rapid pace of the new democratic process. Used to the inertia of the socialist regime, party leaders and activists were overwhelmed with piles of literature and pamphlets, all in English, Dutch, or German, that flooded their offices from Western green parties and organizations eager to support their Eastern Bloc cousins. It certainly was true that in only two years the party had passed through conflicts that had taken many Western green parties over ten years to develop and to resolve. They also pointed out that ecology, as a political issue, had all but disappeared from public opinion polls.

The first post-communist fissures among Slovak environmentalists involved both symmetrical separations, where different political vehicles are chosen to fight for similar doctrines, and complementary divisions, where a heretical group (nationalists) distances itself from an orthodox parent political organization (federalists). This second type of break, manifested in the Green Party's fracturing, indicated a fundamental realignment of the communist landscape. Not only was the state capable of refashioning communist-era projects and selling them to the public, but the political branch of the ecology movement felt it had no choice but to support this new reconfiguration. Ecology, at least in a formal political arena, now had to conform to ethnic discourses. The fate of the other branch, manifested as a lumbering and lost post-socialist social movement, also faced the conundrum of cultural and political reconfigurations.

The Union's battle against Gabčíkovo also exposed an intimate discursive courtship between nature and ethnicity. Czechoslovakia's "divorce" thus appeared to have given birth to new relationships among people, place, and politics, indicating the emergence of an ethnicized environmentality. Although it involved an unprecedented realignment of power systems, from socialist to democratic, this new environmentality was comprised of a relatively simple project of space-making (Hughes 2005). With the collapse of communism and with the establishment of the republic as an independent state, Slovaks were now framed as national subjects inhabiting a nature preserve writ large. In this reconfiguration, the landscape becomes an imperative and notions of place become primary: making a claim on "our part of the Danube," no matter what the condition of the river may be. The conversations of socialism had shifted significantly, from how to make protest even possible to performing a new post-socialist *proxemics*—a new cultural use of space. Slovakia was no longer a polluted wasteland of socialism, but a possession and a symbol of the people: the nation.

5 Argonauts of the Eastern Bloc

FREEDOM IS LIKE AN OPEN SEA. WHILE ONE HAS THE CHOICE to go in any direction, there is also the possibility of losing one's way. If, by the end of 1992, freedom had emboldened Slovaks to part ways with their Czech partners, freedom also brought widespread and remarkable changes to the newly independent state. In this new world, the frustrating incongruities of the transition from socialism were thrown into sharp relief. On the one hand, the slow but irreversible creep of capitalism mesmerized a citizenry used to saving and reusing practically everything. Bratislava residents who had once headed out without distraction to their daily appointments were now often delayed by frequent stops to gaze upon new window displays crowded with kitchen appliances, portable washing machines, and countless electronic gadgets. Western books, previously unavailable, lined the shelves of new bookshops and now-ubiquitous sidewalk bookstalls. Very few of these titles, however, were printed in Slovak, as most foreign publishers produced only Czech-language translations. Austrian day-trippers, hunting for East European bargains, maneuvered their enormous Land Rovers past the locals' tiny Czech-made Škoda sedans on Bratislava's narrow streets. The American retail chain Kmart brightened up the capital city with its purchase of Prior, the drab, state-owned department store in the center of town, transforming the grim concrete structure into a mosaic of materialism and convenience.[1] Where in the past Slovaks had to carry their own canvas sacks to state-owned shops and wait in long lines for basic foodstuffs, the Western-style superstore offered smiling employees sporting pins announcing "We're here to serve you!" These friendly clerks helped bewildered shoppers negotiate aisles of consumer goods, now easier to haul away with Kmart's limitless supply of complimentary plastic bags. If under communism a beleaguered Slovak, exhausted from standing all day in queues, had to make do with a snack of greasy *langoš* (fried bread) wrapped in thin brown paper from an outdoor kiosk—no napkins in sight—he or she now could, with almost no waiting, pick up a Little Caesar's pizza neatly packaged in a colorful box complete with disposable plastic utensils.[2]

On the other hand, alongside capitalism's sometimes disorienting, sometimes delightful offerings, there reappeared the icons of a history and culture that had been denounced by the regime. Street names were changed after the Velvet Revolution from names referring to Czechoslovakia's efforts to build international socialism to names commemorating the places and personalities of Slovakia's long struggle for independence. On occasion, this return to Slovak history partnered intimately with market consumerism and produced what appeared to some Western observers to be bizarre hybrid cultural conflations (Garcia-Canclini 1996). For example, at one Saturday evening *country bal*, Slovaks line danced to an American-style country-and-western band following a medieval sword fight performance sponsored by Coca-Cola. Other cultural conflations incorporated the symbols of Slovak national consciousness into Stalinist-era development. A 1991 boat trip down the Vah River, engineered by the Ministry of Water Management and the state-owned construction company Hydrostav, included hired actors dressed as the nineteenth-century national fathers, Ludovit Štur and Antonin Bernolak, to advertise, in all seriousness, a set of hydroelectric power projects that had, until the Velvet Revolution, been a centerpiece of socialist planning.

Still other transformations of the landscape exposed enduring internal political conflicts and tensions simmering within Slovak identity. At a 1995 May Day celebration, sponsored by the Communist Party of Slovakia, a group of elderly Slovaks, whose average age could not have been under 60, danced to lively polka music beneath a large red banner announcing in bold white letters, "Freedom Came from the East." Above the dancers towered an enormous metal sculpture commemorating the 1944 anti-fascist Slovak National Uprising: a young peasant-partisan standing triumphantly with weapon in hand. Across town, on the same day, the Party of the Democratic Left (SDL), a new post-socialist incarnation of the old Communist Party, sponsored their own festival to celebrate the traditional socialist holiday. The SDL event, held in a city garden in the historic Castle district, featured gigantic images of Peter Weiss, the party's handsome young chairman. One poster-size photo depicted Weiss firmly shaking hands with the country's newly rich private entrepreneurs. Regardless of the fact that SDL's economic platform embraced heavy state control of market reforms, the message of these new communists seemed to be that if liberation from fascism had come from the East, prosperity could come only from Western investment.

Slovak nationalism, however, looked neither East nor West but inward, to the very center of the country. Matica slovenská, the cultural organization that first pushed for independence from the Czechs, was based in Martin, some 400 kilometers east of Slovakia's capital. After 1989, nationalists in HZDS and the Slovak National Party began to shift the target of their accusations of political corruption from Prague to Bratislava. As a Danube River city, sharing a border with Austria, Bratislava had indeed been a historically diverse center of power, with significant Jewish and Hungarian influences, and it now played host to increasingly large numbers of international visitors, as well as to growing Gypsy and South Asian guest worker populations. In 1993, Ján Slota, the chairman of the Slovak National Party, even proposed moving the capital to the more central town of Banská Bystrica, implying that Bratislava did not effectively represent the Slovak people, their heritage, or their history.

Whether the country's politicians were old or repackaged communists, nationalists, populists, or Christian Democrats, it seemed to many Slovaks that political elites shamelessly used Eastern-style power networks and patronage to lead blatantly Western consumer lifestyles, and citizens found it increasingly difficult to thoroughly trust any of them. Likewise, the inverted post-socialist political spectrum, where right meant liberal and democratic and left signified totalitarianism, confused voters and foreign observers alike. Amid the confusion, the authoritarian governmental style of Vladimir Mečiar dominated Slovak politics for most of the 1990s and delayed the country's move to join the European Union.

In what was proving to be Slovakia's lengthy and unique transition from communism, the freedom to open up new public discourses also demanded that environmental activists more clearly define the world that they wanted to save. This task turned out to be quite a difficult one, since people did not seem certain anymore as to who was or was not an environmentalist. After the very limited gains made by the Green Party, and after the failure of SZOPK's demonstrations to stop Gabčíkovo, many *ochranári* began to suspect that some of their "green" leaders had pursued ecological issues more as a strategy to oppose the regime than as a long-term commitment to environmental advocacy. They submitted as evidence the fact that none of the major personalities of 1989, like Ján Budaj, Milan Knažko, and many others who went on to hold important positions in government or society, appeared to champion the environment in any way. Despite the new freedom of public debate, the issue of ecology had plummeted to nearly last place in opinion polls, replaced at the top of most surveys with national independence, ethnic minorities, and growing concerns about social security, unemployment, and rising crime (Fric 1991). Moreover, new state leaders, such as Mečiar and Čarnogurský, appeared to have learned from communism's quick demise the crucial need to control public media and to repackage state paternalism and monopoly with images of cultural pride.

As I will explain below, in the upheavals and dramas of the transition, SZOPK activists either turned inward to redefine the organization or left the Union to create new ones. This process was in part the result of the growing influence of Western and international organizations in the region. Throughout Eastern Europe, environmental organizations also started to professionalize and to narrow their ecological agendas (Glinski 2001). However, as the cases of Gabčíkovo and the Green Party indicate, the creation of new Slovak environmental organizations occurred much slower than in other post-socialist states. Once these organizations appeared, their development unfolded during an intense period of national revitalization in which politicians viewed cooperation with Western ecological groups with suspicion. At the same time, Slovakia's separation from the Czech Republic attracted the growing attention and criticism of the international environmental community. Within this framework, a new generation of young Slovak activists arrived on the scene, many of whom were too young to have experienced a life of repression under socialism and who brought a fresh perspective on ecological politics, with their own version of radical activism and with a decidedly confrontational approach to public protest. But this energetic group, along with older activists, also had to contend with the Slovak state's attempts to weaken civic organizations, a battle which used up valuable and shrinking resources.

All of these developments served to further marginalize green activism in the new state, and highlight a shifting environmentality in Slovakia's transition from communism. This new environmentality fostered a repositioning of citizens as nation builders and the *ethnicization* of places and resources. By *ethnicizing* I mean the employment of primordialist framings of ethnic identity in order to assert political, economic, or social power (Snajdr 2007). Along with these new relationships, the state continued to maintain a paternalist model of economic management and the control of public media and political discourse. Through all of these repositionings and reiterations of post-socialism, the one subject that seemed to slip from the grasp of new environmental organizations was the voice of the Slovak public itself, a process aptly illustrated by the village of Slatinka, when activists sought to defend its residents, whose homes faced destruction in the wake of a government-sponsored dam project.

THE SLATINKA DAM: A PICTURE OF THE OLD WORLD

In late July of 1995, in the town of Zvoleň in Central Slovakia, Vodohospodarska Vystavba, a state construction company specializing in large water projects, held a public hearing for the residents of the nearby village of Slatinka. Slatinka was marked for obliteration with the construction of a new dam and reservoir project in the Slatinka valley. Activists from the Slatinka Association, an ad hoc environmental group that included several Slovak environmental organizations, also showed up for the midsummer meeting in hopes of representing the village and defending its residents against the state. The Slatinka Association was the brainchild of Juraj Zamkovský, a former *ochranár* from zo 6, and his new organization, the Center for Public Advocacy (CPA). Zamkovský had taken the lead among activists in moving out from under the roof of szopk. After a brief visit to the U.S. in 1992, where he worked with American environmental groups, he decided to create the CPA, with the aim to better educate both citizens and activists about lobbying the Slovak government and utilizing the law to fight for environmental issues. Joining Zamkovský in the Slatinka Association was an impressive array of new NGOs that now comprised Slovakia's environmental movement, including the Society for Sustainable Living, the Slovak Rivers Network, People and Water, and Wolf (VLK). Also among the activists in the Association were Slovak members of the global environmental organization Greenpeace, which had opened up a Bratislava branch in early 1993.

On the day of the hearing, the activists gathered outside Zvoleň's House of Culture, where the meeting was to take place. As he waited outside the building, Pavol Mišiga, a member of Zamkovský's CPA, summarized the situation. "[The villagers] signed an agreement with the state to get compensation for their property, which the government would flood with a reservoir resulting from the Slatinka Dam. This reservoir will supply water for the Mochovce plant down south. You see how these things are all connected?" The Mochovce nuclear power plant was a new state energy project near Levica, some 100 kilometers to the southeast. The project was well under way, but had stalled due to a shortage of government funding. Mišiga insisted that Slatinka was not only important as a case of local environmental justice, in the sense of the villagers' well-being, but also as a battle in the struggle over the larger issue of nuclear energy and safety in Slovakia. By protecting the villagers of Slatinka from losing their land, environmentalists also hoped to block the completion of the Mochovce nuclear plant, which, activists pointed out, utilized inadequate Chernobyl-era safety technology.

At six o'clock in the evening, a bus carrying some 25 villagers from Slatinka pulled up in front of the crowd of activists. They had been brought to the hearing by state officials. As the villagers stepped slowly out of the vehicle, it was clear that they were old. Their average age appeared to be well over 65, and they reminded me immediately of the elderly Slovaks who were the controversial subjects in Dušan Hanák's film *Pictures of the Old World*, which the former regime had banned but which I had recently seen at a film festival in Čadca sponsored by the Ethnology Department of the Slovak Academy of Sciences. Mišiga went on to describe the problem further.

> The agreement that the state offered them wasn't fair. If they signed the agreement, they would get 20 crowns (80 cents) for 1 square meter of their land. If they did not sign the agreement, the state would give them 40 *haliers* (about 5 cents) compensation per square meter. Last year a new EIA [Environmental Impact Assessment] Law was enacted by the government. But it has never been tested. Institutional "traditions" have been keeping it from being properly enforced. This law, which was made available to us, was never mentioned to these residents whose village will be completely ruined by the dam. Our association will try to use this case as a precedent for the new law. I don't know how it will turn out.[3]

The villagers wore their Sunday best to the hearing. The men sported black suits and hats. Women had donned the black kerchiefs and dark dresses with elaborate lace trim usually worn to Catholic mass. The stately villagers filed past the casually and colorfully dressed activists. Some were in bright yellow T-shirts with the words "Stop Mochovce!" Others wore sweaters and jeans. One activist had on a black shirt bearing what I recognized as an icon of the radical American environmental group Earth-First! Emblazoned in bold white letters above an image of a monkey wrench crossed with a Native American tomahawk was the designation "Eco-Warrior." While the activists clutched folders containing talking points, environmental studies, and promotional literature, the villagers entered the meeting hall empty-handed. Mišaga continued his briefing.

> It is most important for them to present their side. We have been personally working with some of the residents. Telling them what their rights are. But we haven't had much time, because the government gives us information at the very last minute, so they can say they follow the laws. We did a survey of the residents, asking them if they wanted to move or not. Eighty percent of them said they wanted to stay.

The hearing opened with a formal presentation by an "expert" panel comprised of engineers from Vodohospodarska Vystavba, a lawyer from the state, and a few other government representatives. Panel members sat at a long table on the stage of the hall's theater. The residents and activists sat in the auditorium seating below the stage. The panel members began by recalling the history of the dam project and describing its construction and technical operation in great detail. According to one engineer the company's goals for the project were to "secure enough water for the effective operation of Mochovce, for the town of Levice, and to provide fishing and recreation for the residents of nearby Zvoleň." At the close of the presentation and before beginning a question and answer session, the panel warned that, although it would consider project alternatives, the "null variant"—i.e., not building the dam—was not an option for discussion.

A microphone for audience questions stood in the auditorium's center aisle. "The residents don't have any information in hand!" began one activist, who had quickly dashed out of his seat as soon as the panel finished its introduction. "It's because they are old that this company comes in and builds a dam here," he went on, "and the guarantees that people will be compensated? How do we know this? This is not too radical a question to ask."

The state lawyer responded to the activist's query with a brief but pointed description of what he called a "gray period between the planning of the project and the formal passage of the EIA law." In 1994, Slovakia adopted the EIA Act, which mandated a transparent public process in the assessment of the environmental impact of large-scale construction projects. The lawyer reminded the audience that since the Slatinká project had been planned well before this environmental law was passed—the plan was first drawn up by the communist regime in 1958—the state was not legally required to fully inform the public about specific environmental impacts. He suggested that the audience was lucky to be getting this kind of hearing in the first place.

Slatinka's mayor, a younger man who had not joined the villagers on the bus but arrived at the hall on his own, rose to speak. "There are two groups here. Older people, who have to leave their homes. Where will they live? This is their concern. And this younger perspective, they obviously want to help, but how can they help? I haven't heard a single concrete recommendation from them. The only thing that I have heard is that the dam shouldn't be built."

As the mayor took his seat, murmurs grew among the activists. Zamkovský then stepped up to the microphone. "People of Slatinka," he said loudly, "you can get out of this agreement if you want. It is your right under the law. You can get out of it if you feel you have an interest to. We are not doing a protest here. We are simply making sure that the state follows procedures according to the current law."

The mayor quickly got back up from his chair and countered Zamkovský's plea with a direct question to the residents. "Do you want to be represented by these people?"

To this, a few of the residents, who had until now remained silent in their seats, shook their heads and answered quietly, as if almost to themselves, "No, no."

One of the elderly villagers slowly stood up and shuffled over to the microphone. "Who is this Slatinka Association?" he asked. "Are you registered somewhere? Who finances you?"

Mišiga approached the stand and calmly began to explain. "Certainly we are here to help, and it is concerning you. Our interest in Slatinka is quite harmless. I want to reassure the citizens of the village."

Ľubica Trubiniova, the head of Greenpeace Slovakia, followed Mišiga. "We are not representing anyone but ourselves. My organization is funded by private gifts, not taxes. The dam is not a problem of just the local community but for all of Slovakia. We don't need it. You [pointing to the villagers, then the panel] don't need it. Why am I here? I am here as someone who pays taxes and who knows that the government and state companies are building needless water dams!" Trubiniova later told me that she recognized the mayor as belonging to HZDS, Slovakia's ruling political party.

A woman from Zvoleň got up, took the microphone, and turned suddenly toward the activists in the audience. "You know, the environment also means people. How are you helping these people? I have heard here tonight very little about help, directly, for these people."

A second Slatinka villager turned to the activists and said: "You are making a lot of trouble for us, you know—having these hearings, this panel. We are old. We just want to live. We just want to make sure we can get a bus from our house to the town so we can get to a store."

The meeting went on like this for an hour, after which the residents of Slatinka had to leave, since this was when the bus was scheduled to take them back to their isolated village. Although several had spoken, most of them had remained silent the entire evening. After they departed, Mišiga somberly concluded,

> They knew they were going to have to move. It does not look good. And one of the mistakes we made was that Zamkovský was not a familiar face to the villagers. Me and Medved [another CPA activist] were the ones who had all the face-to-face contact in the village. And the people we spoke with— people who told us they did not want this dam—were afraid to get up. I could see it. We'll have to wait and see.

The Slatinka case was one of hundreds of campaigns and actions throughout the 1990s that comprised Slovakia's post-socialist environmental movement. Yet from it we see a number of features that define this movement and that mark its transformations since the collapse of communism. Most conspicuous is the absence of the once-famous Union of Nature and Landscape Protectors and its highly popular Bratislava branch and local group ZO 6. Another theme is the presence of a varied array of new organizations with new names and new objectives, groups that did not and could not have existed under communism. Among these new groups we also see the appearance of a young and apparently aggressive cohort of activists, not shy about displaying the emblems of foreign environmental groups. Below I describe the emergence of these specific features as Slovakia's environmental movement attempted to continue its confrontation with state power. Following this I will discuss how the Slatinka case reveals the new relationships evident in post-socialist environmentality: a novel combination of state paternalism, free market discourse, nationalist ideology, and public acquiescence. Together these features indicate a political and cultural landscape in which neither the environment nor environmentalists can articulate a common message about place and identity.

BACKLASH

The process by which new environmental organizations emerged in Slovakia was at first quite slow and linked in part to both the internal situation of the greens and Slovakia's status on the international stage. The Green Party experiment and the Union's popularity and sheer dominance immediately after communism's collapse clearly delayed the appearance of new organizations. Yet, after SZOPK's confrontation with the government over Gabčíkovo, the Union came under pressure from some of its more conservative members to be less critical of the state and more explicitly engaged with decidedly nonpolitical environmental topics such as nature education or wildlife conservation. Members in the countryside, who were tending to support nationally oriented parties such as HZDS and SNS, began to express a concern that more radical factions from Bratislava had driven the Union's agenda. This shift away from controversy was actually expedited by the Union's revolutionary reorganization while under the leadership of *ochranári* from ZO 6. Before 1989, Central Committee leadership could be chosen based entirely on the popular vote, which had been, at that time, significantly skewed by large numbers of activists in the Union's Bratislava organization. In 1990, the membership voted to encourage more democratic representation of local branches from all regions of the country, which ironically gave the Union's more conservative ranks a stronger voice. Union members also decided to change the name of their monthly periodical, again in a spirit of becoming more democratic, from the imperative slogan *Poznaj a Chráň* (Know and Protect) to the more inclusive and perhaps less confrontational *Ekopanorama*, which better reflected the diversity and decentralized character of the Union's local organizations. An issue from summer 1992, for example, offered articles on fishing, how to dispose of old batteries, the threat of acid rain, skin cancer and ultraviolet light, recycling tips, and a recent Bratislava dog show (SZOPK, *Ekopanorama* 7, 1992).

As the Union "democratized" itself, the government decreased its portion of funding from the state budget. In 1991, the Union's annual budget was 6 million crowns (the equivalent of $160,000 in U.S. dollars), which it used to pay full-time staff members, to support the *Zelené Slovensko* news insert, and to publish the newly renamed monthly *Ekopanorama*. In 1992, however, this state support diminished significantly. By 1993, funds had been slashed by the government to 2 million crowns (about $55,500). Activists who had led SZOPK's campaign against the Gabčíkovo Dam complained that these cutbacks were made because of the Union's prominent role in fighting the project. They believed that state funding now came at the price of political loyalty. As one activist put it:

> SZOPK's role in the Stop Gabčíkovo campaign showed the government that the Union would be dangerous. The state never said it openly, but it cut its budget because it was against the project. They told us, "We simply don't have enough money for the Union this year." But it wasn't that simple.

In fact, rather than being a form of indirect punishment for its activism, SZOPK's loss of funds was likely the result of an overall decline in state revenues. Kirschbaum (2005:261) notes that while government coffers totaled 18.8 billion crowns in 1988, they nearly evaporated, down to 2.1 billion, in 1991. Regardless of the real reason for the funding cuts, activists feared that any additional criticism by SZOPK of major energy issues might be met the next time with more than just fiscal penalties. In 1994, the state further whittled down its support for the Union to 650,000 crowns (roughly $18,000), forcing the Central Committee to cut staff and to reduce the quality of its periodical. *Ekopanorama*'s glossy, full-color photographs were replaced in 1994 with black and white photos, there were fewer pages, and the nonmember price, 4 crowns from 1991 to 1993, increased to 10 crowns.

Along with its funding, the Union's membership was steadily dropping. One of the largest and perhaps most obvious decreases occurred just after 1989, when thousands of people disappeared from the organization's meetings and actions. Activists conjectured that these members had joined SZOPK as an opportunity to make a statement of defiance against the regime at a time when no other confrontational groups existed. But in 1992 and 1993, the Union's rosters continued to shrink. Between 1985 and 1988, SZOPK membership had almost doubled. Yet only two years after the Velvet Revolution, the ranks of the organization had fallen by nearly three-quarters (table 5.1).

If the Union's openness had been its major strength in the 1980s, its tolerance of multiple viewpoints the hook that had drawn in hundreds of new members, this same inclusive approach seemed to work against SZOPK in the transition period. The collage of issues and activities that comprised the Union's vision of ecology now held less appeal to a population that was free to pursue special interests in the newly opened society.

Even more ironically, for young Slovaks interested in ecology and environmental activism, the conservation organization that during the regime had provided so many people with fresh and progressive ideas now appeared to represent the past. One college student recalled that when she went to her first SZOPK meeting in 1992

> All they did there was talk. I thought it was too formal. Besides, even though it wasn't a communist organization, there were lots of things about it that were, you know, communist. Like, there had to be a person in charge, with a title. And there was a committee. There was always a committee.

She stopped going because the Union's structure reflected, for her at least, the manner and style of the old regime. Although the regime was gone, people did not shed the habits and styles that it had cultivated among the population for almost fifty years. What the younger generation described as "the communist mentality" was still evident in the mannerisms and almost unconscious rituals that older citizens performed. Prior to 1989, SZOPK had pushed the boundaries of socialist *proxemics*, what anthropologists call the cultural use of space (Hall 1973). They stood in public squares to promote their cause. They issued proclamations— a daring move under normalization. They cared for neglected meadows or riverbanks or abandoned buildings. They volunteered their own resources to help others than themselves. Under socialism, such behavior was anomalous, suspicious, and liberating. Yet their meetings, even after the Revolution, still retained structure. Following the familiar format of Party proxemics, they had a "leader" who introduced items for discussion. There was a lot of talk-

TABLE 5.1 National Membership in SZOPK, 1985–94

Year	Members
1985	13,000
1988	28,000
1992	7,000
1994	5,000

Source: Compiled from *Poznaj a Chráň* and *Ekopanorama*

ing, but people took turns speaking, and often stood when they spoke. These procedures of socialist discourse had been learned since grade school, and were still present in public meetings and gatherings throughout Eastern Europe. For younger people who were interested in doing and protesting, and confronting and shouting, the Union was no longer the right place, particularly after the Gabčíkovo demonstrations. Done with protests and spectacles, the Union returned to the meeting room format, to organizing film festivals and planning summer brigades.

In fact, by 1995, SZOPK, as a national-level environmental organization, played almost no direct or openly confrontational role in fighting for environmental issues that did not resonate with the wider public. Some viewed the Union as obsolete, or simply too large and too diverse—a group without consensus, and thus without a strong voice. Some activists, like Pavel Šremer and Juraj Podoba, both of whom had been authors of *Bratislava/nahlas*, ended up leaving the movement altogether.[4] But the Union had little control of its voice or the voice of others, as the opening up of society attracted a growing interest on the part of international environmental groups in Slovakia's position and that of other formerly communist states in Europe. These groups, with external funding and the potential for new partnerships, gave many SZOPK activists new opportunities to move beyond the boundaries of the communist-era movement.

THE SEARCH FOR A NEW SLOVAK ECOLOGY

Before 1989, like most Slovaks, very few SZOPK activists had traveled anywhere beyond the Eastern Bloc states. Some *ochranári*, like Ján Budaj, had fostered clandestine and quite limited relationships with Western activists and environmental experts. Not surprisingly, Mikuláš Huba, despite (or perhaps because of) his popularity within the Union, had by 1989 visited only neighboring Austria, and then only as a faculty member of the Slovak Academy of Sciences.[5] Even in the first decade of the transition, people's passports may no longer have been restricted, but they still lacked the financial means to travel to the West. In fact, only a handful of SZOPK members were able to see the world beyond the Eastern Bloc in the period just after the fall of communism. These rare opportunities were possible through highly competitive study visits and brief networking trips abroad sponsored by Western aid programs. During these dizzying excursions, the lucky travelers met with representatives from dozens of environmental NGOs, such as Friends of the Earth, the Sierra

Club, and Greenpeace, all of which enjoyed relatively large memberships, commanded seemingly endless resources, and had gained, at least at the time, a degree of success on a number of environmental issues. Through these fortunate yet brief experiences, *ochranári* reported back to their colleagues an exciting world of grassroots organizations connected through an impressive network of personal relationships and advanced technology. Paradoxically, perhaps, they also brought back critical accounts of the rampant consumer societies that had given rise to the very groups that inspired their work in Slovakia. For example, after a short visit to the U.S. in 1992, Juraj Zamkovský, in an article published in *Ekopanorama*, described America as

> a sick country, which it alone proudly placed itself as the most mature among the rest. We saw the structural, legislative, economic, environmental, and physical racism of blacks and poor whites, Indians and women, who penetrated the haze of consumer propaganda . . . We also saw the systematic, industrial destruction of every alternative . . . toxic waste dumps among the poorest and most uneducated communities in the Southern states (Zamkovský 1992:14).

Zamkovský revealed a world of sharp contrasts which he himself viewed through a double lens of political naïvety and communist-era experience. On the one hand, he glimpsed a society where it was possible to lobby the government, attract supporters, and affect policy. On the other hand, Zamkovský witnessed a culture saturated with materialism, rife with ethnic injustice, and under assault from pollution comparable to the industrial maladies for which he had condemned the Czechoslovak regime. While the Western world generated the inspirational global discourses produced by what had been to him almost legendary environmental organizations, it was, in his view, by no means a greener world.

Even to those not fortunate enough to experience the world outside, however, the outside world eventually came. All throughout the first half of the 1990s, foreign environmentalists, consultants, and international personalities visited Slovakia, along with the rest of East Europe. Soon, what seemed to be an endless stream of invitations to foreign-sponsored conferences, expert seminars, and working lunches filled *ochranári* mailboxes. Some of these new visitors, such as the Australian ecologist John Seed, the director of the Worldwatch Institute, and even the U.S. politician Gary Hart, gave generously of their time and knowledge, holding open public lectures, professional workshops, and private meetings on global policy issues and the legislative process of democratic societies (Huba 1994:115–21). A few foreigners perhaps came more for the novelty of taking a peek behind the Iron Curtain to experience the chaos of a newly opened totalitarian state than to actually establish any sort of long-term partnerships. Among the wave of international visitors, the most sought after were representatives of foundations and granting agencies who brought with them the promise of financial assistance for environmental causes.

Among those who benefited early on from these new visitors and took the lead in moving out from under the roof of SZOPK were those *ochranári* who had been lucky enough to take short trips abroad. For example, Juraj Zamkovský capitalized on the contacts he made on his trip to America and opened the Center for Public Advocacy with support from the U.S. German Marshall Fund. Zamkovský wasted no time in applying what he'd seen of environmental lobbying in the U.S. to a CPA action targeting Istrochem, a state-owned chemical plant, which had been dumping waste products near the small village of Budmerice.[6] But his new organization also began to train other activists and to provide small grants to create new environmental initiatives. Like Zamkovský, Juraj Mesík, the upstart medical student who tried to form the independent group Ekotrend under communism, also took advantage of a visit to the U.S. and became the director of the Environmental Partnership for Central Europe, a network of Western donors devoted to establishing independent environmental organizations throughout post-communist East Europe. Other grant-making vehicles arrived on Slovak soil, including the Regional Environmental Center, which, although headquartered in Hungary, offered a small grant program to environmental groups in Central Europe, with resources from U.S. and Western European states.

Through these new funding opportunities, a few ambitious *ochranári* working in local branches of SZOPK helped their organizations acquire essentially independent identities. This process was expedited through the specific task of writing out grant proposals, which most Western-backed organizations required from applicants before awarding any money. The goals of the group needed to be spelled out along with detailed descriptions of the activities it would undertake for the entire year. Proposal writing of this nature demanded long-term planning and agenda setting; clear descriptions of one's basic organization, to distinguish it from others; and justifications of the group's activities and mission for a review board, just to be eligible to compete for funds. Group independence, then, was an inevitable outcome of this process. Even though a basic organization that had been awarded external money might still have held on to SZOPK member status, it became effectively self-sufficient upon winning the grant. One example was a SZOPK organization called Ĺudia a voda (People and Water), created by Michal Krávčik, a young engineer who had criticized the Gabčíkovo Dam project. Krávčik's vision was to introduce post-socialist society to new concepts in water management using Slovakia's existing waterways, particularly in the hilly topography of northeastern Slovakia. If Krávčik and his fellow activists could not stop the construction of large dams, like Gabčíkovo, his organization proposed to try to show Slovaks how networks of small dams could prevent flooding and generate power. Another SZOPK organization that came out from under the Union's umbrella was VLK (Wolf), a Prešov-based group led by Juraj Lukač. Wolf defined its main goal as protecting Slovakia's wolf population through education, monitoring, as well as demanding limitations on tree harvesting, an objective that would require vigorous lobbying of Slovakia's Department of Forestry and Water Management.

As separate segments of SZOPK sought and won external money, they were significantly transformed not only in terms of clarifying specific goals and issues which set them apart from other groups, but also in terms of gaining control of previously unavailable resources for activism. With even a small amount of foreign assistance, groups were able to acquire the vital equipment for lobbying the state and communicating with the public. Many of these tools, such as telephones, computers, and fax machines, were secondhand. For example, most of the PCs that groups purchased still ran on DOS systems. But this technology was far better than the carbon paper and mimeograph machines that had been used only a couple of years earlier, under communism. Fax machines gave organizations new networking capabilities, and operated surprisingly well, given the highly unreliable socialist-period phone system that continued to frustrate Slovaks long after the collapse of the regime. Nevertheless, money offered through Western assistance remained quite limited throughout the first half of the 1990s, and even the most competitive grants rarely exceeded a few thousand dollars.

New legislation allowing independent NGOs, associations, and foundations also encouraged activists to establish new organizations. For example, the Slovak Rivers Network (SRS), founded in 1993 by two members of SZOPK in Bratislava, hoped to serve as a lobbying and technical expertise center which would carry out longitudinal studies and propose new state policies on the care and management of Slovakia's water systems. Its network, in turn, pulled several local SZOPK organizations, including the Ipel River Union on the Hungarian border, the Vah River Union in Central Slovakia, and People and Water in Eastern Slovakia, further away from the Union's influence.

Mikuláš Huba, who had been so instrumental in shaping SZOPK under communism, also created a new NGO, the Society for Sustainable Living (STUŽ). Huba envisioned that STUŽ, which was completely independent from the Union, would be at the forefront of Slovakia's post-socialist environmental community by providing a framework for collaboration among a variety of activists, ecologists, and natural and social scientists. Huba's Czech colleague and longtime friend, Jozef Vavroušek, who had served as Czechoslovakia's Federal Minister for the Environment in 1990 and 1991, created a similar organization in the Czech Republic. The two veterans of the communist-era green movement still held out hope that Czechs and Slovaks would work together on the problem of ecology in the post-socialist world.

In fact, after 1993, the Union itself had reached out to Western and international conservation groups. For example, the International Union for the Conservation of Nature (IUCN), a global NGO focused on the protection of natural resources and wildlife, set up a Project Coordination Unit in Bratislava. The IUCN's long-range goal was to work with SZOPK to create natural conservation "corridors" throughout the country. With the cooperation of SZOPK leadership, the World Wildlife Fund (WWF) began an educational partnership with Strom Života, the formerly communist environmental youth organization. And Friends of the Earth, the well-known U.S.-based conservation group, invited SZOPK's Central Committee to join its global partnership network.[7]

If there was an overarching yet unique eco-philosophy emerging from among these new Slovak environmental organizations and partnerships, it was the concept of "sustainable living." Sustainable living was a term, promoted mainly by Huba and which his new organization was named after, that was generally adopted by new NGOs as a basic orientation expressing their broader goals and objectives. Sustainable living borrowed from the prevailing global environmental paradigm of sustainable development but incorporated, and tried to resolve, the specific political and cultural experiences of communism. The concept of "sustainable development" was first articulated in the 1987 Bruntland Commission's report *Our Common Future* and later adopted at the 1992 Earth Summit in Rio de Janeiro. From there, the paradigm provided a framework within which the international community of states and NGOs could pursue ecologically sound legislation and policy on a global scale (Liefferink and Andersen 1998:80). A key pillar of sustainable development was the decentralization of the energy sector, which, the plan's proponents argued, would allow for more effective local management of resource consumption. Sustainable development, it was suggested, would hold all consumers of energy, whether in the private, public, or corporate spheres, to the same standards of efficiency in use. In addition, the paradigm required international cooperation. That is, governments needed to work together to design and implement legislative and policy measures that more effectively conserved natural resources, more responsibly disposed of waste, and more cooperatively solved transboundary pollution issues. These were two of the main components of the Kyoto agreement of 1997, which focused on the problem of global warming.

In refashioning this paradigm, new Slovak NGOs hoped to contribute a unique perspective on sustainability as a movement born under totalitarianism. An obvious first step, in their eyes, was to revise terminology which, for many, evoked the old system. Development, Huba argued,

> was such a reminder of the old regime's approach to society. We wanted to emphasize the idea that there really was a third road of using the things we had, the villages, the infrastructure, and the people. [Sustainable living] meant true decentralization without the need to make more and more.

Under the new banner of "sustainable living," STUŽ and other NGOs sought to promote the idea that Slovakia itself, which had been historically less industrialized than its Czech or Polish neighbors, represented a viable alternative model for both Europe and the world. Huba imagined that Slovakia's still-bucolic countryside would become a model of sustainability not only for post-communist societies, but for post-capitalist and developing countries as well. Like the nationalist politicians in the Mečiar government who had proudly described the new state as being the Heart of Europe, Huba also drew on this geographic theme. This suggested, he argued, that as Europe's new geographic center, Slovak economy and society should remain reasonably small and, thus, sustainable. As a staunch opponent of the breakup of Czechoslovakia, however, Huba was careful to avoid nation as a trope in his ecological model. Yet he did not hesitate to draw heavily on traditional Slovak culture as an example of a post-socialist society in harmony with nature. Huba was aware of how other nativist models, such as the Chipko movement and indigenous activism in the Amazon Basin, had contributed to global environmental discourses, and through his new organization he hoped to show how Slovakia could serve as an ideal case for the integration of Europe.

INTERNATIONAL NGOS: "STOP NUCLEAR ENERGY" AND "SAVE THE ANIMALS!"

It was not a new Slovak eco-philosophy, crafted amid the inefficiently grinding gears of socialist industrialization, that brought the new country to the attention of powerful international and West European environmental organizations. The local problems articulated by STUŽ and other Slovak NGOs within their framework of sustainable living, such as water management, emissions reductions, and forest preservation, all took a back seat to what the international green community considered to be the most important legacy of communism: nuclear energy. This issue had certain immediacy in the minds of many West European green groups, particularly in light of the Chernobyl accident in Ukraine in 1986. Moreover, environmental activism in Russia, Ukraine, Lithuania, and Armenia had all crystallized under state socialism around the topic of nuclear energy and safety (Dawson 1996). While many of these groups had lost their popularity once regimes collapsed, several new NGOs in these countries continued to combat the issue and looked to Chernobyl as primary evidence in their struggles (Dawson 1996). This communist-era environmental disaster was also still a fresh experience for West Europeans, and reiterated throughout the 1990s in new media coverage of long-term health problems of the disaster's victims which were only now showing up. Organizations such as Greenpeace International; For Mother Earth, in Holland; and Global 2000, in Austria looked to the former Eastern Bloc countries as a key battleground in their anti–nuclear energy campaigns.

Thus, during a period when new Slovak NGOs attempted to link cultural discourses to the global paradigm of sustainability, several powerful international and European environmental groups seemed little interested in applying broad models of ecology to the new state. Instead, they sought to sharply narrow the narrative regarding Slovakia's role in the global ecological crisis, and hoped to take over the discursive arena of activism in the process (table 5.2). In 1993, as soon as Slovakia became an inde-

TABLE 5.2 New Slovak NGOs and Environmental Issue Focus

Issue	Nuclear Energy	Water Mgmt.	Biodiversity	Conservation	Public Advocacy
Society for Sustainable Living (STUŽ)	X	X	X	X	X
Slovak Rivers Network (SRS)		X			
International Union for the Conservation of Nature (IUCN)			X	X	
Horsky Park Association				X	
Center for Environmental Public Advocacy (CEPA)					X
Greenpeace Slovakia	X				

pendent state, Greenpeace opened an office in Bratislava and found a local Slovak director, an energetic and outspoken activist named Ľubica Trubiniova, to head its Slovak operations.[8] Greenpeace focused on only one issue in Slovakia, namely, the half-completed nuclear power plant at Mochovce. The new Slovak government had run out of funding to finish the project, and in the early 1990s had appealed to the European Bank for Reconstruction and Development (EBRD) to provide financing to get the plant operational. Greenpeace, and other anti-nuclear groups, warned that the Mochovce project utilized Chernobyl-style safety technology and posed a serious transborder threat to Western Europe. In the summer of 1994, a band of Greenpeace activists scaled the cooling towers of the Mochovce plant and unfurled a gigantic banner that demanded, in English, "Stop Mochovce!" Trubiniova remained on the grounds outside Mochovce's security fence to brief the news reporters she had alerted of the event. The demonstrators remained at the top of the enormous towers for several hours, finally surrendering themselves to frustrated police and plant guards. Photographs of the action appeared on the front page of every Slovak newspaper on sale at Bratislava kiosks the following day.

Other anti-nuclear groups, such as Austria's Global 2000, also tried to inspire new Slovak NGOs to highlight nuclear safety as a major ecological issue for the new country. But rather than setting up a satellite office, this organization marshaled support for its cause within the Austrian parliament, pushing the Mochovce project into the realm of an international dispute similar to the Gabčíkovo Dam battle between Slovakia and Hungary. Slovak NGOs, understandably, were reluctant to align themselves with the international activist community on this issue. While most groups, including the Union, listed Mochovce among their topics of environmental concern, nuclear energy was never at the top of the agenda.

Another international organization that set up a Bratislava office with serious impact on the public face of post-socialist activism in Slovakia was PETA. This Western-based animal rights group, known for its provocative demonstrations and confrontationally graphic images of animal testing, like Greenpeace hired Slovak directors who then orchestrated a series of local protests, under the name Sloboda Zvierat (Free the Animals), that coincided with PETA's global campaigns. Some of these actions targeted consumers of fur coats, others focused on discouraging Slovaks from buying new convenience goods manufactured by multinational corporations, such as Gillette disposable razors. Still others targeted the meat industry, promoting vegetarianism by exposing the cruelties of mass food production. Through highly public demonstrations, PETA actions appeared in newspapers almost every week.

In addition to stealing media space from Slovak groups, these international organizations attracted young Slovaks in significant numbers to the cause of ecology. At Greenpeace's daring Mochovce action, none of the Slovak activists, with the exception of Trubiniova, were over the age of twenty (Snajdr 1998). The Slovak PETA directors were barely out of high school. At Sloboda Zvierat rallies, crowds of young people (sometimes several hundred) would gather to watch, listen, and take fliers home. Many PETA supporters and activists during the 1995 campaigns were no older than ten. If one did the math, all of these new Western groups were attracting people who at best were teenagers during the Velvet Revolution.

Along with the wave of new NGOs breaking away from SZOPK in 1993 and 1994, new Slovak groups, including Deti Zeme (Children of the Earth) and Za Matku Zem (For Mother Earth), were appearing whose members were mostly students in high school or college. Za Matku Zem began as a breakaway group from Greenpeace, when several young Greenpeace activists became disillusioned by the international organization's heavy focus on nuclear energy in Slovakia. Although both Za Matku Zem and Deti Zeme had international headquarters in Western Europe, the parent organization, unlike Greenpeace, allowed local organizations substantial autonomy in crafting activism and choosing issues. This autonomy, not surprisingly, also meant almost no financial support for local activists. Nevertheless, both Deti Zeme and Za Matku Zem, as well as Greenpeace and Sloboda Zvierat, began to operate alongside new NGOs from the old Union.

As the communist regime fades further into history, two distinct branches of Slovak activism develop within parallel but distinct currents of post-socialist activism. On the one hand is the old guard, who, despite their refashioning into new organizations, attempt to remain instrumental in their orientation to activism. On the other hand, younger activists, many of whom were too young to have been part of SZOPK under socialism, and who are led by agendas formulated from outside of Slovakia, choose to be symbolic. Notably, these different approaches appear intimately related to their proponents' experiences in a changing political system. Instrumental activism is the pragmatic attempt to eradicate ecological maladies through legislation, lobbying, and ethical prescriptions for social action based on a model of "good citizenship." By contrast, symbolic activism, perhaps far from practical, attempts to vividly express a critical view of the social order (see figures 5.1, 5.2, and 5.3). Such a view of pollution involves, to paraphrase Mary Douglas (1966), reflecting on the relationship between order and disorder in society. The goal of symbolic activism is to capture the attention of the public by presenting a society in crisis, where the particular issue is, itself, articulated in a manner "out of place," or outside of social and political norms.

Ironically, the new generation of activists appearing on the scene seemed, in a sense, to be returning to some of the powerful tactics used by their predecessors from the communist period. In 1987, *Bratislava/nahlas* symbolized a corrupt regime's neglect of the country's poor health and polluted environment. The discursive power of this report was in part generated by its illegality, its symbolic placement as a polluting element of an ordered and functioning communist system. *Bratislava/nahlas* exposed the very real disorder of Slovakia's environment and socialism's failure on multiple levels. After the collapse of communism, the new incarnations of the old movement proceeded to work instrumentally—and legally—to promote effective environmental policies. They researched and wrote about ecological problems and attempted to translate "sustainability" into a Slovak vernacular. At the same time, they lost much of the symbolic force of their movement and its previously articulate and intimate connection to the social fabric.

Young greens, on the other hand, continued to push symbols into the path of the public gaze and boldly reconfigured the environment as in a state of immediate crisis. After the spectacular Greenpeace demonstration at Mochovce, various Slovak newspapers sensationally described the "protest" as an act of "terrorism" (*Pravda*, July 8, 1994) and accused Trubiniova of "manipulating children" (*Práca*, July 8, 1994) in a campaign of "anti-propaganda against our own state" (*Slovenská Republika*, July 7, 1994). But the media also acknowledged that the Greenpeace activists who scaled the power plant's fence and towers had been more organized than the stunned police and security guards who tried, but of course failed, to stop them (*Sme*, July 8, 1994). Members of Greenpeace considered such press as an indication that the action had been a resounding success.

In contrast to the limited and rather makeshift media efforts of older greens, such as *Zelené Slovensko*, that often ended up exposing internal debates and factionalism more than engaging the public with a unified message, young activists quickly learned to use the entire spectrum of the post-socialist press to their advantage. Despite the state's ongoing control of major newspapers and television, young greens' symbolic activism allowed them to effectively utilize even unreliable post-socialist media.[9] By holding colorful demonstrations focused primarily on a specific ecological issue, the members of Za Matku Zem and Greenpeace challenged the media not to miss an event on which other papers would likely report. This discursive strategy effectively increased the coverage of both the organization and the issue it promoted. Through their experience with public protest actions and the international community, young activists learned to produce sharp and concise press releases and to forge relationships with specific journalists in order to get their demonstrations covered. By

FIG. 5.1 A new generation of activism. Juraj "Rizo" Rizman, a seventeen-year-old high school student and founder of Za Matku Zem (For Mother Earth), a radical ecology organization formed in 1994. Rizman venerates the U.S. ecoterrorist group Earth First! He was twelve years old during the Velvet Revolution.

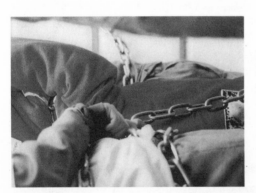

FIG. 5.2 Direct action protests. Activists from Za Matku Zem and Greenpeace Slovakia demonstrate against nuclear energy by chaining themselves to a government office, Bratislava, 1995.

FIG. 5.4 Going to extremes. Young activists march down the tram line in downtown Bratislava in an animal rights demonstration. The banner reads, "We'd rather go naked than wear fur!"

FIG. 5.5 Dangerous message. Slovak activists and international greens marching against nuclear energy, on a rural road outside Jaslovske Bohunice power plant. Behind the banner (upper left corner), which makes English language reference to the plant's Soviet-era safety system, a curious elderly villager looks on.

FIG. 5.3 *(Facing page, bottom)* Taking on international issues. Za Matku Zem members handcuff themselves to the French Embassy in Bratislava, protesting French nuclear weapons testing in the Pacific Ocean, 1995.

alerting journalists to upcoming actions and sending out faxes explaining the background and significance of their protests, the new greens provided newspapers with instant stories. Moreover, pithy, clever, often sensational slogans or phrases painted on huge banners offered observers and photographers an instant message, easily recorded, about dams, power plants, or the dangers of freon (see figures 5.4 and 5.5). Often, news coverage of such events appeared in papers only as a photograph with a caption. Through both independent and pro-government media, spectacular demonstrations got free state-wide public exposure and advertising.[10] During the year 1995, each of several major Slovak dailies ran an average of two stories a week featuring the environment. And credit for such exposure undoubtedly belongs largely to the efforts of young demonstrators.

In addition to calling attention to the environment in a spectacular manner, the symbolic power of public demonstrations also served as presentations of disorder that challenged citizens to confront the broader norms and practices of society. The actions of young activists compelled Slovaks to ask themselves, "Why are people walking through my village with banners?" or "Why are children climbing cooling towers at great risk to themselves?" These performances were also meant to remind the public that the incipient post-socialist political transformation left a system still in need of repair. Through a combination of symbolic demonstrations and focused lobbying, young Slovak greens attempted to engage both the political process and the public mind.

At the same time, young greens exhibited a political sensitivity to the conservative character of their Slovak audience and were not averse to adjusting their image as need arose in the course of their campaigns. In August 1995, for example, Za Matku Zem organized an *ekotabor* (ecology camp), during which they incorporated more traditional conservation vocabulary targeted especially for media consumption. Every day, communist-style brigades picked up garbage in a nearby village and along roadsides. As bands of activists strolled through town with sacks and bags picking up stray paper and cans, Juraj Rizman, the group's seventeen-year-old leader, greeted onlooking villagers with his best formal Slovak *"Dobre ráno Vám prajem* [I wish you a good morning]!" Za Matku Zem activists invited older, more established environmentalists to give lectures and provide information on more traditional aspects of ecology. Not surprisingly, media coverage of the camp depicted both the organization and its activities in a positive vein, as these public actions were the only ones local and visiting reporters were allowed to observe. They were not, of course, invited to attend the sabotage lectures or direct action training sessions, which were held later in the evenings or in secluded areas far from public view.

In addition to maintaining flexibility in the creation of public images for media consumption, Za Matku Zem also showed itself to be sensitive to nationalist politics. So, for example, while it was committed along with Greenpeace to creating public discourse critiquing nuclear energy in Slovakia, the group did not hesitate to take this issue beyond Slovak borders. In 1995, a group of international activists walked across Europe from Brussels to Moscow to protest nuclear energy. Za Matku Zem led the group on the Slovakian leg of this trip. On this journey and on dozens of local protest marches, blockades, and at international demonstrations, Za Matku Zem activists made certain that they also waved the new Slovak flag.

ENVIRONMENTALISM IN THE MARGINS

In spite of their post-socialist upbringings, their highly visible presence in the media, and their occasional flexibility in directing environmental discourse away from their own nation, young Slovak NGOs remained, along with their older counterparts, a marginalized community. This marginality was no doubt a result of their increasing connection to the international environmental community and the controversial subjects which they relentlessly targeted. Other features of the new movement, however, contributed equally to this marginal condition, including a lack of financial support, a dependency on charismatic leadership, and confusion among the public about their identity.

Perhaps it is not surprising that when protest and political representation are free, protestors tend to cling to the issues with which they most identify. Hence the new state of the nation left environmental NGOs somewhat underpopulated. The independent NGO sector had only a sixth the membership of the more conservative, conservationist-oriented SZOPK (see table 5.3). The largest organizations had the youngest members, most of them university or high school students with limits on the availability of their time. Their ability to survive also depended on the skills of individual leaders to develop a consistent and continuous funding base, whether foreign or local. Such a support base, however, had not yet been developed by any of the new NGOs by 1995. Young activists shared with the older generation a serious lack of financial support from their own

TABLE 5.3 SZOPK and New NGO Membership, 1995

SZOPK*		Independent**	
Bratislava	450	Greenpeace	50
Košice	271	Deti Zeme	145
Lipt. Mik.	446	STUŽ	50
Pov. Byst.	322	Ipel U.	42
Prievidza	200		
Others	1,593	Others	149
Total	3,092	Total	536

*Not including members of the UV
**Not including the animal rights group *Sloboda Zvierat*

society. While groups attempted to raise money through contribution campaigns, by mailing fliers and pamphlets, response was minimal. Competition among NGOs was intense, and foreign funding sources often meant limitations on the issues pursued and the format of activities to promote them.[11]

Limited resources encouraged intergroup cooperation, where one organization allowed another to share office space. For example, the Slovak Rivers Network set up operations at Gorkého 6, where the Central Committee of SZOPK had its main office. The Bratislava MV SZOPK let Greenpeace Slovakia have one of the three rooms in its small *domček* in the castle district. But this situation also meant cramped quarters. This same building now served as the headquarters of the MV SZOPK, the section for folk architecture, and the meeting space for all the rest of the Union's Bratislava organizations, as well as for STUŽ. The *domček* had only two phone lines, one copy machine, a few secondhand chairs and desks, and two aging computers. When Greenpeace moved in, the small cottage bustled with young students who stopped by after school to volunteer their time. In this claustrophobic atmosphere, tensions mounted between SZOPK members and Greenpeace Slovakia. Older *ochranári* complained of the disorder that the younger activists created in the office, the result of banner paintings, post-protest parties, and the sheer volume of material that Greenpeace had accumulated. Ironically, the clustering of different NGOs under the same roof in an attempt to support each other amplified a general confusion among the public over what group stood for which issues and which activists belonged to what group.

One morning in 1995, Katka, the City Committee secretary of SZOPK, arrived to find painted on the office door, "*Zeleni do riti* [Greens go fuck yourselves]!" She hoped that this vulgar graffiti referred to Greenpeace

TABLE 5.4 New NGOs in Slovakia 1989–93

Year	Number	Percent
1989	1	3
1990	67	18.5
1991	85	23.5
1992	102	28.2
No year*	107	29.5
Total	362	100.0

*These NGOs did not provide the year they were established, but they certainly did not exist before 1990.
Source: Second Stupava Conference 1994

activists' anti-Mochovce campaign, but ultimately could never be certain of this as the Gorkého office had also been the headquarters of the Gabčíkovo Dam campaign several years before. Neither of these issues had won much sympathy from Slovaks.

On top of all of this, all new environmental NGOs, along with other organizations and associations that comprised Slovakia's post-socialist civil society, became the political targets of members of the HZDS-led government, which saw them as a threat to the country's power and stability. This perception on the part of Mečiar's ruling coalition, which included the far right Slovak National Party, began to emerge as early as 1993, when the leaders of several new environmental NGOs, along with the heads of various civic foundations and groups, decided to establish a loosely organized network of all NGOs in Slovakia, referred to as the Third Sector. NGO leadership figured that, since the number of NGOs had grown so dramatically (see table 5.4), an umbrella organization representing all of these groups could act as a lobby for more financial aid, for better public awareness, and for improved intergroup coordination. Members of the ruling coalition read this emerging network as a new political movement, a view that was only confirmed as several opposition politicians, among them Pavol Demeš, a vocal critic of Mečiar's heavy-handed approach to governing, openly supported the Third Sector initiative. In October of 1995, Roman Hofbauer, a deputy for HZDS and the chairman of the Slovak National Council, launched a negative campaign against the Third Sector, calling for greater financial disclosure of independent foundations in Slovakia. Hofbauer argued that many NGOs had not fully disclosed their accounting practices or their funding sources to the Ministry of the Interior. In fact, there was no requirement that they do so; they only needed to be legally registered. He further suggested that these groups were contributing to the "political chaos" of Slovak society, claiming that "groups and associations . . . with seminars, symposia and congresses are more anti-Slovak and slander the state" (*Slovenská Republika*, October 4, 1995). In addition to demanding financial disclosure, Hofbauer's party introduced a bill to establish a governmental administrative body whose purpose would be to evaluate the aims and goals of foundations and associations. This body would determine whether a group's "activities [were] directed to providing services and activities potentially beneficial to all citizens" (*Navrh* c. 4082/95–60 1995).

Hofbauer's proposal was interpreted by environmental activists not only as a blatant attack on the Third Sector, but as yet another attempt to discredit and control ecological groups that had dared to take on large state-owned companies such as Hydrostav and Vodohospodarska Vystavba with direct interests in continuing Stalinist-type megaprojects, regardless of whether the projects still seemed to have any value. While other foundations and associations, such as those assisting persons with disabilities, youth service programs, and associations for the aged, would be included in Hofbauer's accountability regime, environmental activists argued that these organizations would have little difficulty in passing a governmental review. Environmental NGOs, on the other hand, given their record on controversial issues like nuclear power plants, water construction projects, and pollution regulations, as well as their growing ties to international groups, could easily be shut down by this proposed legal organ. Beginning in 1996, Third Sector member groups began to collaborate in fighting the bill through demonstrations, news conferences, and petitions, an effort which drained many activists' resources and time. This struggle continued for three more years, until 1998, when Mečiar fell from power. Mečiar was replaced by a broad coalition government under the leadership of Mikuláš Džurinda. Much of the credit for Džurinda's victory went to the work of foreign and Slovak NGOs to mobilize an urban electorate and place the country back on a path to democratic reforms (Kirschbaum 2005:297). Although the battle to squelch a repressive governmental measure was an experience that united many green activists who had not worked together on a common goal for several years, the struggle was not to benefit the environment. Rather, it was a battle for many environmental organizations' very survival.

Returning to the case of the Slatinka dam hearing in Zvoleň, in the end, the villagers signed the government agreement and lost their village. In February 1999, Vodohospodarska Vystavba expropriated the property of the residents of Slatinka. The state water management company, still short on money, now planned to utilize European Union funds to finance the as yet to be constructed Slatinka dam. If the new *ochranári* of Slovakia had won their right to survive in a young and troubled post-socialist democracy, they had not been able to save the victims of the megaprojects of the old regime.

POST-ECOLOGY: A PICTURE OF THE NEW WORLD

From state socialism into the transition and beyond, we see how political and cultural processes can conspire to propel, dismantle, and reshape ecological activism as well as reformulate environmentalities in what might be considered the emerging post-ecological condition of post-socialist Slovakia. By this I mean a world where Marxist ideologies that governed environmental subjects shift, but do not altogether disappear. Alongside an environmentality of communism emerge new models of ethnic nation-state authoritarianism that resituate nature as a symbolic resource for the mobilization of culture and capital. Within this highly unstable political context, Slovak environmental activists were well positioned to reformulate the green agenda after the Velvet Revolution but failed to work against the very symbols (of nation and of nature) that challenged their legitimacy.

In this emerging post-ecological condition the movement was, itself, involved in a series of shifts. First, the movement changed from a monolithic volunteer Union to specialized and professionalizing expert organizations. Interestingly, the year in which most new NGOs were established, 1993, was the year that Slovakia became independent from the Czechs (see table 5.5). Prior to this period, Slovakia had been a second-class recipient of Western aid to East Europe, with most assistance finding its way to Prague and the Czech Republic. This was not only the case with foreign capital investments, but also with efforts to help establish Third Sec-

TABLE 5.5 Number of Environmental NGOs
Founded in Slovakia, 1989–94

Year	Number	Percent
1989	1	1.6
1990	10	15.8
1991	10	15.8
1992	15	23.8
1993	26	41.4
1994	1	1.6
Total	63	100.0

tor associations focused on promoting democracy, improving education, and developing social services. If many Slovaks were disillusioned by the breakup of Czechoslovakia, the Velvet Divorce actually drew more international attention and increased assistance to the newly autonomous state. This was not just the case with European development funding from agencies such as the European Bank for Reconstruction and Development, which the Slovak government lobbied to help it finance large energy projects, but also with resources available for environmental organizations and other Third Sector groups.

Second, the movement shifted from informal, organic collective action to more formal, expert-based and issue-based operations. The impact and momentum of the communist period SZOPK depended significantly on the quality of volunteer leadership and on the degree of commitment of particular individuals to provide such leadership. Such authority, what Max Weber describes as "charismatic," is based on the ability of individuals to inspire a sense of "devotion to the possessor of the quality, arising out of enthusiasm, or of despair and hope" among followers (Weber 1978:242). Green leadership under communism was informal and situational and almost entirely based on an individual's ability to persuade members to action. Leading by example, authority figures like Huba, Tatár, Budaj, and Podoba, who often personally carried out a significant amount of the planning and administrative work essential to so many of the group's projects, had been quite successful in wielding and sustaining the necessary levels of charismatic authority within the movement. As some of these leaders left for other pursuits, group enthusiasm diminished. Even in cases where a few charismatic and inspirational figures tried to maintain their membership in the Union, their leadership abilities lost potency due to overextended responsibilities and commitments outside of the group. For example, Mikuláš Huba, although he never left SZOPK, over the course of the first three years in the transition served on the Slovak Commission for the Environment (an advisory body created right after the Revolution), attended sessions of parliament as a Green Party deputy, and juggled his post at the Academy of Sciences with his duties as a leader of the new Society for Sustainable Living.

Third, in the face of the rapid displacement of ecology by issues such as the pace of privatization, which was fundamentally integrated with identity politics, Slovak environmental NGOs faced the daunting task of creating a clear and relevant ecological message in the cacophony of post-socialist society. Only greens in the younger generation, through single-issue symbolic demonstrations, went directly after this goal. In this sense younger activists were willing to work within the nascent system, creating new activist roles in the process. Unlike their predecessors, these "children of the greens" were determined to adapt to the particular cultural and political situation of post-socialism, even in their attempt to change it. Yet, since most of these new organizations were controlled by the agendas of international environmental organizations, their impact on the public, though highly visible, was largely negative.

Fourth, while Slovak activists had plenty of experience in pushing their message in more cosmopolitan settings such as Bratislava, they were much less effective in reaching out to rural, and particularly older, Slovaks. In the case of Slatinka, new environmental groups had indeed prepared themselves (and showed up in force) to confront the state on specific issues and on current policy. However, they apparently overlooked the need to adequately prepare, and even to fully understand the needs and concerns of the people most directly affected by the project in question. Instead, activists from the Center for Public Advocacy figured that their own discourse would suffice as an act of resistance, and, evidently, assumed the inability of subalterns to speak (Spivak 1988). By speaking for the residents, activists actually failed to win the trust of the very people they tried to rescue.

Finally, and no less importantly, we see elements of both communist-period and transition-era environmentalities in the state's efforts to reshape Slovakia's landscape. On the one hand, we can see in the Slatinka case how the government understood very well how and where to take advantage of public passivity. Vodohospodarska Vystavba representatives knew where to target large projects to serve the company's own ends, to exert its power where counterdiscourses were unlikely to be articulated.

Although the Slatinka project would wipe out an entire village, it would cause only limited social upheaval. This "inconvenience" of a "state affair" would be felt only among those Slovaks who were easily appeased with a few crowns for their land and forced relocation to an apartment complex in Zvoleň. On the other hand, the post-socialist landscape itself had been transformed to become an ethnic nation where old projects of socialism, rather than being vestiges of totalitarianism, now appeared as vital symbols of independence. In the end, the villagers of Slatinka in no way resembled Hanak's communist-period cinematic portraits of the subversiveness of elderly, rural Slovaks, tenaciously independent, the keepers of cultural tradition in villages far from the socialist city. Rather, the villagers of Slatinka represented the submissive subjectivities of the socialist landscape of normalization, not wanting to make waves, not rising above the crowd to question authority or to speak in a recalcitrant, independent voice. The old world was still quite present in the new.

6 Returning to the Landscape

IF SLOVAKIA'S LANDSCAPES HAD CHANGED SIGNIFICANTLY since 1989, one thing remained the same: in the summer Slovaks still left the city for rest and relaxation. Like elsewhere throughout East Europe, in Slovakia August is the traditional vacation month. A visitor to the capital city during this month, perhaps on a side trip from Vienna, just thirty minutes away by bus, will find many shops in town with signs on their doors reading "*zatvorené: na dovolenku* [closed for vacation]." During the time of my field research in the mid-1990s, only a small group of newly profit-minded merchants remained in Bratislava to take advantage of the fledgling tourist market. Everyone else, it seemed, had headed for the countryside.

Only a few years had passed since the flood of East Germans, crammed in their cars, descended on Hungary in the summer of 1989, just after the country opened its borders to the West. This August migration of "vacationers" had marked the beginning of the end for the communist regimes in Eastern Europe. That same August, three months before the Velvet Revolution, Bratislava itself was virtually empty. But rather than daring to join the droves of East Germans fleeing the communist bloc, Slovaks made their own private escapes. A common destination was the man-made lakes of Senec, about thirty kilometers outside the city. Here Bratislavans spent the month in their bathing suits, sitting in beach chairs and sleeping in small wooden vacation huts along the water. Others swarmed to the Tatra and Fatra mountains for hiking and trekking. Small villages throughout the country filled up with urbanites eager to relax with their extended families for a few weeks. No one knew that only four months later they would be free to go wherever they wished for vacation.

That same summer of 1989, the *ochranári* had also escaped Bratislava's streets to continue their work in the Kvačian Valley near Liptovský Mikuláš. It was the summer before their surprising takeover over of the Central Committee of szopk, and the summer after they issued their Earth Day Proclamation, which had boldly announced their new role as the environmental conscience of the nation. The 1989 brigade to the valley managed to construct a new water wheel for the upper mill. It took eleven people just to lift it up and onto the wooden axle. But there were plenty of activists on this brigade. After all, it was 1989, and zo 6 of szopk had over 500 members in its ranks.

Six years later, in 1995, the conservation of cultural monuments, a practice that had become the cornerstone of the volunteer environmental movement under socialism, was still alive in Slovakia. The Bratislava City Committee of szopk continued to work at the lower mill in the Kvačian Valley. Some 50 kilometers further west, Mikuláš Huba and his brother Marko, along with other members of the old zo 6, were putting a new roof on a small *chata* at Podšíp. And much further east, in Brdarka, a small village not far from the Ukrainian border, a fledgling environmental ngo was having a brigade of its own. In the summer of 1995, I was invited to all three of these projects by the people who organized them. Each had encouraged me to come observe and contribute to the volunteer practice of preserving Slovakia's heritage and landscape. But I quickly discovered that *ochranárstvo* had developed along different paths. The *ochranári*'s brand of landscape preservation, which thrived under totalitarianism as an escape from the gray life of the communist city and which evolved into a surprisingly effective critique of the regime, experienced some significant transitions of its own. Among older activists, the volunteer preservation of cultural landscapes no longer served as a point of confrontation with state power. Instead, it remained a form of recreation and a sort of withdrawal from and introspection about the post-socialist world. For a group of younger conservationists, however, the once quite subversive practice of historical preservation became a new expression of patriotism and ethnic consciousness in a post-communist Europe grappling with increasing tensions of identity politics.

The three conservation projects to which I was invited in the summer of 1995 serve to illustrate this transformation. In comparing these, what appear to be similar practices of landscape preservation in fact represent quite different and competing ideas about nature, place, and identity in Slovakia's overlapping discourses of post-socialist culture change. In one project there appears to be a new discursive community emerging from the ranks of SZOPK within the framework of Slovak independence. Some activists referred to this new movement as "ecotourism." Others called it "eco-fascism." However it was viewed, and whatever its different messages were, volunteer *ochranárstvo* remained a local and grassroots attempt to wrest the project of legibility (Scott 1990) from the hands of the state.

THE MILL AT KVAČIAN

On an early August evening I arrived at the edge of the Kvačian Valley by the last bus from Liptovský Mikuláš. It was too late to head down the long trail through the woods without a flashlight. "The trail goes right along the edge of a cliff," warned the owner of a nearby hostel. I stayed the night in one of his rooms, all of which had been rented by hikers the night before. "It's vacation time, you know, you're lucky to get a bed," the owner remarked. The next day I trekked along the winding paths between the valley's ravines and, after about an hour and a half, came upon the clearing in which the mills of SZOPK sat nestled deep at the valley's bottom. Katka, the secretary of the City Committee of SZOPK in Bratislava, was staying at the lower mill. She was with her two children. Andrej, a young man doing his civil service duty[1] with the City Committee, was staying in the upper mill, just a few hundred yards up the valley's gentle slope.[2]

SZOPK had maintained both mills as a museum for tourists. During the week that I was there, Katka and Andrej helped look after the properties, keeping them clean, doing minor repairs, and handing out literature to hikers who passed by on the many trails through the valley. The lower mill at Kvačian was a long-term project and a showpiece of SZOPK, representing the type of careful and meticulous preservation work that the old guard *ochranári* in ZO 6 carried out during the 1980s. Though renovation of the mill was completed in 1989, the structure required ongoing maintenance. Around the sides of the lower mill were piles of lichen and mosses that were to be put between aging boards in order to seal up gaps that formed over time. Tourists were welcome to stay in the mill, which had goose-feather beds and a functioning wood stove. But most visitors who came by that week just sat and talked for a while with Katka or Andrej and then continued on their way. In midweek, one couple from

Moravia, who had arrived at dusk, slept near the lower mill, outside under twinkling stars.

A few days after I arrived, Peter Špörer, a journalist from the independent newspaper *Narodná Obroda*, came to stay at the lower mill with his daughter. Špörer had been a member of ZO 6 in the 1980s and had gained a reputation as a "green journalist" before the Velvet Revolution. Under socialism, particularly after the appearance of *Bratislava/nahlas*, Špörer had boldly covered environmental problems in the state press. However, six years into the transition, he now explained that his role as a reporter was to take on new stories.

> I don't write about just the environment now. At the beginning of 1990 it was the most popular thing. Everybody wanted to find out about the problems that the communists let develop under our noses. Today, there is too much else going on. My editors expect me to write about everything. I have to. I am still interested in these topics though, the problems of nature and pollution, etc. I try to put a piece in here and there.

In fact, Špörer had recently written one environmental piece for his paper. But in it his message to the public was far from positive. In September he published a short memorial to the late Jozef Vavroušek, Czechoslovakia's first (and last) post-communist Minister of the Environment, who had died in a tragic accident that spring while hiking in the Tatra Mountains. Špörer's article was entitled "The Lone Environmentalists." Špörer noted that ecologists were now rejected as "enemies of progress" and "enemies of Slovakia," and that they had certainly failed in the political arena (*Narodná Obroda*, September 1995). Though he offered no answer, his text asked whether there was any chance for nature activists to have an impact in Slovak society as it leapt into the world of consumerism and the pursuit of prosperity, a world that seemed to suggest the death of ecology.

While his daughter played with Katka's children, Špörer visited with Katka, who had been his colleague during his days with ZO 6. The mill was a piece of Slovak history that Špörer himself had helped to reconstruct over the years, and which he now used to decompress from the modern bustle of post-socialism. He reiterated, "I came here to relax. It is my vacation. The work that I do the rest of the year is exhausting. There are so many problems in society, so much to worry about. This valley is only stars and the trees on the hills." This August, Špörer was not at Kvačian as an *ochranár* or even as a journalist. He was there only to enjoy the quiet benefits of hard work done long ago, in another summer, in another Slovakia.

If the Kvačian mill had survived the changing landscape of post-socialism, the City Committee of szopk was on the edge of extinction. This once remarkably vibrant conservation organization, which had supported the rebuilding of hundreds of monuments of pre-communist culture, and whose members later unexpectedly rose to public power during the Velvet Revolution, was itself in need of salvation. Katka complained that

> there is no money for the City Committee. No money at all. I'm not even sure if we have enough to do the *Ekofilm* this fall . . . But what am I going to do? I have looked for some kind of grant. And Andrej has tried to help. But even if we get money for the *Ekofilm*, what else do we need? And where is the money supposed to come from?

Katka looked tired and worried. It had been a long year, and she had hoped the mill would give her some peace and rest. Throughout 1995, the City Committee had spent a great amount of its human energy, which was almost all it had left as a resource, in an effort to connect with international environmental organizations. Among Katka and Andrej's ideas was to try to attract a Peace Corps volunteer, as other organizations in the Third Sector had successfully done in 1993 and 1994. One volunteer had been assigned to the Ipel River Union, a new NGO in Šahy, a town on the Hungarian border. Through this American volunteer's help and expertise, the Ipel River Union won foreign grants, reorganized its database, and forged stronger contacts with ecological groups throughout Central Europe. But there were only so many Peace Corps volunteers to go around in Slovakia, a country low on the priority list for the U.S. in the context of ongoing violence in the former Yugoslavia, and the abundance of other states, such as Romania and Bulgaria, which were also slow to democratize their governments and privatize their economies.[3]

Katka's personal connection to the Peace Corps was Pavel Šremer, the Czech dissident who had been with szopk since its founding in 1969. But since the split of Czechoslovakia in 1993, Šremer was now in an independent and disconnected Czech Republic. His Peace Corps post in Prague was limited to servicing Czech NGOs. By the time Katka applied in Bratislava, the deadline had passed. Like most other old-school environmentalists, Katka was spread too thin as an activist. For example, she had been helping Huba's new group, STUŽ, on a Slovak translation of a several-hundred-page European Council document outlining concepts of sustainability for the European Union. This document had only been available to environmental groups in East Europe in its English version. On top of her work with the City Committee, she also occasionally served as STUŽ's secretary. The Bratislava City Committee of SZOPK would not get an American Peace Corps volunteer this year.

Before I left the Kvačian Valley, I went with Katka to the *chata* of Peter Kresánek, another *ochranár* of the older generation but currently Bratislava's embattled mayor. Kresánek had been essential in initiating, along with Huba, the first *ochranárstvo* brigades in the 1980s. After studying architecture at university, Kresánek became an outspoken proponent of historical monument protection and was a local champion of the city of Bratislava during the Velvet Revolution. He wrote a chapter for *Bratislava/nahlas* outlining the neglect or total destruction of the city's pre-communist monuments. As an *ochranár* he had also been on hundreds of weekend and summer brigades.

Kresánek's *chata*, at the edge of a nearby village, was a nineteenth-century dwelling that had been rescued from almost complete decay. That August his wife and kids were there, playing in the tall grasses around the cozy wooden cabin. Katka asked Mrs. Kresánek if Peter was going to make it out this summer. "No, I'm afraid not," she replied. She then lowered her voice, as if wary of being overheard. "The office is so stressed over the budget cuts, and he isn't even sure if the public transportation system will be able to survive without renovation funds. He doesn't know if there will even be enough money to keep the street lights on." In 1995, as part of a move to strengthen his power base in the center regions of the country, the state authorities under Mečiar severely cut Bratislava's budget through a clever tax law passed by the HZDS-dominated parliament. Young and old greens alike saw this as a personal attack on Kresánek, who had recently won a second term as mayor after defeating an HZDS challenger in local elections.

It was beginning to look as if the original activists of the past had been swallowed up by politics and divided by special interests, something that Ján Budaj, the dissident publisher of *Bratislava/nahlas*, writing in 1989, claimed would never happen.

> Conservation is and has to remain altruistic. It has to be competent, of course, but altruism I take differently than might be seen from outside. The altruism of the *ochranári* is currently in their common relationships, thanks only

to the fact that among the *ochranári* rules tolerance. Tolerance is stronger than any individual. They are not rivals with each other, regardless of the kind of attack on the community. It is possible to say that *ochranári* stand together and hold together (SZOPK, *Ochranca Prírody* 1989:4).

The *ochranári*, however, had not held together at all in the new system. Budaj himself had left the conservation movement entirely. He was now working full time as a political consultant and fundraiser for a new party, the Democratic Union.

In Slovakia's new society it seemed that those *ochranári* who became public officials had no time to do anything for environmental causes that they had once championed. These activists, like Kresánek, were too busy challenging, or perhaps more truthfully just surviving, the heavy hand of Mečiar's populism to be able to go on conservation brigades, let alone summer vacations.

RESTING AT PODŠÍP

After staying at Kvačian for a week, I went by train to the eastern edge of the Malá Fatra Mountains and disembarked at a village called Stankovaný. I was supposed to meet up with Mikuláš Huba, who had invited me to see some of the results of his conservation work. Huba was spending the summer with his brother Marko at a small cluster of *drevenice* at Podšíp, a plateau just below Šíp Mountain. It was early afternoon when I stepped off the train, and I asked a local storekeeper in town how to get there. "Where?" he asked.

"Podšíp," I repeated.

"Oh, oh yeah, there's a few people gone up there two days before. You just go along the railroad and head up the trail to the right."

The "trail" turned out to be a narrow dirt furrow that quickly disappeared into deep woods which covered a steep slope. The storekeeper told me it was only a kilometer up the hill. He was correct, but the grade went up more than 800 meters. This almost vertical journey took over two hours, the path climbing treacherously up beneath a dark deciduous forest. Before my legs gave way, and as the sun was quickly setting, I reached a more level clearing surrounded by wispy pines. I followed the sounds of hammering and the smell of wood smoke emanating from a barely visible group of *chaty* huddled beneath the dramatic rocky peak of Šíp Mountain in the distance.

"Podšíp was a settlement (*osada*) in the nineteenth century," Huba explained in a quiet but authoritative voice. "No one really knows exactly when it was abandoned. But herders lived here, away from repression and warfare." The settlement had a dozen *drevenice*, all single-room cabins, the traditional dwelling of Habsburg-era Slovak mountain peasants. Save for a couple of buildings, they were in excellent condition. Huba, his brother, and their friend Kajo were hammering freshly cut wooden shingles, carved from native pines with small hatchets (*sekerky*). They had been re-roofing one of the cabins all afternoon.

During the next few days, the *ochranári* planed off small wooden support beams, cut shingles, hammered them onto the beams with the backs of their *sekerky*, and chopped still more shingles from a pile of wood on the ground. In the evenings they sat around a small wooden table, drank homemade *slivovica*, and talked underneath the stars. People rose in the early morning to start this cycle of work and leisure all over again.

"I don't see my work here like some kind of expression of national identity," Marko said. "It is my art." After thinking for a moment, he went on with his analysis.

> It is paradoxical, though, that we are being labeled "enemies of Slovakia." Many of the people today who present themselves as "great Slovaks" really do actually very little—even nothing. They want money, they want power. From my point of view, the ideal thing is to do practical work. I see my work as preserving a cultural past. But more than this, I come here to be close to nature, to be on vacation from the city. And to do something that I love to do.

Marko was a sculptor and an art teacher at a Bratislava high school, where he taught, among other subjects, the craft of woodworking. Several of his students had arrived at Podšíp a couple of days after I did to learn *ochranárstvo* from their teacher. None of them were members of any of Slovakia's environmental organizations. Rather, they all aspired to study architecture at university.

Later on in the week, Igor Halama arrived from Bratislava with his wife, Darina. Igor was the current chairman of ZO 6, the SZOPK branch that Huba had founded with Marko and Kajo. Igor had come to work on the *drevenice*, but also to relax. The next day, I joined Igor and Darina on a day's hike up to the rocky peak of Šíp. At the top, Igor quietly assessed the organization which had been so well known and of which he now was in charge.

There aren't many of us anymore in ZO 6. All of the personalities, the people who really put their heart and soul into it, are gone. Even Huba has this new STUŽ. We still have meetings, every month. Sometimes four people show up, sometimes more. But there are only maybe 20 of us now. In fact the last meeting, I could not make it. I had to stay late at work. But every summer we try to make a trip somewhere. Sometimes it's here, sometimes to Kvačian.

Knowing that Greenpeace had more or less taken over the building in which ZO 6 held their meetings, I asked him about these new environmental groups in Slovakia.

I can't say that Greenpeace is all that bad. But they are too radical for me. I don't like people doing things that are dangerous like they did at Mochovce [nuclear power plant]. I am not for nuclear energy, but I'm also against trespassing. Also, this Greenpeace is for young people. People who are older don't make demonstrations.

It was true that older activists did not make demonstrations. Only one demonstration out of the thirty I had attended over the past year included a Slovak over the age of thirty-five.[4] Rather than take to the streets in protest, older environmentalists preferred press releases and public seminars. They translated English language environmental literature into Slovak and analyzed environmental laws and policies proposed by Western organizations. Of course these were things that their younger colleagues did as well. In the remnants of SZOPK, however, *ochranárstvo* remained the central agenda, albeit a practice that more and more frequently coincided only with vacation time.

In 1988, ZO 6 members had enjoyed a growing reputation of heroism among the public, which they did not hesitate at that time to emphasize in their own writing. That year, a caption to a full-page photograph of a Habsburg-era house published in the City Committee's magazine, *Ochranca Prírody*, read:

A monumental object in the middle of the city's so-called historic preserve, Green Street No. 10, found itself in the fall of 1987 on the brink of collapse. Professional firms refused to even enter it. So the Bratislava *ochranári* took care of it. Under the direction of Juraj Flamik, and in the course of several Saturdays, they managed to save it from complete ruin (SZOPK, *OP* 1–2 1988).

By 1995, however, the vibrant organization that grew up around the practice of saving public places and preserving a culture's residential history had shrunk in size from hundreds in 1989 to a couple of dozen members. Even for Mikuláš Huba, who pioneered the practice as a volunteer effort, *ochranárstvo* was no longer a central environmental issue. STUŽ of course listed it among its many projects and priorities in pursuit of sustainable living.

But in practice, in the shadow of Šip peak, saving old structures had been relegated to mere recreation. The preservation of culture, which under socialism had discursively given birth to a social movement, became akin to the socialist-era vacation, where individuals could seek solace from the city. But this time, it appeared that people were fleeing from the challenges and uncertainties of a new, post-communist society.

THE SPRING AT BRDARKA

After my stay at Podšíp, I traveled by train, and then by bus, to the tiny village of Brdarka in the Gemer region of southeast Slovakia. During what felt to be an endless ride sitting beside a pair of Roma (Gypsy) women, each clutching a squawking hen in one hand and a squirming child in the other, the lurching bus wound slowly around barely paved roads beneath towering trees. As the road appeared to give way to dust clouds, we arrived at a remote village of some 40 old houses, several of which were clearly abandoned, with broken window panes and cracks in their exterior walls. It was here, in this tiny place called Brdarka, that a new NGO, the Return to the Landscape Foundation (Nadácia Navraty ku Krajiny), was holding a summer brigade.

The Return to the Landscape Foundation was established in 1992. It was founded by a small group of university students in their late teens and early twenties who had been members of ZO 6 and who had worked on its brigades in the late 1980s. After the Velvet Revolution, these junior *ochranári* broke away from ZO 6 and formed an independent organization. Peter Smežiansky, one of the Foundation's leaders, explained:

> We wanted to do something. We wanted to do it on our own, outside of ZO 6. And Mikuláš Huba realized this and he told us to go to Kysicka Huta, a small settlement in the Low Tatras. In the summer of 1992 we decided that we would do a brigade. There were about 20 of us. We found an abandoned house and put up a roof. It took us two weeks.

Like SZOPK, the Foundation devoted itself to recreational *ochranárstvo*. Its mission was to assist in "the cultural and economic development of the countryside on the basis of sustainable use of local cultural and natural heritage" (*Nadácia navraty ku krajíny* 1995). To achieve this goal, however, the Foundation developed its own version of what has become known as ecotourism. One of the first environmental groups in Slovakia to believe that people with the means to travel might want to spend free time doing something other than snorkeling or sunbathing at a beach resort, the Foundation arranged for ecotourists to help reconstruct decaying villages and, presumably, in the process of carrying out their work give a much-needed boost to the local economy. That summer, the Foundation was realizing this idea through a long-term project in the isolated and clearly struggling village of Brdarka. Its members had chosen this site through personal ties. One of the group's founders, Peter András, an architecture student from Bratislava, had family roots in the Gemer region, and had bought one of the dilapidated buildings in the village. After refurbishing it, he moved in with his wife.

When I arrived in Brdarka, the brigade had already been underway for more than a week, and Foundation members, along with a large and lively group of foreign tourists, had already completed the frame of a 15–meter-high wooden pavilion over the village spring. The spring was in the center of the village, and flowed from a spigot which had been encased in an enormous concrete block during the communist period. The foreign participants included tourists from the United States, Switzerland, France, Spain, Holland, Poland, and Morocco. Among them were also a few Slovaks from Bratislava and several from Košice, the country's eastern urban center. In all, more than 100 people had joined the Brdarka brigade. The international guests slept in local houses that the aging residents rented out to them for a truly nominal fee of a few crowns. Being able to see "the real Slovakia" was a feature of the brigade highlighted in the Foundation's full-color catalog, which advertised the excursion as a unique opportunity "to experience Slovak traditional village life." The accommodations certainly delivered on this promise. The houses in which the guests stayed had no indoor plumbing. Chickens scurried about in the courtyards of the dwellings, and cows and sheep grazed in nearby pastures. The mattresses on which people slept were made from straw stuffed into linen covers.

Along with the rugged conditions of Slovak rural life, all of the participants shared in the experience of doing renovation work. Some people cut shingles from pieces of wood with *sekerky*. Others used old-fashioned planes to shave down the shingles for a proper fit. For reasons of safety, however, Foundation members took on the task of hammering shingles onto the high support beams of the pavilion roof. In addition to the pavilion, the Foundation had started repairs on an old church perched on a hill above the houses. The Foundation members had only begun to tackle this task before their foreign guests arrived, because it required quite a bit of knowledge of stonemasonry. After first cutting drainage grooves into the church's saturated walls, the entire brigade pitched in to repair the timber roof, which had been on the brink of collapse.

Along with this construction work, the Foundation's camp included daily meals and evening "cultural programs," both of which brought out a more rigid division of labor along gender lines. While both men and women helped with the woodworking, mostly women prepared food and cleaned up afterwards. Women also brought tea and watermelon slices to the workers in the afternoons. The cultural programs consisted of live folk music and singing, which were led by the young male Foundation activists who were also accomplished musicians. One evening, an activist pulled out a *gajda*, traditional Slovak bagpipes made from sheep gut, and performed a series of mournful folk songs with the prowess of a Slovak shepherd. In keeping with the mission of showing foreign guests the "real" Slovak countryside, Foundation members also organized a couple of excursions to places of interest in the surrounding region. A shopping trip to Košice, where ecotourists could buy traditional pottery, leather goods, and other crafts, was followed a few days later by a visit to nearby ice caves, buried deep under the rolling hills of the Gemer Valley, which were themselves covered with the region's famous cherry trees.

The Foundation had also invited a few journalists to join the brigade, and a reporter from *Narodná Obroda*, a national newspaper, wrote the event up as a heartwarming experience of cultural revitalization.

During free time we carved brushwood, modeled clay and listened to lectures. On Saturday, there was a small, improvisational folklore festival, to which 500 people came from the surrounding hillsides. There had never been such a thing here. For the first time in 14 years the village celebrated. Brdarka, revitalized with young blood and with the mental concord of all interested, got up on its feet (*Narodná Obroda*, August 28, 1995).

The village had certainly been rejuvenated. While the tourists worked, villagers frequently came by to observe the group's progress and to chat. They were very pleased by the fact that the Foundation was doing this for "their village." "This is just great," said one villager, gazing on the workers. "And it is really something that that young one moved here. We are all old here. It's nice to see these young people."

Earlier in the year, Peter András, the Foundation member who had become a village resident, had built a new bus stop for the villagers. The bus from Rožňava, the closest town, came only three times a day, and one often had to wait in the hot sun for its arrival. One of the members, who had been interviewed by the reporter from *Narodná Obroda*, explained the philosophy of the Foundation.

> We don't want to do this work as only a hobby or for relaxation, where we repair something and then do nothing else the entire year. We want to provide people some instruction for their continued livelihood. To teach them how to use the materials they have, and of course to help them raise up their lives (*Narodná Obroda*, August 28, 1995).

This mission to raise up their lives had not been so easy to accomplish when the group first started after the Velvet Revolution. Similar to the Slatinka residents' reaction to environmental activists who wanted to help them, local villagers at first viewed the Foundation's work suspiciously as an incursion by "outsiders." Smežiansky recalled how, when they began their work in Kysicka Huta, they tried to reassure residents by proposing to sign an agreement with the town.

> The older people there didn't believe what these young people were doing. They thought we had some other motives, I don't know. I mean, I really don't know why but the town government went back on their decision [to sign the agreement]. And we weren't allowed to fix up anything.

In light of the reluctance on the part of local villagers, the Foundation decided that their next brigade would be more organized. Rather than just showing up in a village with their tools and heading for the first abandoned house, they explained, "we drew up a strategy for our group. We made a brochure. And we applied for a grant. We received our first grant in 1993 from ProSlovakia, a funding institution for nongovernmental organizations focused on culture."

The Foundation used this seed money to make a longer-term connection to villagers in places such as Brdarka. For example, they would show residents photographs of the buildings they had restored and explain to them their commitment to helping the local economy. To protect and help the nation, the Foundation learned that it had to get to know the nation, and what the community wanted.

The Foundation's approach was quite unlike other environmental NGOs, that looked to serve, somewhat paternalistically, as liaisons between the state and local communities. The organization was listed alongside these other NGOs in SZOPK's annual directory of environmental groups. The Foundation's work was also advertised in the City Committee's monthly newsletter.[5] In its promotional literature, the Return to the Landscape Foundation also prominently included the term "sustainable." Upon closer inspection, however, and after talking with other activists in Bratislava, it appeared that the environment with which this new organization was concerned was perhaps not the same environment that other post-socialist ecological NGOs were trying to save.

THE DOUBLE-EDGED HATCHET

Shortly after visiting their brigade, I came across another article that featured the Foundation's work. To my surprise, the piece had appeared in *Zmena* (Change), an openly anti-Semitic and extremely nationalist weekly. The article, entitled "The Renaissance of the *Drevenice?*" suggested the motivating factor of renovation work in the countryside should be commercial development, part of a rural tourist industry for which Slovakia offered a "'paradise on Earth' that was still possible to find" (*Zmena*, March 15–21, 1995). The *Zmena* article notably omitted any mention of other organizations doing similar work on *drevenice*, and conspicuously featured the Return to the Landscape Foundation. Beside the article was a large color photograph showing members of the organization standing beside their early work, an isolated shepherd's cabin in the Vajskova Valley in the Low Tatras. The article was written as a public relations piece for the Foundation.

The other articles in *Zmena* were, as I expected, clearly xenophobic. For example, the cover piece bore the title "The Muslim Invasion of Western Europe," featuring a color illustration of a cross-eyed, turban-wearing, rifle-carrying Arab riding a camel and framed by other racist and Orientalized representations of people from the African continent (*Zmena*,

March 1–7, 1995). This "report" documented the threat of non-white peoples, noting the shrinking native populations of the European Union and Slavic world. There was also a story about global tourism which opened with the following:

> In the widely connected global problems of our planet, the activities of ecological organizations of the Greenpeace type or the tragicomic fight of eco-fanatics from various world "green" parties certainly make an impression. . . . if greens were to genuinely be for ecology, they must go after the real reasons for world ecological devastation and not just politically profit from the indications of its outcomes. For example, just look at the campaign against Mochovce and the Slovak Republic (*Zmena*, April 1–7, 1995).

Not only was *Zmena* anti-Semitic, racist, and extremely far to the right, it also seemed to be anti-green, particularly against the new wave of Slovak activists, like STUŽ and Za Matku Zem, which promoted a global discourse of sustainability.

When I mentioned to older *ochranári* that I had visited the Foundation and attended one of their brigades, they cautioned that the organization, in their opinion, was oriented in a nationalist direction, and had supported splitting from the Czechs. Upon learning that I had attended one of the Foundation's projects, a Greenpeace activist replied "Oh, you went to the fascist camp. They are fascists!" In their post-socialist experience, Greenpeace activists and members of Za Matku Zem were beginning to develop their political identities as young but engaged citizens. In terms of political ideology, they placed themselves far to the left of the traditional spectrum, a position represented by the anarchist Free Alternative group. Free Alternative's leader, Juraj Hipš, had also been a Greenpeace activist, but quit to form this new nongovernmental organization. If they were not "real" anarchists, that is, in the classic Western European sense—they were, after all, only high school students—they nevertheless tried to protest, as visibly and as often as possible, against what they considered to be fascism, which they believed to be the true threat of the post-communist world. To combat what they saw as growing evidence of what they called "fascist intolerance" throughout their city— racist graffiti, skinheads in bomber jackets picking fights around bars and taverns or kicking Gypsies and harassing street musicians—they marked up public spaces with anti-skinhead graffiti and held concerts for peace and diversity.

FIG. 6.1 Battling identity politics with direct action. Za Matku Zem members join anarchists in blocking the entrance to a museum featuring a Jozef Tiso exhibit. Tiso led Slovakia's clerico-fascist independent state, allied with Nazi Germany during the Second World War.

The Free Alternative also tried to discredit any sort of public veneration of Father Tiso, the leader of wartime Slovakia, which the anarchists characterized as a puppet state for Hitler. For example, Hipš organized a demonstration in front of the Matica slovenská museum in Bratislava, which had been showing an exhibition on the life of Tiso (see figure 6.1). Joined by friends from Greenpeace and Za Matku Zem (but who did not explicitly represent these organizations), Free Alternative members dressed up as Nazi SS troops and Hlinka Guards, from Slovakia's native fascist movement. The activist "soldiers" stood at either side of the museum door while three activists, one dressed as a Gypsy, one as a Jew, and one as a Slovak woman, lay on the sidewalk blocking the entrance.[6] In order to go into the museum one had to step over these "victims of fascism." The activists had also poured ketchup on the sidewalk around them to symbolize the victims' blood. The soldiers held up a large white banner that read "This is the True Picture of the Slovak State" in bold scarlet and blue lettering. Another activist clutched a similar sign commanding, "Don't Abuse God and Nation!"

Within moments after this scene was put in place a large crowd gathered, some in support of the anarchists, others enraged that the Tiso exhibit was being criticized in such a way. "For shame!" one woman said. "You should be proud of your country!"

"I am!" replied one activist. "But I am not proud of some of the things it has done. And I don't want others to pretend that these things never happened!"

After about an hour, two police cars and a paddy wagon pulled up. For a while, officers just stood around watching the crowd that was watching the performance. Then, without warning, the police descended on the demonstrators and piled them into their waiting van. The activists were held that evening for a few hours in the station and then released. Free Alternative had possessed a legal permit from City Hall for the demonstration, which Hipš had shown to one officer when they arrived at the action. Surprisingly, the police explained that they had detained the demonstrators despite this permission because they saw their protest "promoting fascism."

In cooperation with Hipš and his anarchists, the young activists in Greenpeace and Za Matku Zem began to expand their environmental activism to include a dialogue with the extreme right and with the proponents of Slovak national identity. They eagerly added new messages regarding political freedom and tolerance of diversity to their ecological activism. Their characterization of the Foundation's version of *ochranárstvo* had developed in light of their understanding of the group's nationalist position, which, they argued, was a form of native fascism.

I later learned that just after the Velvet Revolution, the members of the Foundation had generated a curious statement, replete with the seeds of a nationalist movement. In March of 1990, during the wave of demonstrations that had sprung up calling for the rights of the Slovak nation within the context of the Czecho-Slovak Federation, the Foundation published the following.

We Have Fears—Appeal of Slovak Students to the Current Situation
They call us the rescuers, the bearers of progress, authors of the future, but we are also after all the heirs of this country and culture. Therefore, we must say: We have fears. Fears that the revolution has ended and the idea of unity has died. Freedom is here . . . We consider [freedom] as an inevitable

component of that which gives our efforts meaning, so that we can be able to direct our efforts toward higher ideals, to higher principles . . . We have fears for a dying country, which without embarrassment we henceforth are destroying. Immediately we must create a new relationship with nature, a new feeling of responsibility toward our surroundings—ourselves—the following generation . . . We have fears that in us has degenerated the power to create the spirit of the nation, to call forward a national identity, and to be acquainted with our own history . . . Our national life must not succumb to consumer morals, the commercialization of culture and the philosophy of money like in the West . . . We declare to the people feelings of responsibility, designate problems, indicate a starting point, try to trace out to where we are marching. Let's erect before society the right ideals and goals. Let's look for lost pride and humility before the nation and life. (reprinted in SZOPK, *Ochranca Prírody* 1990:21)

This declaration, which was not unlike the statements that other groups issued during those revolutionary days in its length and emotion, did not appear to invoke an explicitly visible fascism. There was no call to intolerance, nor any other directly chauvinistic philosophy expressed in its words. Yet phrases such as "lost pride" and "our own history" were similar to the calls of hard-line nationalists who pushed for Slovak autonomy, or the themes that consistently appeared in xenophobic weeklies such as *Zmena*. During an interview I conducted after the Foundation's brigade at Brdarka, Martin Brunovský, one of the group's founders, explained his position as an activist and revealed a bit more about his views on the environment and his country.

> I was a member in ZO 6 for six or seven years, but after the revolution I became active in many other things. Well, actually, I really no longer agreed with that group of people. The key people especially, their political thinking. All of these people, Marko Huba, and others. I'm not interested in 90 percent of these groups, these volunteer organizations, these activists like Greenpeace, Huba, Trubiniova. I don't agree with them.

I asked him to elaborate.

> They supported the Federation and were against the division of the country. And they did not support a separate Slovak state. I am a supporter of the creation of an independent Slovak Republic. I think it is better for us to

work, in my view, in a Slovak system. The independence of Slovakia is the best solution for leading the Slovak nation. From an economic view, from a cultural point of view, and the environment is part of this whole spectrum. And the state will function better and the nation will function better as a community in their own state. The key point is that being a nation was the whole thing. For me the number one problem was not the environment but this.

Brunovský then reiterated the goals of his Foundation.

We are trying to preserve Slovak historical structures. We are trying to develop rural ecotourism. This means that tourists can spend their vacations in the houses of villagers, they can work on the farms. This type of tourism is not as damaging for the environment.

While these goals did not seem far from the work of other *ochranári*, his views on large-scale energy projects sharply diverged from those of other environmental groups in the country.

I was against Gabčíkovo at the beginning. But now I think it was a mistake. Now I am a supporter of it. Of course, if they would just be starting the dam now I'd be against it. In my opinion Greenpeace and these others are amateurs. To be against the Gabčíkovo Dam when it was 95 percent finished is complete stupidity. And Mochovce [nuclear power plant]? What is the solution for Slovakia? If somebody would show me some replacement I would talk about it. But what is there? Nothing.

My opinion is that Slovakia doesn't have any serious environmental issues. There are some hot spots, but there is no need to be nervous. There are no radical solutions. More investment, the development of our economy, when these things happen we will be able to deal with whatever problems we have.

Brunovský's Foundation fit nicely into a prevailing nationalist worldview. Regardless of the fact that it was listed, together with the rest of the country's new green NGOs, in the environmental movement's directory of civic organizations, and despite its strategy to use foreigners to do its work, far-right elements of Slovak society, such as those who subscribed to the newspaper *Zmena*, were certainly listening to and allying themselves with its uniquely nativist environmental discourse.

So was the Foundation "fascist" like the skinheads against whom the

Anarchist Association wanted to do battle? Slovak skinheads appeared to espouse a hybrid post-socialist fascism where young Slavic kids with Slovak flags on their bomber jackets also wore Nazi crosses. Rather than propagating conspiracies about the evils of wealthy Jewry, they beat up poor Roma in back alleys. They sat and drank beer in the very same pub where some of the founders of Public Against Violence had gathered to organize and to plot anti-regime strategies in the name of tolerance and freedom during the Velvet Revolution. Unlike the coy and literary greens, these young Slovaks would raise their arms boldly in jeering Nazi salutes to confront Bolivian street musicians, innocently returning home from a long day of performances. In the eyes of skinheads, these "*černoši*" (blacks)—which they openly called them—were making more money than they, and stealing "their" Slovak women, who sometimes dated these talented migrant musicians from Latin America. On public walls and in city parks, skinheads brazenly spray-painted the words "Gypsies to the gas chambers!" But unlike their mid-century predecessors in Central Europe, fascists who were backed by powerful states and political machines, these kids were adolescent and aimless. They had no living leaders to command them. Instead, they had to rely on the veneration of long-dead Slovaks, like Fathers Tiso and Hlinka.

If the Foundation members were indeed fascists, as some young eco-activists charged, they exercised an unassuming and subtle fascism, concealed in the countryside. Their brand of fascism did not combine open intolerance with expressions of national heritage. Nor did it involve public marches featuring pictures of Tiso or Nazi crosses. The organization's fascism unfolded through practical work, far from the city, using, ironically, the manpower of foreigners. They were perhaps no more fascist than Greenpeace activists were truly anarchist. Yet both of these post-socialist identities were nonetheless present within the new dialogues that each group promoted about Slovak nature and place.

GRASSROOTS LEGIBILITY

The *sekerka* can be used to repair something old or to build something completely new. Throughout the 1980s *ochranári* only repaired what had been built before, and continued to maintain the buildings they had saved. Yet the *ochranári*'s post-socialist conservation efforts were now mostly for recreation. In contrast, the Foundation used the hatchet in an act of national re-creation, to help a village become a viable part of the revival of an independent state. These different goals are ultimately represented by the very structures upon which both groups worked, and underline the malleability of *ochranárstvo* as a tradition. On the surface, the scenes produced by each group are interchangeable: volunteer activists using their summer vacations to work on protecting a cultural landscape (compare figure 6.2 with figure 2.1). Both the projects of the Foundation and those of the *ochranári* suggest a process of saving a cultural authenticity that responds to what Eric Gabler and Richard Handler (1996:569), in their analysis of Colonial Williamsburg in Virginia, refer to as a modernist anxiety over "[a] 'lost world' . . . in need of 'preservation.'" If the *ochranári*'s mill at Kvačian was an authentic structure of the past, the pavilion at Brdarka was, like Williamsburg, a political space, a pseudo-historical public monument, refashioned as authentic and essential identity. The traditional style of the pavilion mimicked the nineteenth-century mill, with its steeply sloping roof of handmade wooden shingles. But unlike the mill, the pavilion had never existed in the past. It was a new architectural feature, invoking a landscape one might have witnessed in history but in some other village, somewhere else in Slovakia.

The *ochranári*'s mill project was a historical and educational site where visitors could find the material remnants of traditional Slovak subsistence and economy. The spring at Brdarka, however, was a new cosmetic feature of the Slovak cultural and national imagination. Anderson suggests that, for national communities, the power of essentialism is not measured by the degree of a community's "falsity [or] genuineness but by the style in which they are imagined" (Anderson 1983:6). The Foundation's pavilion is authentic in the sense that its style faithfully reproduces the details of the past. Brdarka's actual historical feature at the pavilion's site was the socialist-period cement spring, which the villagers said had "always been there." The spring brought water closer to the residents as part of a local Party campaign to improve village infrastructure.

The Foundation's pavilion, which now towers over the old spring, is a *reinvented* landscape. Such landscapes are built through volunteer work, a practice which sought during communism to inculcate cultural norms with new values. The effort to preserve the mill in Kvačian became a symbolic struggle in an emerging fight with socialism. *Ochranárstvo* was thus a private, somewhat romantic, and ultimately subversive response to an anti-historical and hyper-rational ideology. Conservation projects back then were an attempt to create an "invented tradition," in Eric Hobsbawm and Terrence Ranger's sense, and to instill through its repetition

FIG. 6.2 Saving the nation. Members of the Return to the Land Foundation, a nationalist group formed from the ranks of SZOPK, repairing *drevenice* (wooden cabins) in 1994. The Foundation promotes what it calls ecotourism, hosting foreign visitors to Slovakia who pay to work on the restoration of folk architecture in rural areas. At the same time, the organization supports large-scale dams and nuclear power plants, considered to be ecologically damaging by other Slovak environmental groups. From *Zmena*.

older cultural values and norms (1982:1). After state socialism, the Foundation's pavilion serves as a project to promote essentialized cultural values through appearances.

But whether the products of *ochranárstvo* were spurious or genuine, foundational or cosmetic, the grassroots practice of volunteer conservation remains a tradition through which people try to wrest a small piece of the project of legibility from the state.[7] Far away from dams and power plants, the megaprojects of state-run space-making, the Foundation and SZOPK struggled to protect and promote two very different landscapes. In one sense, these landscapes of a past world, one real, one imagined, suggest a clash of cultural worldviews, each working from a unique historical perspective, what Marshall Sahlins (1985) has called the *struc-*

ture of the conjuncture. A structure of the conjuncture forms when historical relationships create new values based on essentialized visions. In Sahlins' example, indigenous Hawaiians interpret the novelty of Captain Cook's multiple visits to their island as a slight revision of their historical cosmology. Cook, the English colonial explorer, performing within his own cultural framework, unwittingly becomes a Hawaiian god. While these events resulted in Cook's murder, his killing was logically initiated and understood by Hawaiians as occurring within an existing cultural value system. Cook's killer, Sahlins suggests, was merely reading Cook's actions according to the Hawaiian cultural mind.

In Slovakia, the culture clash at stake within the tradition of historical preservation is, unlike Sahlins' case, not grand or globally pivotal. It is not between societies from opposite ends of the earth, involving leaders with power, and with implications for the way maps are to be drawn. Nor is it a direct physical clash involving violence and bloodshed, the stuff of meaningful history or good fiction. Rather, it is a grassroots conjuncture expressed through everyday structures built or rebuilt by very different generations that are each the product of a historical disjuncture. The mill symbolizes the *ochranári*'s broader ecological goals and facilitated the discourse of a global environmental movement prescribing that its activists "think globally and act locally." The *ochranári*'s projects under the regime were practical symbols of the paradigm of sustainable living, a paradigm suggesting that cultures should conform to a limited and fragile nature.

The Foundation's eco-philosophy inverts this international green credo, suggesting the imperative to "think locally and act globally." Its brand of *ochranárstvo* literally utilizes global labor, in the form of international tourists, to advance a localized project of nation-building. The Foundation's full-color catalog listed hundreds of places where visitors could work and, at the same time, discover "the long history of Slovakia . . . present in every town and village" (*Nadácia navraty ku krajíny* 1995). The Foundation characterized this history as that of a "nation living at the crossroads of a variety of cultures, absorbing fascinating diversity and transforming it into a new and unique way of perceiving the world" (ibid.).

The Foundation, viewing its young nation as endangered, attempts to fashion Slovakia with cultural monuments that never existed. Its members are part of the grassroots refashioning of post-socialist environmentality. The *ochranári* of socialism, still reading the landscape as threatened by totalitarianism, and still coming to terms with their new marginality, maintain their lonely *drevenice* safe from the challenges of a post-socialist politics in which their ecological values never took hold. Both discursive communities make their mark, if subtly and without great fanfare, on the landscape. But they are marks nonetheless of Slovakia's post-ecological condition.

Slovakia in an Age of Post-Ecology

IN THE EARLY MORNING HOURS OF A SEPTEMBER SATURDAY IN 1995, a line of people waited patiently on the edge of a sleepy Bratislava square for Eduscho, a new Austrian-owned coffee chain, to open. They had responded to an advertisement in a city weekly for free packets of coffee, which the store was offering to promote its new location. Without warning, a band of activists from Za Matku Zem, one of Slovakia's newest environmental organizations, charged out of an alley toward the French embassy, across from the coffee shop. The two-story, bright yellow building had been recently renovated, and stood out among the many tired and decrepit structures of Bratislava's Staré Mesto, the small historic district in the city's center. The young activists, none of whom was older than eighteen, first converged on the embassy's front entrance, handcuffing their wrists to the wrought-iron latches of two large, medieval wooden doors. Seconds later, and in a similar fashion, other activists locked themselves to a smaller side door. Still more activists joined their arms through metal tubes, essentially forming an unbreakable human chain around the embassy. The people waiting in line at Eduscho contorted their torsos and strained their necks to see what was happening. A large tree in the middle of the square blocked the view for some. Though clearly curious about the spectacle across the square, no one wanted to give up a place in the queue for free coffee. As more Slovak shoppers joined the long line at Eduscho, a few tossed quick smiles at the frustrated embassy staffers, who by this time had arrived for work.

The Za Matku Zem activists spent the entire day chained to the French embassy, in a standoff with a squadron of Slovak police officers. It was the same day that France had embarked on a new round of underwater nuclear tests in the Pacific Ocean. The blockade, and the growing numbers of police, attracted a crowd of onlookers, eventually including dozens of reporters and cameras. Of course, the day before, Za Matku Zem had called a couple of "friendly" journalists from papers such as *Sme*, which generally targeted a younger readership. The whole ordeal lasted about eight hours. Occasionally, a few police officers roughed up some of the demonstrators. One protestor—who had not been chained to the building—was handcuffed by a group of four policemen and shoved into a squad car, which quickly drove off, its tires rumbling over the old cobblestones of the square. French embassy employees, several of whom were visibly upset, stood by helplessly.

The action ended when Juraj Rizman, Za Matku Zem's young spokesperson, approached the press, flanked on either side by police and embassy employees. "We have delivered a petition to the French Chargé d'Affaires. He has assured us that our views on nuclear testing will be heard by the French government," Rizman announced to a circle of television cameras and microphones. With the blockade over, the demonstrators unlocked their human chain and carried away their equipment. The square quickly returned to the quiet landscape it had been at the beginning of the day. The other "human chain," lined up for coffee at Eduscho, had disappeared as well, in fact, hours before Za Matku Zem's demonstration had finished. The free coffee special had ended, as advertised, at noon.

As the first direct-action protest carried out solely by a homegrown Slovak environmental group, Za Matku Zem's blockade of the French Embassy marks a significant turn in the narrative of post-socialist ecological protest in the young state.[1] In this demonstration, for the first time, Za Matku Zem did not target its own government but rather tried to show the public that Slovakia could and would make environmental demands of other countries as well. At the same time, the blockade signals yet another shift in an emerging post-communist environmentality. Za Matku Zem measured the success of the action not by its impact on the French government, but by how many papers and television news channels covered the story the following day. The specific demands of the demonstrators were secondary to local media representations of the event itself, a prevailing orientation within Western environmental activism which Kevin DeLuca (1999) calls *image politics*. DeLuca argues that among environmental activist groups in the U.S., the success of demonstrations is now measured by media portrayals of the protest, what he terms the *image event*, rather than any actual change of policy or practice. With the appearance of groups like Za Matku Zem, at least one narrative strand of Slovak ecology after socialism seemed now to be promoting a particular Western form of environmental discourse.

Totalitarian environmentality unwittingly imbued ecology with an accessible, if at times covert, discursive unity. It was an arena of power in which apparently harmless behaviors, like interest in landscapes or walking in the woods, took on a poignantly critical character. Post-socialism, by contrast, highlights how easily and how quickly ideas about nature and the environment can be repositioned, recycled, reinterpreted, and unresolved. In the transition, we see on several levels a post-ecological moment at play in the Slovak political and cultural landscape after communism.

SLOVAKIA'S POST-ECOLOGICAL CONDITION

By following Slovakia's ecology movement through more than a decade—from socialism through its collapse and into the transition—we see how environmentalism is indeed comprised of several narratives which speak about the politics of identity and of place as much as they are driven by the existence of pollution or guided by fundamental ideas about nature. On the one hand, the narrative certainly suggests the discursive power of ecology to unite disparate voices and interests. From scientists and students to artists and homemakers, Slovak activists under communism attracted a mosaic membership that in many respects represented society at large. Under the banner of ecology, these citizen volunteers conceptualized and articulated an intimate and meaningful relationship among a wide spectrum of issues, from the condition of cultural monuments to mercury levels in public drinking water.

At the same time, ecology's unifying power was also the result of discursive weaknesses in the regime's aspirations to totalitarianism. Within the framework of a distinct environmentality, communism had relegated nature to a marginal space, and state authorities allowed volunteer activists to take care of a subject to which the regime assigned relatively little importance. Through their work, SZOPK activists shifted the place of nature from the margins to the center.[2] Nature, which Marxist ideology conceptualized as a passive space within which humans act, thus became an active subject to which humans needed to react and respond. This simple discursive move of taking something the regime barely thought about and constructing it as just that—something that the regime barely thought about—succeeded in bringing public attention both to Slovakia's neglected environment and to the neglectful regime. This message was effective not only because it confronted socialist ideology with reality, but because it exposed to the public that it was a reality the regime refused, at first, to acknowledge. In this social dialogue, nature became more than just a victim that needed to be rescued; nature began to represent the oppression of culture. Thus it was within an ironically "safe" and overlooked contestatory space—one that the regime itself had created—that SZOPK activists engineered an articulate message of opposition.

Slovakia's post-ecological narrative emerges precisely at the nexus of new messages generated by those who assumed power, messages which were all but ignored by old-guard activists. First, symbols of socialism, such as dams and power plants, became cultural icons of independence, essentially new forms of "space-making," without altering much of the original socialist space at all (Hughes 2005). In their fight against the Gabčíkovo Dam project, SZOPK activists failed to see this transformation, and in doing so missed an opportunity to characterize the dam as a threat to a native Slovak landscape, or to argue for the inherent value of a diverse ecosystem to a nation's health or identity. Instead, activists continued to push the unremarkable message of the project's obvious totalitarian heritage on a public that they assumed still felt oppressed by Stalinist-style megalomania. Second, in order to survive in the political arena, the Slovak Green Party had to attach itself to an emerging master narrative of ethnicity, changing its shade from green (eco-centric) to brown (nationalist) in the process. At the time, conventional parties were also slipping environmental planks into election platforms with more clearly defined political positions on the economy and on identity. Yet, the survivalist mode of Green Party activists appeared to *ochranári* outside the party as merely the revelation of the organization's spuriousness.

Alongside these missed messages, efforts to save historical architecture transferred seamlessly into essentialized environments of national identity. The Return to the Landscape Foundation approved of the continuation of Stalinist models of state-controlled economic development at the same time as they created their own environmental market for eco-tourism. Slovakia's new status as an independent state in turn attracted international antinuclear groups such as Greenpeace, which had ignored it in the past.

In 1995, a cartoon appeared in the HZDS daily *Slovenská Republika*, depicting a young Slovak wearing a Greenpeace T-shirt and holding a lantern. The caption read, "I will lead you on the road to Europe." Ironically, in 1997, Julius Binder, the fledgling country's greatest proponent of the Gabčíkovo Dam, publicly admitted that the project was a child of Soviet-style planning and should not have been built (*Sme*, March 12, 1997:2). Despite this belated assessment, Binder had successfully recycled Gabčíkovo as an essential part of the Slovak landscape, a key step in the young country's post-socialist mission to become a real nation. From Gabčíkovo to Za Matku Zem, we see in the narrative of post-ecological Slovakia several environmentalities.

When asked to articulate what had been the most important environmental problem immediately after the Velvet Revolution, most *ochranári* gave muddled answers similar to the following response of one SZOPK activist.

It is a hard question, because all of the problems . . . to narrow it down to one problem would be hard. But I think it is important to create among the younger generation some kind of relationship to the environment—to love Nature, because when they love Nature, they will be able to sacrifice things or at least ponder questions about the environment that they will consider important. Of course there are also real problems like Gabčíkovo and Mochovce. But what is important? These are questions about solutions to particular things. But you need to construct a relationship of awareness about the larger environment in order to even begin to talk about these things, and this is the most important problem.

Answers like these, tangled in complexity and accentuated with uncertainty, proved to be no match for the simple words of proponents of Slovakia's energy independence.

Along with discursive disjunctures, the post-ecological narrative also reminds us that in the framework of dynamic environmentalities, various ideas and symbols of ecology remain personal and fragmented performances. Whether under communism or during the post-socialist transition, an essential green identity never existed. Instead we see a shifting pattern of private *bricolage*, or what Claude Lévi-Strauss described as "making do with whatever is at hand" (Lévi-Strauss 1963:16). For Mikuláš Huba, who pushed the boundaries of volunteer conservation, ecology meant recognizing a harmony between natural and historical landscapes and a blueprint for a tolerant and sustainable society. For Juraj

Podoba, one of the founders and now an ex-member of the Green Party, ecology invoked the possibility of a new environmental politics that could carry the energy of grassroots volunteerism to the halls of government. For Ján Budaj, the dissident *ochranár*, ecology symbolized the ability to choose one's battles, and the freedom to think independently and to speak out collectively against the interconnected problems of socialism. Socialism, of course, united these different perspectives in an alliance of common purpose, encouraging Huba to optimistically personify nature as one of the primary "actors" in the demise of communism (*Pravda*, July 13, 1990). In the wake of the Velvet Revolution, Budaj proudly described ecology as "the key that opened the dungeon of totalitarianism." After communism's collapse, however, alliances between these visions disintegrated. Huba worried that "Nature had not felt the Revolution" (*Ochranca Prírody* 1990), and Podoba cynically and ironically concluded that "freedom killed volunteer environmentalism in Slovakia."

If freedom destroyed Podoba's version of ecology, it gave others the opportunity to craft their own visions, inverting existing ones in the process. For young activists like the members of the Foundation, ecology meant embracing large-scale development—even at the price of the destruction of unique environments—as long as one recreated a rural national landscape elsewhere in the country. Through ecotourism, the Foundation inverted the international credo of global thinking and local action. By inviting foreigners to help preserve Slovak culture, they performed globally to create a local landscape, imagined as essential and timeless.

For teenage radicals such as Rizo, the founder of Za Matku Zem, ecology involved other types of post-socialist inversions of the past. For his generation, the *ochranári* of the Velvet Revolution represented an outdated generation. It was a generation that had been constrained by socialism, confined to conservation brigades and reluctant to open confrontation. Rizo's peers in international NGOs, with whom he often worked, were constant reminders of the relative backwardness of Slovak greens. In Rizo's eyes, in the 1970s, while Western organizations such as Friends of the Earth and Greenpeace were saving whales and fighting lawmakers, Slovak *ochranári* were merely cleaning up forests. In the 1980s, when green parties were changing parliamentary politics and direct-action campaigns halted the construction of highways in Western Europe (Bramwell 1994; Lowe and Rudig 1986), Slovaks were fixing up cabins and writing reports.

Rizo's generation assumed the public identity of *aktivisti* (activists) to per-form their allegiance to a Western environmentality and to distance them-selves from both the communist past and the politically contentious present. For the older generation of *ochranári*, that these new organizations—from ecotourists in the Return to the Landscape Foundation to the ecoterror-ists of Greenpeace and Za Matku Zem—existed at all was in fact quite remarkable, for none of these iterations of ecology could have been imag-ined within a communist environmentality.

NEW ENVIRONMENTALITIES OF POST-SOCIALISM

If Slovakia represents a particularly vivid case of the effect that post-ecological conditions have on activism, it is precisely because of the promi-nent role that greens played during late socialism and the opportunity they had to reposition the green agenda after the collapse of communism. In cases where environmentalism played important, but not central, roles in regime change, we see the appearance of opportunities for more pos-itive reformulations of environmental politics. These may be shaped by a society's particular experience with market capitalism. For example, Krista Harper (2005) shows how in Hungary, greens have reconditioned the dialogue about environmental activism to focus on the threat of unreg-ulated multinational corporations in an ethnicized landscape—a narra-tive which resonates among a relatively homogeneous Mađar population. Hungary's fight against socialist dams on the Danube shifted, with little upheaval for the movement, to a battle against "wild capitalism." As Harper observes, post-socialist Hungarian politicians "enthusiastically took up the mantle (if not the actual political commitments) of environ-mentalism as part of their new identity" (Harper 2005:228). The recent economic and political crisis in Hungary over financial instability and underemployment has reignited East-West dialogues within the society about the motives of foreign investors (of whose funds Hungary was by far one of the biggest recipients).

Other reformulations of environmentality may be marked by long-term engagements between local agricultural communities and transna-tional NGOs in settings where environmental activism played little part in the collapse of communism, as Barbara Cellarius (2004) indicates for post-socialist Bulgaria. Jane Dawson (1996) shows us yet another post-ecological nexus in formerly socialist Lithuania, where nationalism and environmentalism were synonymous. In the transition from Soviet domination, nationalists shed their green surrogate. The implications are, to say the least, delicately troubling, as the new state assumes ownership of the very nuclear power facilities for the destruction of which it claimed it needed independence from Soviet Russia. Overshadowing these transformations, however, is the transnational reach of Western environmental NGOs, which promote what Timothy Luke (1997) calls a "hegemonic eco-critique." It remains to be seen whether East European environmentalism has any impact on the environmentality of capitalism (Wapner 1996).

In East Europe's post-socialist transition, the ecology issue is not the only discourse undergoing a process of structuring and restructuring cultural and symbolic relationships. Other aspects of social, economic, sexual, and political life have unfolded in a series of inversions and reinventions. Katherine Verdery (1996) has explored some of these inversions in Romanian land reclamation projects following collectivization, and in new pyramid schemes that preyed on anxious citizens eager to join but uncertain about nascent capitalist markets. Gail Kligman (1998) and other scholars have tracked the changing relations of social, symbolic, and personal power within the subject of reproductive rights, from access to abortion under socialism to pro-natal policies restricting women's health services. These shifts do not just reconfigure land ownership and sexual rights, but also labor relations (Dunn 2004) and concepts of citizenship (Bakić-Hayden 1995; Gray 2003).

The new symbolic geographies of Europe after the transition, in which formerly socialist states have only recently joined the West, beg new questions concerning their status and stability in the future. For example, Vaclav Klaus, the Czech prime minister, recently questioned both his country's and Slovakia's membership in the EU, claiming that after three years there had "been no measurable impact on the economic growth of Slovakia or the Czech Republic." Klaus also "criticized [a] recently adopted EU policy, known as REACH, that binds member countries to examine the effects of chemicals on human health and the environment" (*International Herald Tribune*, January 11, 2007). By joining Europe in the hope of improving their economies, Slovakia and the Czech Republic may find themselves forced to shut certain industrial sectors down. Like the shift in environmentality after communism, these new inversions and reinventions of post-socialist East Europe involve competing ideologies that reconfigure concepts of pollution and purity, essentialism and fabrication, and desires for order in the face of disorder (Douglas 1966).

POST-ECOLOGICAL SHIFTS AND THE FUTURE OF ECOLOGY

Returning to the case of Za Matku Zem's blockade of the French embassy, we also see a shift in the process of ethnicizing the post-socialist landscape. Through the direct-action blockade, Za Matku Zem represents a Slovak attack on a sovereign state. Emerging from the embassy, the young Slovak tells France, a nuclear power, what to do. In one sense, this dimension of Za Matku Zem's image-making strategy (DeLuca 1999) also recalls the rather limited expectations of the communist-era *ochranári* as they published *Bratislava/nahlas*: to create only an image, while not imagining that anything will change. The *ochranári*'s perceived limitation, however, was shaped by the fundamental relationships fostered under communist environmentality. Za Matku Zem's expectations, by contrast, are multiple, and involve both a new twist on ethnicizing the ecological voice—against a Western power—and an embracing of the image as commodity, thereby taking away press space from the group's own nationalist government.

Do the experiences of environmental activists in Slovakia signal the initial moments of an impending global post-ecological age, one in which the marginalization of nature discourse has been the outcome of major cultural shifts toward both global consumerism and security-based identity politics? Now, over a decade after the fall of communism, global environmentalism appears to be no match for an expanding global consumerism hell-bent on destroying local variation and diversity. In this new post-ecological world, ecology, once configured as an ideology focused on the interconnectedness of people and place and the need to protect this interconnection, has been professionalized and disconnected from local practices. We see this disconnected outcome of professionalization in James Fairhead and Melissa Leach's (1996) analysis of the disjuncture of ecologies in Guinea, where expert policy making has overtaken and rejected modalities of indigenous farming practices. We see it as well in the fate of European green parties, which, rather than transform the structures of participatory political systems, have instead been forced to compromise fundamental ecological goals and to conform to the norms of coalition power sharing in parliamentary systems (Bramwell

1994). We also see the results of professionalization in so-called Southern ecological "resistance movements," with ties to indigenous communities fighting foreign development programs and internal exploitation, that are appropriating the expertise culture of Northern environmentalism (Taylor 1995).

Northern movements in turn have reified themselves and, as Beth Conklin (1997) has suggested, have exoticized others, using the imagery of indigenous communities as resources for their own image-making politics. And the image itself—the skinless animal corpse, the twisted and malformed bodies of the children of Chernobyl—while making for good spectacle, often does little to advance dialogues about either sustainable policies or practices. The piecemeal and partial consensus created through the 1992 United Nations Earth Summit in Rio, the 1997 Kyoto meetings, and the 2002 Johannesburg summit indicate that "the prospects for transnational unity on environmental matters are not favourable" (Yearley 1996:151). Exacerbating this discursive dissonance, the recent rise of international terrorism and religious extremist activism has swept aside discourses of nature with hegemonic narratives of safety and place through cultural sectarianism. In such an era, hard-won environmental laws and reforms of past decades have been casually rolled back or sidestepped by states prioritizing national security alongside the less-promoted agenda of economic growth. Within post-ecological conditions, the key elements that are vital to social movement formation—a common identity, the possibility of mass mobilization, the defense of society (Scott 1990)—have become the very political spaces which contemporary global communities have contested. These contests also have implications for the stability and sustainability of specific environmentalities.

At the same time, these very post-ecological moments may also be important opportunities for the establishment of new and intuitively unlikely power relationships. Returning to Za Matku Zem's protest of French nuclear testing, we see a shift in interlocutors of place and purpose. By changing its target from the Slovak state to European nuclear chauvinism, the young ecology organization attempted to gain new cachet in the eyes of its own pro-state public. Whether or not the move was successful (it was, to a degree) matters little. A post-ecological condition is a moment in which local movements can and must engage structural relations of power in unique and divergent ways.

Devon Peña (2005) suggests as much regarding the unique cultural experiences and corresponding environmental challenges faced by U.S.

ethnic minorities, specifically the Mexican-American community. Peña shows how potentially powerful the idea of what I will call an *immigration ecology*—which both produces and resists an ethnicized ecological subject—can be on several levels. In terms of repositioning community self-awareness, Mexican-American environmentalism can be a point of discovery of previously unknown or unarticulated forms of discrimination. It may be a portal through which people can gain greater voice as a collective, using existing regulatory regimes which historically have applied to other communities. Whether Norteño land-use practices were once sustainable and now are not, or if ancestral lands were really owned by ancestors, as Peña describes, is beside the question. After all, Haripriya Rangan (2001), in revisiting Chipko activism in India, finds that the myth of a movement can be just as powerful as actual direct-action protests in sustaining new practices or configuring relationships between people, place, and land. Regardless of the veracity of ethnic mythologies, which are of little concern to nationalist communities (Anderson 1983), the narratives of Mexican-American ecological subjectivity are attempts to engage with power relationships in unique ways, not only by calling into question the efficacy of mainstream approaches to environmental activism, but also by repositioning identity formations within new dialogues. "Ethnicized ecologists" working within local-level "ethnoscapes" (Appadurai 1991) may yet yield unforeseen approaches to transborder environmental policy making.

Another very different example of a post-ecological shift can be seen in the recent dramatic turn toward environmental problems among the American Evangelical community. Despite traditional alliances with big business and social conservatism in the U.S., a growing number of Evangelical Christians are promoting a form of scripture-based environmentalism termed, among other things, "creation stewardship" (DeWitt 1998). This turn toward a reconsideration of the tenets of Christianity, particularly within a community which focuses heavily on conversion and proselytizing, presents an unexpected potentially transformative opportunity for the mainstream (and largely secular) environmental community.[3] Cooperation between these two "communities of faith" may go well beyond the socialist-era religious/environmental alliances that emerged in Slovakia (between the *ochranári* and the Secret Church) or in East Germany (among Lutherans and antinuclear peace activists) by drawing on both the integrity of science (and its accompanying professional associations) and the intensity of spirituality (and its enormous, grassroots community networks) to develop enormously powerful social mobilizations regarding pollution, climate change, and environmental rights.[4] Such cooperation would no doubt create a significant challenge to the power of the state in terms of setting environmental priorities and policies.

Back in Slovakia, and in lieu of clear predictions, a set of disjunctive and conflicting conceptions of culture and place comprise, for the moment, Slovakia's post-socialist vernaculars of ecology. These vernaculars seem unlikely to ever coalesce or unite again in the spirit of *Bratislava/nahlas*, at least not in Slovakia. Less than a decade after the Velvet Revolution, what united Slovakia's diverse ecological voices came only in the form of memorials. In the fall of 1995, Mikuláš Huba held a meeting in the Tatra Mountains to honor the late Jozef Vavroušek, former Czechoslovak Minister of the Environment, and his daughter. The pair had died tragically in an avalanche while on a hiking trip that spring. Over sixty people attended the remote and informal memorial service for their friend and fellow activist. The group included some of the prominent personalities of the Velvet Revolution. Among them were the writer Fedor Gál, who had fled Slovakia to live in Prague after anti-Semitic threats to his life; Pavel Šremer, who had signed Charter 77; and Juraj Podoba, the ethnographer who helped form the Green Party. The attendees hiked up the steep ravine to the remote site where the father and daughter had met their untimely fate. The air was brisk for early autumn, and it rained steadily. In the ravine, two lonely piles of stones, a makeshift wooden cross in the center of each, rose above a motionless stream of rocks and boulders. The small mounds lay within several meters of each other, marking the places where the bodies of a loving father and his daughter were found after the snows had thawed. The group looked on in silent sadness (figure 7.1).

Vavroušek's passing was not only a deep personal loss for those who knew him as a friend and colleague, but also a loss for the environmental movement, of someone who, during the transition from communism, was an articulate and vocal advocate for the environment. Vavroušek had been the Slovak environmental movement's transborder link with NGOs in the Czech Republic and a bridge to the network of international organizations that funded projects, supported research, and sponsored conferences in the formerly communist states of East Europe.

After the makeshift mountain ceremony for Vavroušek, Huba convened a meeting of the Society for Sustainable Living at a small mountain resort

FIG. 7.1 Disillusioned old guard. While hiking in the High Tatras in 1995, Jozef Vavroušek, Czechoslovakia's first Minister of the Environment, died along with his daughter in an avalanche. Here, Mikuláš Huba, leader of szopk under communism, former head of Slovak Council for the Environment, and an ex-Green Party deputy, lays stones at the site where his Czech friend and colleague perished.

not far from the site of his friend's fatal fall. Noting the group's small numbers, Juraj Flamík, one of the founders of zo 13, who was now living in the Czech Republic, remarked that "we cannot infiltrate the political structure with people, only with ideas." Other members posed a series of disjointed and wandering questions. Perhaps the *ochranári* should have supported the Green Party more strongly, they mused. How could the organization do grassroots fundraising when prices had recently tripled despite salaries remaining at pre-revolution levels? Despite their frustrations, many stuž activists appeared to be thoughtful critics of their own experience. Budaj, who had himself left the movement long before, concluded that the *ochranári* looked for the values of freedom and openness in their activism. But when the prison was destroyed they did not realize these values. Instead they began a polemics about values, and about the social contract. And this sphere concerns more than just conserving nature, but conserving all of Slovakia.

Also realizing that Slovakia, itself, was now a new place, the old-guard greens asked themselves, "Who are we? Where are we going?" They felt a need for a more articulate voice, something they had searched for since the first moments of their internal revolution under socialism (*Ochranca Prírody* 1–2 1989a:1). Slovak environmentalism, however, did not suffer from a lack of articulation. Rather, it refused to see a post-ecological moment, which demanded disengagement from a dialogue with a system that no longer existed. The regime's demise, like Vavroušek's, marked the closing of an old, familiar conversation and, for the time being, the end of ecology.

NOTES

INTRODUCTION

1. All acronyms for Slovak organizations are in the Slovak language.

2. I will be using the terms *communism, socialism,* and *state socialism* interchangeably throughout the text. In East European states, as well as in the Soviet Union, socialism was the official term for the ideology of Marxism-Leninism, while communism was commonly used by Western states to describe the implementation of this ideology by the party-regimes in power.

3. Environmentalists were also part of the growing opposition to communism in the Czech Lands in the 1980s. However, the conservation movement was quite small and significantly co-opted by the regime. I discuss this more fully in chapter 1. During the Velvet Revolution, Czech greens, along with almost all other issue-based groups, were more or less completely overshadowed by the popularity and charismatic presence of Vaclav Havel.

4. Weigle and Butterfield's full definition of civil society reads, "the independent self-organization of society, the constituent parts of which voluntarily engage in public activity to pursue individual, group, or national interests, within the context of a legally defined state-society relationship" (Weigle and Butterfield 1992:3). Their definition refers specifically to the emerging public sector after communism's collapse. Civil society was, in fact, a notion conceptualized much earlier, under socialism, by East European intellectuals and dissidents who were concerned with opening up segments of public life to independent groups and associations and who saw in this sphere the emergence of regime opposition and the possibility of social, political, and economic reform (Arato 1981; Keane 1988; Tismaneanu 1990). Free associations, interest groups, watch dog groups, volunteer organizations, and other nongovernmental entities all fall under the concept of civil society. See, for example, Cellarius and Staddon (2002) and Grunberg (2000).

5. Agrawal is not the first scholar to use this term, and he gives credit to Timothy Luke (1995) for its coinage. He further points out that his conceptualization of the term *environmentality* differs from Luke's in that with it he attempts to "examine more insistently the shifts in subjectivities that accompany new forms of regulation rather than seeing regulation as an attempt mainly to control or dominate" (Agrawal 2005:232). Luke, on the other hand, employs environmentality as a sort of paradigm that transnational environmental organizations follow in order to dominate environmental policy and activities around the world. I would argue that Agrawal's conceptualization of the term can also incorporate Luke's narrower meaning.

6. Slovaks are a western Slavic people (a group that also includes Czech and Poles) whose origins have been traced back to ninth-century Europe.

7. Stanley Kirschbaum interprets this troubling period in Slovakia's history as a strategy for survival in the face of German aggression (Kirschbaum 2005: 185–89).

8. These earlier works in the anthropology of East Europe, with the possible exception of Simic (1973), reflect the interests and limitations of their time, when anthropologists commonly studied people in small-scale societies, inhabiting relatively fixed geographic locations (Goodale 1971; Lee 1979) or making up an economically bounded part of a larger complex population (Pilcher 1972; Williams 1981). Anthropologists working in the post-socialist period in East Europe and the former Soviet Union are revealing the remarkable cultural and political diversity of a region that has otherwise shared a long and common experience with totalitarian rule and the domination of Marxist ideology (Mandel and Humphrey 2002).

9. Markowitz's (2001) conceptualization of this sphere of field research is in turn drawn from Laura Nader's research on political elites in the U.S. (1972).

10. Anthropologists conceptualize *community* as any "site where one experiences social life," with any range of common behaviors and beliefs in group activities, such as worship or economic transactions (Cohen 1985:15). In place of physical boundaries, some types of communities may be constructed "symbolically, making [them] resource[s] and repositor[ies] of meaning" (Cohen 1985:17). The members of such communities create boundaries by displaying their interests and beliefs as a public act, similar to what Roy Rappaport, following Durkheim, defined as a *congregation*, "an aggregate of individuals who regard their collective well-being to be dependent on a common body of ritual performances"(1984:1).

11. There is a vast social science literature on social movement history and theory as well as new approaches to social and collective action, and on public discourse movements in the fields of cultural studies and ethnic and gender studies. My discussion here does not intend to be exhaustive. See for example McAdam and Snow (2007); Tilly (2004); and McAdam, Tarrow, and Tilly (2001) for good surveys of specific issues in the field.

12. Milton suggests that "environmentalists often intend to imply more by this label than just a concern to protect the environment" (Milton 1996:35). For example, they may be protecting a lifestyle in addition to the environment.

13. In *Traces on the Rhodian Shore*, Clarence Glacken (1967) reaches back to ancient Greek culture to present a history of environmental thought in Europe through to the Enlightenment. Even more ambitious, Max Oelschlaeger (1989) begins speculatively in the Paleolithic, moving quickly into the modern period and American culture, to track the idea of "wilderness." Both scholars approach environmental thought as an exercise in classification. Lynn White Jr. (1967) was one of the first historians to argue that an environmental ethics of one form or another has always existed within any cultural system, and has been intimately linked with this system.

14. Scholarship in the United States focuses heavily on the grassroots mobilization and issue-bound character of American environmentalism. While much of this sociological research is based on surveys of organizations, more ethnography is appearing on the subject. U.S. environmental sociology tends to rely on responses from leaders of environmental organizations. Some anthropologists have also begun to examine the different approaches to environmentalism evident among ethnic groups in the United States (Lynch 1993; Peña 2005).

15. These case studies also describe the perceptions that residential communities have of large-scale development projects. North American and British approaches have also focused on individual ecological conflicts, producing a wealth of data contributing to a micro-historical perspective of certain environmental campaigns (Egginton 1980; Lowe et al. 1985; Smith 1975). One of the problems with the case-study approach, however, has been the tendency to choose more formal, well-established organizations over spontaneous, informal groups that emerge and then disappear either when the conflict is resolved or when campaigns fail to achieve their goals (Lowe and Rudig 1986:527).

16. Anthropologists have described globalization as a process where cultural boundaries are crossed over by countless individuals in a world system that is more extensively (if not intensively) connected by technology than ever before (Appadurai 1992).

1   COMMUNIST ENVIRONMENTALITY

1. Anthropology tells us that all human societies separate nature and culture in some way (Ortner 1974). This divide between nature and culture is of course variously constructed. Agricultural populations rely on nature's patterns and try to negotiate or balance its uncertainties (Netting 1981). By contrast, industrial and post-industrial societies generally view the natural world as a sphere to be used in the service of human development. Even the members of hunting and gathering cultures, which have been described as existing "closer to the land" or

in harmony with local ecosystems, recognize and maintain distinct human and natural realms (Warner 1958).

2. This process of modernizing and rationalizing production also involved the large-scale collectivization of agriculture, which took place in Russia in the 1930s and in East Europe in the 1950s. See for example Bell (1984); Kideckel (1976); Maday and Hollos (1983); and Winner (1972).

3. There are several ethnographic studies on the socialist city, including, for example, French and Hamilton (1979); Sampson (1982). Using Belgrade as a model, Andrei Simic (1973) demonstrates the urban-rural linkages that persisted throughout East Europe's communist period.

4. Roma throughout Europe have been routinely criminalized and marginalized. At the same time, many Gypsy communities in Eastern Europe, along with providing traveling entertainment, handicrafts, and music, often did survive, in part, on illicit activity, such as begging or picking pockets. For a comprehensive examination of Roma social organization and ethnic identity formation, see Belton (2004).

5. Spas and special care facilities, however, did cost more. These types of special health services were much less accessible to the average worker (Lovenduski and Woodall 1987:380).

6. For accounts of the Prague Spring and its aftermath see Pehe (1988) and Williams (1997).

7. The report, titled "Report on the State of the Environment in Czechoslovakia," was "leaked to the Czech dissident group Charter 77 and consequently published in the Western press in 1984" (Jehlicka and Smith n.d.:7). The Slovak public, except for a few cases within the scientific community and the volunteer conservation movement, knew little about the study.

8. Although Drakulić writes about Yugoslavia, the details of communism's ecology of poverty were similarly present in every East European country and in the Soviet states. Drakulić reminds her readers how strongly this notion of saving and recycling endures in the transition as a key cultural practice throughout the region. One of her interviewees admits to her that even years after the collapse of the state socialist system "I just collect [containers], God knows why. I guess nowadays collecting doesn't reflect the state of facts as much as the state of our minds" (Drakulić 1993:186).

9. This situation is similar to what Douglas Weiner (2002) has found for Soviet Russia, where professional scientific organizations were free to pursue alternative environmental paradigms.

10. It is interesting to note that Aladar Randik, the Union's historian, admits that SZOPK did not at first have sufficient membership to support all of its planned sections and committees (1989). This disjuncture is a theme that repeats itself throughout the Slovak ecology movement's experience and is perhaps the prod-

uct of the enduring elements of the socialist imagination, obsessed with planning despite the realities of limited resources.

11. Despite this formal Czech and Slovak divide, this was not a strict rule in any way. Although it was not common, a few Slovaks joined CSOP, and several Czechs also participated in Strom Života. In some rare cases, individuals joined both groups.

2 HATCHETS VERSUS THE HAMMER AND SICKLE

1. Dissidents did not summarily or even openly reject socialism, but rather challenged its contemporary manifestation (Connor 1980). See also Havel (1978) on dissidence in Czechoslovakia, Gilligan (2003) on dissent in the Soviet Union, and Joppke (1995) on the East German dissident movement.

2. Many of the materials by East Europeans published in the *East European Reporter* were *samizdat* literature smuggled out of their home countries. In some cases, *samizdat* included translations of Western materials brought in by foreign visitors. These writings ranged from published articles to draft essays or even college lecture notes (Day 1999:100–122).

3. Secret police agencies throughout East Europe, modeled after the notorious KGB in the Soviet Union, focused their attention on anyone who seemed remotely seditious. At the same time, hundreds of thousands became unofficial "employees" of these state bodies, "paid" through favors or privileges granted them, so long as they provided information of value to the state. No one knew for certain whether a person was a spy or an informer, but everyone imagined that they knew who particular agents were according to their appearance, probing manner, and undivided attention. For an account of the intimacy of the secret police relationship with the public, see Drakulić (1993).

4. By the 1980s, more than 1000 people signed the Charter, but only a few signatories were from Slovakia. Among them were the writer Dominik Tatarka and the former Communist Party member Miroslav Kusý. Milan Šimečka, the political theorist who was fired from his post at Comenius University, although certainly considered a dissident, did not sign Charter 77 (Day 1999:225). Antonin Liehm (1973) provides English translations of several essays by Chartists other than Havel.

5. David Doellinger (2002) also describes how, after 1987, young believers and supporters of the Secret Church began to organize pilgrimages to religious sites throughout the country. Although these groups were at times large, they were not tightly organized, and often had little direct connection with Secret Church leaders in Bratislava such as Ján Čarnogurský, one of Slovakia's future prime ministers.

6. Traditional peasant architecture was simple and functional. Several

anthropologists working in East Europe and Russia during the 1960s focused a significant part of their ethnographic research on material culture, including detailed description of rural dwellings. For example, see Dunn and Dunn (1967:111–17) on peasant houses in Central Russia and the Halperns' research in rural Yugoslavia (Halpern and Kerewsky-Halpern 1972). Jozef Obrebski, a student of Malinowski, published some of the earliest ethnography on peasant communities in the marshlands of Belarus following his prewar fieldwork in the 1930s.

7. Instead of hammers, SZOPK members used the backs of *sekerky* to hammer nails.

8. Real names are used with quoted text in cases where individuals are public figures, published authors, or leaders of organizations or political parties. Otherwise, informants being quoted remain anonymous, except in cases where individuals requested that their names be used.

9. I use the Slovak term *ochranár* (singular; *ochranári*, plural), which means "protector" or "conservationist," throughout the book. Other activists, as well as laypersons, routinely used this traditional Slovak term during socialism, instead of *aktivista* (activist).

10. This informant uses the term "*starý ľudia*," which in this context means "people of the past." The term in Slovak literally means "old people."

11. Krista Harper (2005) examines this controversial project of late socialism and its post-socialist aftermath from the perspective of Hungarian activists. The Union's post-revolution fight against Gabčíkovo is described in detail in chapter 5.

12. This power of sanction, however, was effective enough to disband Ekotrend in Banská Bystrica. In this case, the committee reprimanded apparently "wayward" university students, who at the same time were threatened by the secret police.

13. Some individuals who joined the group were suspected of being agents of the secret police. But the membership carried out most of their work openly. After the Velvet Revolution, some of these suspected individuals (and a few unlikely members) were discovered to have been informants for state authorities (see chapter 3).

14. Gale Stokes characterizes state socialism as an experiment in hyper-rationality, an ideology that went beyond mere rational economic planning to embrace reason as a "transcendent law of society that justified a totalitarian regime" (1993:5). Hyper-rationalism backed an effort to "direct all aspects of society because [it was a] correct, or 'scientific,' understanding of the laws of human development which [the Communists put] to use to conquer nature and to create a truly human society" (Stokes 1993:5).

15. In the early twentieth century, conservation in the U.S. emerged from highly educated upper-class intellectual groups that provided a model for future NGOs (Hays 1958). This critique was amplified after the publication of Rachel

Carson's groundbreaking *Silent Spring* (1962) and gained additional momentum from a growing counter-culture movement throughout the late sixties.

16. These organizations later incorporated a constellation of integrated issues (e.g., alternative energy, population growth, and biodiversity) as they grew in membership base and financial contributions as well as initial legislative lobbying success (Sale 1993).

3 "BRATISLAVA ALOUD"

1. Meeting minutes were kept by an appointed secretary and then circulated among members of the group. Technically, they were not intended for public consumption. The *ochranári*'s report, although released in October, was identified as minutes to a meeting held on June 4 in honor of the UN's International Day of the Environment.

2. The chapters of the report were divided into three parts. Parts 1 and 2 covered conditions in the natural environment, including air, water, land, radioactivity, and noise pollution; and in the urban environment, including industry, transportation, and buildings. Part 3 described the situation facing the social environment, including social and cultural infrastructure, services, health, and social groups.

3. Many informants told me that this kind of publication gymnastics was common with dissident literature, and not unknown to those in the organization who considered themselves to be a part of the underground publishing world.

4. Voice of America is the official international radio broadcasting service of the United States federal government. As part of the U.S. Cold War strategy, Voice of America began to transmit radio broadcasts into the Eastern Bloc and Soviet Union in the late 1940s and early 1950s.

5. A bloc of Communist Party loyalists at first challenged the outcome. They protested that the newly elected committee should itself vote for leadership positions, regardless of the popular vote totals. The new committee then met in Zvoleň on December 7, at the height of the Velvet Revolution but before the outcome of the mass demonstrations was clear. One of SZOPK's old guard, Professor Midriak, declared that the November elections had been manipulated. But when the voting continued, Huba was again chosen as chairman, and a young biologist named Jozef Gregor was picked as the Union's secretary. Gregor's victory was actually a compromise between the Union's old cadre and the new reformers from Bratislava. As a traditional conservationist, Gregor was acceptable to SZOPK's older generation. But Gregor was a non-communist as well, and symbolized for the Bratislava *ochranári* a new spirit of freedom and openness. The members of the MV also knew that Gregor was sympathetic to Huba's views and would support his leadership, particularly with respect to the group's desire to establish better contacts with international environmental organizations.

6. One example was the creation of *Lidové Noviny* (People's News) in Prague, which was also made available to a few Slovaks in Bratislava. Launched in January of 1988, it contained "uncensored material about East-West disarmament talks and the Soviet role in Afghanistan" (Ramet 1995:133). The newspaper was edited by, among others, Vaclav Havel and Jiři Dienstbier.

7. Interestingly, Mikuláš Huba had been away on a short study trip to Austria during most of the Bratislava demonstrations. As national chairman of szoPK, he formally offered vPN the Union's full assistance.

8. In 1987, Husák stepped aside to allow "younger" communists to lead Czechoslovakia. Miloš Jakeš became Party Secretary, and Adamec assumed the office of prime minister of the federation. This change in no way altered the state's level of repression. Jakeš was a solid hardliner, and had led the purges of reform communists after the Prague Spring.

9. For a thorough account of the events during the Velvet Revolution see Bradley (1992). For an eyewitness account by a Westerner see Garton Ash (1990). A good visual "diary" of the revolution in Slovakia is *Z tých (revolucných) dňi* (Moravčik 1990). For an account of the collapse of the regimes throughout East Europe see Stokes (1993).

There is a vast literature on the many factors leading up to and influencing the fall of communism in East Europe in 1989 and the Soviet Union in 1991, a comprehensive analysis of which is beyond the scope of this book. Among these influences and factors are severely strained economic systems; an unbeatable escalation in the Cold War security sector on the part of the U.S., coupled with significant prosperity and economic growth in the West; a growing lack of legitimacy on the part of communist leadership and formal institutions; the growth of opposition currents; a failed Soviet war in Afghanistan; counter models of consumer society which became increasingly available to East European and Soviet societies through Western media; as well as others. See Castells (2003), Beissinger (2002), White (2001), and Edwards (1999). Cipkowski (1991) provides an earlier analysis of regime collapse in East European states as well as the Soviet Union.

10. One activist recalled that this was a time "when no one had time for anything and everything needed to be done."

11. *Lustrácia*, or lustration, began officially in October 1991 and continues in the present period. Lustration throughout Central Europe "entailed the screening of bureaucrats and political leaders to ascertain who had collaborated with the communist-era secret police. Collaborators lost their government positions. East Germany and Czechoslovakia led the region in adopting lustration laws" (Calhoun 2002:494). In Slovakia, newspapers published the names of individuals who had been on the ŠtB's list of "informants." This list provided no information as to what the nature of the "collaboration" had been, but under legislation passed by the new parliaments, all individuals who appeared on this list were barred from public office for five years. Or, at least, it was supposed to

work this way. In Budaj's case, he had been singled out because of his highly public role during the Revolution. He admitted that in the late seventies he had signed a paper as an "informant" for the ŠtB in order to gain a passport to travel to Italy.

12. Budaj became a journalist and essayist, writing for the weekly *Slobodný Piatok* in the mid-1990s. In 1995, he re-entered politics as a member of the Democratic Union (DU), a moderate reform party.

13. In November 1990 the sz won 15 mayoral elections and gained a total of 464 seats in local councils. However, many of these candidates ran as part of various coalitions with other political parties against local communists who attempted to maintain their hold on power.

14. *Zelené Slovensko* appeared nationally, first in *Smena*, then *Práca*. The articles appearing in this insert were written by Green Party members and *ochranári* from szopk. Most of the money for publishing *Zelené Slovensko* was provided by the newspapers in which it appeared, since very little funding was available through state sponsorship. In 1992, *Zelené Slovensko* ran out of money. By this time, the Green Party had split, and the Union was losing financial support from the state (see chapter 4).

4   NATION OVER NATURE

1. Most of these parties were serious efforts, such as the Party of the Democratic Left and the Christian Democrats. A few, however, such as the often mentioned Friends of Beer Party, were perhaps the product of a new free expression and experimentation rather than any sustained intention to continue in the political arena.

2. The actual separation of the two republics was officially decided by their respective heads of state at the time and not by popular referendum. Mečiar (Slovakia's prime minister) and Vaclav Klaus (the Czech prime minister) met in July of 1992 and negotiated the split. Regardless of the actual process of separation, disagreements between the two republics over the pace of reform appeared to be irresolvable, and would likely have resulted in the separation of Czechoslovakia at some point in the future. There remains, however, significant disagreement about the Velvet Divorce among scholars and citizens alike (Kirschbaum 2005:270).

3. Štur relied on Bernolak's foundational work in the late 1700s to produce, in 1850, the first dictionary of literary Slovak grammar.

4. In 1993, zo Podunajsko began to work in cooperation with a new Slovak NGO, the Slovak Rivers Network (see chapter 5).

5. Binder began his involvement with the dam project during socialism, as an employee of Hydrostav, the state-owned company responsible for its construction.

6. Other countries also have well-established green parties, e.g., Finland (1983), Luxembourg (1984), Portugal (1983), Ireland (1989), and Britain (1986).

The Green Party in Britain, while very popular in the polls, has failed to win seats on the national level due to the structure of the British voting system, which successfully blocks small parties from parliament (Rudig 1991). The initial electoral success of European green parties in Switzerland, Sweden, Belgium, and, most impressively, in West Germany in 1983, led political scientists and sociologists to turn their gaze on what they thought marked a "more fundamental political change" rather than the emergence of new issues within traditional political structures (Lowe and Rudig 1986:513). This theory gained even more support when these parties made a successful showing in the June 1990 elections to the European Parliament (Rudig 1991). Active green parties in Western Europe certainly generated a new environmental politics and offered political scientists both quantifiable data showing popular support for ecological issues (Barker and Keating 1977; Lowe and Goyder 1983; Muller-Rommel 1982) and qualitative legislative and policy records of green deputies participating in the formal arena (Kitschelt 1989). West European green parties were regarded as significantly new political movements, challenging not only traditional left/right orientations but also the organizational logic and mobilization tactics of political parties, and even suggested a deeper critique of parliamentary systems (Bramwell 1994; Frankland 1995; Rudig 1986).

7. Stanley Kirschbaum points out that there are two terms in Slovak meaning sovereignty. "*Zvrchovanosť* referred to the sovereignty of the nation, that is to say its right to pursue its own national life. The second, *suverenita*, meant state sovereignty as understood in international law" (Kirschbaum 2005:263). Nationalists used *zvrchovanosť* somewhat ambiguously, intending to suggest a range of solutions in the debate over the future of the Czecho-Slovak state: from autonomy, which was terribly vague, to independence, which was not.

8. Gregory Bateson (1958) identifies two general types of schism that can occur within social and political collectivities. He terms the first type "symmetrical," where different groups promote the same doctrine but do so using separate and competing politics. In the second type of schism, which Bateson calls "complementary," divergent groups acquire doctrines antagonistic to those of a parent group. Bateson's concept of *schismogenesis* has its analogs in religious sectarianism, where its symmetrical form produces sects of the same doctrine and its complementary form results in a heretical organization separating from the parent group. Unlike religious sectarianism, in the process of schismogenesis among the greens, the "orthodoxy" from which separations are made is a contested and variously interpreted doctrine.

9. Opinion polls throughout 1993 and 1994 showed SZS carrying about 3 to 4 percent (FOCUS 1994). Perhaps even more interesting was the fact that SZS consistently received a high percentage of support as a second-choice party among Slovaks in any given election. Of course such a statistic is no consolation in the political arena. Yet weak but consistent representation is not actually far from

the current picture of green politics in Western Europe (Rudig 1991). SZS's coalition with SDL and other left parties in 1994 suggests a political path similar to West European green parties active throughout the 1980s (Kitschelt 1989). Supporters of the original federally oriented Green Party (SZ) did not entirely abandon the Slovak political scene but took up new positions within the Democratic Party (DS), which assumed the old Green Party's environmental platform, and with this its small support base, for the 1994 elections.

10. The SZA sought a centrist economic program, at the same time enjoying the safety of running with a highly popular coalition partner. One of its members invoked nationalism and the former regime's poor ecological record in defining the new party: "The members of Slovak Green Alternative are nationally oriented and do not want to be on the candidate list of [SDL], a party that has the greatest reputation of environmental devastation in Slovakia" (Pokorný 1995).

11. The only individual from the pre-revolutionary Bratislava *ochranári* who supported the SZA was a Canadian-Slovak who returned to Slovakia in 1986 and who had been involved with *Bratislava/nahlas* before the revolution.

12. Anna Bramwell (1994), however, represented a more cautious view, but worried that the emergence of green politics in Eastern Europe might weaken the political fortunes of West European green parties. As the ecological horrors of state socialist systems were exposed, she reasoned, the traditional affiliation of these West European parties with socialism perhaps undermined their parliamentary power and "strengthened the hands of environmental pressure groups" (Bramwell 1994:202).

5   ARGONAUTS OF THE EASTERN BLOC

1. In 1994 Kmart was the largest U.S. investor in Slovakia. The Czech Republic received over 80 percent of total foreign investment in Czechoslovakia in 1992.

2. This transformation was quite slow compared with other East European countries like Poland (Dunn 2004) or the Czech Republic. Slovakia's reluctance to embrace market reforms at first discouraged foreign investment. For example, while Prague had three McDonald's chain stores by 1993, the first Slovak franchise opened only in 1995, in, of all places, Banská Bystrica, the center of Slovak nationalism. For other accounts of economic and social change following the collapse of communism in East Europe see Kideckel (1993), Nagengast (1991), Poznanski (1992), and Szalai (2000).

3. Roman Havlíček, a colleague of Mišiga's, later outlined the specifics of the government's offer. "The purchase procedure was as follows: the Water Management Construction had expert opinions made and property price determined by official assessors. They proposed those prices to the owners by letter with an attached warning that if they did not agree with the purchase price, their property would be expropriated. Nobody explained to the people that in the case of

expropriation they would receive the same compensation, and that unlike selling the property, expropriation gave them the possibility of demanding back their property if construction on the dam did not begin by two years hence . . . For example, the price for house gardens was set at 4 crowns per square meter at that time. Immediately after purchasing, Vodohospodarska Vystavba leased such land to the original owners for an annual rent of 1 crown per square meter. Since 1991, the original owners have paid back twice as much in rent for their gardens as they received when they sold it" (Havlíček 2000:21).

4. Pavel Šremer, whose signature on Charter 77 had exiled him to Bratislava in the first place and brought him to the Union, returned to Prague in 1993. There he began working for the Czech Republic's Peace Corps Program, which focused mostly on English language training and placing Western volunteers with fledgling NGOs working on economic development, media, and democratization. Among other things, Šremer had helped form the Green Party, protested against Gabčíkovo, and served as an advisor to Jozef Vavroušek, the Czech Minister of the Environment. Although he became a member of the Czech STUŽ, his participation in the ecology movement was constrained by his new duties in the Peace Corps. Juraj Podoba, another longtime *ochranár* with ZO 6, began gradually to distance himself from the movement. In 1993, Podoba, also a disillusioned Green Party founder, cynically concluded that Slovakia was "not ready for a Green Party . . . [and] not even ready for green politics. The Green Party was a mistake. It should never have been established." Podoba, a professional ethnologist with the Academy of Sciences, had also been offered an opportunity to study at Cambridge, which took him out of the country and away from the movement altogether.

5. As a result of his visit to Austria, Huba missed the first few days of the Velvet Revolution. By the time he returned to Bratislava from Vienna, the major positions in VPN had been already filled. That VPN did not offer him the post of environmental commissioner sparked conspiracy theories among a few activists, who suspected that ZO 6 had been infiltrated by the secret police long before *Bratislava/nahlas* and that the Velvet Revolution had been engineered by the communists.

6. During the Velvet Revolution, Zamkovský had informed people living in Budmerice about Istrochem's dumping practices, and advised the residents on existing Czechoslovak federal laws regarding such pollution. In 1991, he tried to organize the villagers to demand a public hearing with government officials and plant administrators. When he took his trip to the U.S., however, the fledgling civic initiative he had started fell apart. Upon learning this, and inspired by local victories against factories in the U.S., Zamkosvký decided to create the advocacy center.

7. Some new groups that left the Union continued to perform the same work

they had pursued as part of szopk. For example, the Horský Park Community (Spoločenstvo Horský Park) was originally a basic organization (zo 7) with the mv szopk in Bratislava. Under socialism, members of zo 7 met every other Saturday to work in Bratislava's Horský Park, a large, heavily forested metro park in the heart of the capital's castle district. zo 7 brigades cleaned up litter that accumulated in the park, managed trails for hikers, built a series of small irrigation ditches to direct water runoff and prevent erosion, and maintained a park *chata*. In its new guise as the Horský Park Community, its members continued to provide these services, but now with funding from both the City of Bratislava and the Regional Environmental Center.

8. Trubiniova came to the ecology movement by way of the Green Party, for which she ran (unsuccessfully) as a candidate on the federal list in 1992. She also was involved in szopk's Gabčíkovo campaign, continuing to push the dam issue at a time when most other activists would not come near the question. When Greenpeace International opened up an office in Bratislava, it beckoned to her aggressive activist spirit, and she left szopk in 1993.

9. See Jiři Pehe (1992:34–38), Ján Obrman (1993:31–32), and Sharon Fisher (1993) on state control of the media in post-socialist Slovakia.

10. Although independent media covered actions more frequently (and more objectively), even pro-government papers often showed up to and covered demonstrations, thus publicizing issues that otherwise might not have been accessible to most Slovak readers.

11. When asked by members of Za Matku Zem whether Greenpeace activists could join them in an action against water issues, Trubiniova, the Greenpeace director, replied apologetically that "We can only focus on nuclear energy right now." Global 2000, the Austrian-based environmental organization, donated computers and printed material as well as provided fax service to Za Matku Zem. But these resources were understood to be for the purpose of Za Matku Zem's anti-nuclear campaign.

6   RETURNING TO THE LANDSCAPE

1. In place of military service, which is mandatory in Slovakia, a male can apply for civil service, which is twice as long as army duty (two years as opposed to one).

2. The upper mill in the valley is owned by the Liptovský Mikuláš town office of nature protection. Renovation on this mill was also carried out by szopk, and its members contribute significantly to its maintenance and management.

3. In December 1995, Croatia and Bosnia signed the Dayton Peace Agreement, ending the ethnic violence which plagued the former Yugoslavia for over five years.

4. There were only a couple of exceptions to this. On the Walk Across Europe for a Nuclear Free World campaign, organized by young activists in Za Matku Zem, several older *ochranári* briefly joined in a series of marches and demonstrations against the Mochovce nuclear plant. Their participation was temporary, and not part of the direct action protests performed by the group of international activists throughout the journey across Slovakia, personally guided by Juraj Rizman of Za Matku Zem.

5. There were several other brigades that month, as well. One coincided with and was only a few kilometers from Katka's work at the mills. A band of university architecture students were reconstructing a nineteenth-century house in the center of the village of Kvačian. This brigade was organized by Boris Hochel. Hochel was also a member of SZOPK, whose primary involvement in the Union was focused on historical preservation.

6. The activists told me that this symbolized the women Nazi soldiers took in as harlots, and later had killed.

7. Christopher Ely (2002) sees this envisioning of land and nation represented in nineteenth-century Russian landscape painting. One might also argue that this conjuncture of place and identity is common in images of the American Wild West.

CONCLUSION

1. Members of Greenpeace also participated in this action, but not officially representing their organization. Activists from the two groups often joined in actions to support each other, with the understanding that only one group would (or even could) take credit for it. For example, if Trubiniova, the Greenpeace director for Slovakia, did not approve of a blockade or demonstration, participating Greenpeace members would not represent themselves as such to the press. This did not prevent them from wearing T-shirts with the organization's logo, however.

2. An example of this kind of repositioning of nature is found in the viewpoint of *deep ecology* (Sessions 1995), which places the natural world at a central position with respect to human life. Deep ecology's biocentrism brings nature into a confrontation with the cultural world, placing it at the top of the agenda of competing human concerns. This environmental philosophy almost completely displaces the human subject with the nonhuman "object" of nature "as a subject," in order to subvert what is perceived as an inherent power relationship between the two.

3. I do not mean to suggest that there has been no prior connection between religious beliefs and environmental ethics, nor do I claim that mainstream environmentalism is an entirely secular position or worldview. Roger Gottlieb (2006) provides a recent and quite thorough treatment of the links between spiritual communities and ecological thought and activism.

4. According to Jim Ball, president of the Evangelical Environmental Network, Evangelicals have been concerned about the environment since the 1960s. This previously fringe component of Christian activism is changing quickly. "We are now experiencing a growing interest within the center of the Evangelical community" (Pardo-Kaplan 2005).

REFERENCES

PRIMARY SOURCES: PAMPHLETS, PERIODICALS, PROCLAMATIONS, AND PRESS ARTICLES

Binder, Julius. 1992. "Damming evidence?" *East European Reporter* 76:3–9.

———. 1993. "Dielo narodný cti a hrdosti." *Slovak v Amerike*, December 12.

Brontosaurus. 1989. *Brontosaurus*. Pamphlet.

Budaj, Ján, ed. 1983. *Cintorínske príbehy*. Bratislava: Samizdat.

———. 1987. *Bratislava/nahlas*. Bratislava: SZOPK ZO 6 and 13.

Butora, Martin. 1988. "Vyvdoruvanie alebo každodennosť postivných deviantov." In *Lesk a bieda každodennosti*, M. Ac. et al. Bratislava.

Butora, M., V. Krívy, and S. Szomolanyiova. 1989. "Positive Deviance: The Career of a Concept in Czecho-Slovakia in the Late 1980s." Manuscript.

Center for Social Research. 1990. *Public Survey*. Bratislava: Center for Social Research.

———. 1991. *Public Survey*. Bratislava: Center for Social Research.

Charter 77. 1986. "Chernobyl Viewed from East Central Europe." Letter to Czechoslovak Government, May 6.

Chorváth, Ľubor. 1986. "Aktivita spoločenských organizácií vochranárskej oblasti." *Poznaj a Chráň* 4:1–2.

Fabian, Pavol. 1992. Personal communication. SZ Archives, Bratislava.

Fedorko, Andrej. 1982. "Zo správy o činnosti SZOPK za rok 1981." *Poznaj a Chráň* 8:21.

FOCUS. 1994. *Aktuálne problémy Slovenska*. Bratislava.

Fric, P. 1991. *Aktualny problemy Slovenskej spolocnosti*. Bratislava: Center for Social Analysis.

Huba, Mikuláš. 1987. "Je študium Ōudovej architektury anachronizmon?" *Ochranca Prírody*. Bratislava: MV SZOPK, 21–26.

————. 1990. *List ku svetového otca*. Reprinted in *Ochranca Prírody* 1990. Bratislava.

————. 1995. *Po-novembrové Slovensko*. Vols. I–II. Bratislava: Euro-Uni Press.

Moravčik, Štefan, ed. 1990. *Z tých (revolučných) dňi*. Bratislava: Biofond.

Nadácia navraty ku krajíny. 1995. *Nadácia navraty ku krajíny*. Brochure. Bratislava.

Pauliniova, Z. 1990. Interview with Juro Flamik. *Ochranca Prírody*. Bratislava: MV SZOPK, 44–46.

Piškorova, M. 1988. *Nič noveho pod slnkom*. Pravda.

Podoba, Juraj. 1992. "Su zeleni ešte zeleny?" *Kulturný Život* 32:1.

Randik, Aladar. 1989. "Dvacat rokov slovenskeho zvazu ochrancov prírody a krajiny." *Poznaj a Chráň*. 3:2–3.

Sabo, Peter. 1990. *List k členstva Strana Zelených*. SZ Archives, Pieštaný.

Šíbl, Jaromir. 1993. *Stop Gabcikovo*. Bratislava: SZOPK.

Socialist Union of Youth. 1989. *The Brontosaurus Movement*. Prague: Socialist Union of Youth.

Štatistická ročenka. 1991. *Štatistická ročenka České a Slovenské Federativni Republiky*. Prague.

————. 1993. *Slovenskej Republiky*. Bratislava.

Strom Života. 1989 and 1994. *Strom Života*. Pamphlet. Bratislava.

SZOPK. 1982. *Poznaj a Chráň* 1. Bratislava: UV SZOPK.

————. 1983. *Poznaj a Chráň* 1. Bratislava: UV SZOPK.

————. 1984. *Poznaj a Chráň* 3–4. Bratislava: UV SZOPK.

————. 1988. *Poznaj a Chráň* 2. Bratislava: UV SZOPK.

————. 1986. *Ochranca Prírody* 1–2. Bratislava: MV SZOPK.

————. 1988a. *Ochranca Prírody* 1. Bratislava: MV SZOPK.

————. 1988b. *Ochranca Prírody* 2. Bratislava: MV SZOPK.

————. 1988c. *Ochranca Prírody* 3–4. Bratislava: MV SZOPK.

————. 1989a. *Ochranca Prírody* 1–2. Bratislava: MV SZOPK.

————. 1989b. *Ochranca Prírody* 3–4. Bratislava: MV SZOPK.

————. 1990. "State Nature Protection in Slovakia." Press release in English. Bratislava: SZOPK.

————. 1991. *Ekopanorama* 1–12. Bratislava: UV SZOPK.

————. 1992. *Ekopanorama* 1–12. Bratislava: UV SZOPK.

————. 1993. *Ekopanorama* 1–12. Bratislava: UV SZOPK.

————. 1994. *Ekopanorama* 1–12. Bratislava: UV SZOPK.

————. 1995. *Ekopanorama* 1–9. Bratislava: UV SZOPK.

SZOPK, MV. 1994. *Zoznám* (Directory of Environmental NGOs in Slovakia). Bratislava: SZOPK.

————. 1989. *Platforma*. Metská Konferencia SZOPK, Bratislava, April 22.

SZOPK, ZO 6. 1984. *Zapicníci*. Bratislava.

Zamkovský, Juraj. 1992. "Otvarený tvar Ameriky." *Ekopanorama* 1:14–15.

Adelman, Jonathan, ed. 1984. *Terror and Communist Politics: The Role of the Secret Police in Communist States.* Boulder, Colo.: Westview Press.

Agrawal, Arun. 2005. *Environmentality: Technologies of Government and the Making of Subjects.* Durham, N.C.: Duke University Press.

Alvarez, Sonia E., Evelina Dagnino, and Arturo Escobar, eds. 1998. *Cultures of Politics/Politics of Cultures: Re-visioning Latin American Social Movements.* Boulder, Colo.: Westview Press.

Anderson, Benedict. 1983. *Imagined Communities.* London: Verso.

Anderson, David G. 2000. *Identity and Ecology in Siberia: The Number One Reindeer Brigade.* Oxford: Oxford University Press.

Anderson, E. N. 1996. *Ecologies of the Heart: Emotion, Belief and the Environment.* Oxford: Oxford University Press.

Andrews, Richard N. L. 1993. "Environmental Policy in the Czech and Slovak Republics." In *Environment and Democratic Transition,* ed. Anna Vari and Pal Tamas. Dordrecht: Kluwer Academic Publishers.

Appadurai, Arjun. 1991. "Global Ethnoscapes: Notes and Queries for a Transnational Anthropology." In *Recapturing Anthropology,* ed. Richard G. Fox, 191–210. Santa Fe, N.Mex.: School of American Research Press.

Arato, Andrew. 1981. "Civil Society against the State: Poland 1980–1981." *Telos* 47: 23–47.

Arensberg, Conrad. 1954. "The Community Study Method." *American Journal of Sociology* 60:109–25.

Auer, Stefan. 2004. *Liberal Nationalism in Central Europe.* London: Routledge.

Bailey, F. G. 1969. *Strategems and Spoils.* London: Basil Blackwell.

Bakić-Hayden, Milica. 1995. "Nesting Orientalisms: The Case of Former Yugoslavia." *Slavic Review* 54:917–31.

Bakhtin, Mikhail. 1986 [1952]. "The Problem of Speech Genres." In *Speech Genres and Other Late Essays,* ed. Caryl Emerson and Michael Holquist, 60–102. Austin: University of Texas Press.

Barker, A., and M. Keating. 1977. "Public Spirits: Amenity Societies and Others." In *Participation in Politics,* ed. C. Crouch, 202–21. British Sociological Yearbook, vol. 3. London: Croom Helm.

Bateson, Gregory. 1958. *Naven.* 2d edition. Stanford: Stanford University Press.

Bauman, Zygmut. 1987. "Intellectuals in East Central Europe: Continuity and Change." *Eastern European Politics and Societies* 1:162–86.

Beissinger, Mark. 2002. *Nationalist Mobilization and the Collapse of the Soviet State.* Cambridge Studies in Comparative Politics. Cambridge: Cambridge University Press.

Bell, P. D. 1984. *Peasants in Socialist Transition: Life in a Collectivized Hungarian Village.* Berkeley: University of California Press.

Belton, Brian. 2004. *Gypsy and Traveller Ethnicity: The Social Generation of an Ethnic Phenomenon*. New York: Routledge.

Berdahl, Daphne, Matti Bunzl, and Martha Lampland, eds. 2000. *Altering States: Ethnographies of Transition in Eastern Europe and the Former Soviet Union*. Ann Arbor: University of Michigan Press.

Blaikie, Piers, and Harold Brookfield. 1987. *Land Degradation and Society*. London: Methuen.

Blazak, Randy. 2001. *Renegade Kids, Suburban Outlaws: From Youth Culture to Delinquency*. New York: Wadsworth Publishing.

Blumer, Herbert G. 1969. "Collective Behavior." In *Principles of Sociology*, ed. Alfred McClung Lee, 65–121. 3d edition. New York: Barnes and Noble Books.

Bollag, Burton. 1991. "Gabcikovo Dam: Protests Mount." *WWF News*, September/October.

Borneman, John. 1992. *Belonging in the Two Berlins*. Cambridge: Cambridge University Press.

Bowie, Katherine A. 2005. "The State and the Right Wing: The Village Scout Movement in Thailand." In *Social Movements: An Anthropological Reader*, ed. June C. Nash. New York: Blackwell.

Bozoki, Andras. 1999. "The Rhetoric of Action: The Language of Regime Change in Hungary." In *Intellectuals and Politics in Central Europe*, ed. Andras Bozoki, 263–76. Budapest: Central European University Press.

———, ed. 1999. *Intellectuals and Politics in Central Europe*. Budapest: Central European University Press.

Bradley, John F. 1992. *Czechslovakia's Velvet Revolution: A Political Analysis*. Boulder: East European Monographs.

Bramwell, Anna. 1994. *The Fading of the Greens*. New Haven: Yale University Press.

Bren, Paulina. 2002. "Weekend Getaway: The Chata, the Tramp, and the Politics of Private Life in Post-1968 Czechoslovakia." In *Socialist Spaces: Sites of Everyday Life in the Eastern Bloc*, ed. David Crowley and Susan E. Reid, 123–40. Oxford: Berg Publishers.

Butora, M., Z. Butorova, and T. Rosova. 1991. "The Hard Birth of Democracy in Slovakia." *Journal of Communist Studies* 7(4):435–59.

Calhoun, Noel. 2002. "The Ideological Dilemma of Lustration in Poland." *East European Politics and Societies* 16(2):494–520.

Carson, Rachel. 1962. *Silent Spring*. New York: Houghton Mifflin.

Carter, Francis, and David Turnock, eds. 1998. *Environmental Problems in East-Central Europe*. London: Routledge.

Castells, Manuel. 2003. *The Collapse of Communism: A View from the Information Society*. Los Angeles: Figueroa Press.

Cellarius, Barbara. 2004. *In the Land of Orpheus: Rural Livelihoods and Nature Conservation in Postsocialist Bulgaria*. Madison: University of Wisconsin Press.

Cellarius, Barbara A., and Caedmon Staddon. 2002. "Environmental Non-governmental Organizations, Civil Society, and Democratization in Bulgaria." *East European Politics and Societies* 16(1):182–222.

Cipkowski, Peter. 1991. *Revolution in Eastern Europe: Understanding the Collapse of Communism in Poland, Hungary, East Germany, Czechoslovakia, Romania and the Soviet Union.* New York: Wiley.

Cohen, Abner. 1974. *Two-Dimensional Man.* Berkeley: University of California Press.

———. 1981. *The Politics of Elite Culture.* Berkeley: University of California Press.

Cohen, Anthony P. 1985. *The Symbolic Construction of Community.* London: Tavistock.

Cohen, E. M. 1981. "Ideology, Interest Group Formation and Protest: The Case of the Clamshell Alliance and the New Left." PhD diss., Harvard University.

Conklin, Beth. 1997. "Body Paint, Feathers and VCRs: Aesthetics and Authenticity in Amazonian Activism." *American Ethnologist* 24(4):711–37.

Connor, Walter D. 1980. "Dissent in Eastern Europe: A New Coalition?" *Problems of Communism* 29(1):15–26.

Creed, Gerald. 2004. "Constituted Through Conflict: Images of Community (and Nation) in Bulgarian Rural Ritual." *American Anthropologist* 106(1):56–70.

Dawisha, Karen, and Bruce Parrott, eds. 1997. *The Consolidation of Democracy in East-Central Europe: Democratization and Authoritarianism in Post-Communist Societies.* Cambridge: Cambridge University Press.

Dawson, Jane. 1996. *Eco-Nationalism.* Durham, N.C.: Duke University Press.

Day, Barbara. 1999. *The Velvet Philosophers.* London: Claridge Press.

DeLuca, Kevin Michael. 1999. *Image Politics: The New Rhetoric of Environmental Activism.* Guilford, UK: Guilford Press.

Devall, W. 1970. *The Governing of a Voluntary Organization: Oligarchy and Democracy in the Sierra Club.* PhD diss., University of Oregon.

DeWitt, Calvin B. 1998. *Earth-Wise: A Biblical Response to Environmental Issues.* Grand Rapids, Mich.: Faith Alive Christian Resources.

Doane, Molly. 2005. "Resilience of Nationalism in a Global Era: Megaprojects in Mexico's South." In *Social Movements: An Anthropological Reader,* ed. June C. Nash. New York: Blackwell.

Doellinger, David. 2002. "From Prayers to Protests: The Impact of Religious-Based Dissent on the Emergence of Civil Society in Slovakia and the GDR." PhD diss., University of Pittsburgh.

Douglas, Mary. 1966. *Purity and Danger.* London: Routledge.

Dowling, Maria. 2002. *Czechoslovakia.* London: Arnold.

Drakulić, Slavenka. 1993. How We Survived Communism and Even Laughed. New York: Harper.

Dunn, Elizabeth C. 2004. *Privatizing Poland: Baby Food, Big Business, and the Remaking of Labor.* Ithaca, N.Y.: Cornell University Press.

Dunn, Stephen P., and Ethel Dunn. 1967. *The Peasants of Central Russia*. New York: Holt, Rinehart and Winston.

Durkheim, Emile. 1915. *The Elementary Forms of the Religious Life*. New York: Free Press.

Edwards, Lee. 1999. *The Collapse of Communism*. Washington, D.C.: Hoover Institution Press.

Egginton, J. 1980. *The Poisoning of Michigan*. New York: Norton.

Ely, Christopher. 2002. *This Meager Nature: Landscape and National Identity in Imperial Russia*. Dekalb, Ill.: Northern Illinois University Press.

Endicott, Marcus L. 1998. "Czechoslovakia." http://www.mendicott.com/bbb form.htm (accessed January 29, 2007).

Escobar, Arturo. 1999. "After Nature: Steps to an Antiessentialist Political Ecology." *Current Anthropology* 40(1):1–30.

Fairhead, James, and Melissa Leach. 1996. *Misreading the African Landscape: Society and Ecology in a Forest-Savanna Mosaic*. Cambridge: Cambridge University Press.

Feshbach, Murray, and Alfred Friendly Jr. 1992. *Ecocide in the USSR: Health and Nature under Siege*. New York: Basic Books.

Fisher, Duncan. 1993. "The Emergence of the Environmental Movement in Eastern Europe and Its Role in the Revolutions of 1989." In *Environmental Action in Eastern Europe*, ed. B. Jancar-Webster, 89–113. Armonk, N.Y.: M. E. Sharpe.

Fisher, Sharon. 1993. "The Gabcikovo-Nagymaros Dam Controversy." *RFE/RL Research Report* 2(37):7–12.

———. 1995. "Backtracking on the Road to Democratic Reform." *Annual Survey*, 25–31. Washington, D.C.: Open Media Research Institute.

Fitzmaurice, John. 1996. *Damming the Danube*. Boulder, Colo.: Westview Press.

Flam, Helena. 1999. "Dissenting Intellectuals and Plain Dissenters: The Cases of Poland and East Germany." In *Intellectuals and Politics in Central Europe*, ed. Andras Bozoki, 19–42. Budapest: Central European University Press.

———, ed. 2001. *Pink, Purple and Green: Women's, Religious, Environmental, and Gay/Lesbian Movements in Central Europe Today*. Boulder, Colo.: East European Monographs.

Flam, Helena, and Debra King, eds. 2005. *Emotions and Social Movements*. New York: Routledge.

Foucault, Michel. 1994 [1972]. *The Order of Things*. New York: Vintage Books.

Frankland, E. G. 1995. "Green Revolutions? The Role of Green Parties in Eastern Europe's Transition, 1989–1994." *East European Quarterly* 24(3):315–45.

French, A., and E. I. Hamilton. 1979. *The Socialist City*. New York: Wiley.

French, Hillary. 1990. *Green Revolutions*. Worldwatch Paper 99. Washington, D.C.: Worldwatch Institute.

Gabler, Eric, and Richard Handler. 1996. "After Authenticity at an American Heritage Site." *American Anthropologist* 98(3):568–91.

Gal, Susan. 1991. "Bartok's Funeral: Representations of Europe in Hungarian Political Rhetoric." *American Ethnologist* 18(3):440–58.

Gal, Susan, and Gail Kligman, eds. 2000. *Reproducing Gender: Politics, Publics, and Everyday Life after Socialism*. Princeton, N.J.: Princeton University Press.

Galambos, Judit. 1993. "An International Environmental Conflict on the Danube: The Gabcikovo-Nagymaros Dams." In *Environment and Democratic Transition*. Boston: Kluwer Academic Publishers.

Garcia-Canclini, Nestor. 1996. *Hybrid Cultures: Strategies for Entering and Leaving Modernity*. Minneapolis: University of Minnesota Press.

Garton Ash, Timothy. 1990. *The Magic Lantern*. New York: Random House.

Geertz, Clifford. 1973. *The Interpretation of Culture*. New York: Basic Books.

Gilligan, Emma. 2003. *Defending Human Rights in Russia*. London: Routledge/Curzon.

Gindl, Eugen. 1989. *Days of Joy. Ochranca Prírody* 3–4:84.

Glacken, Clarence. 1967. *Traces on the Rhodian Shore*. Berkeley: University of California Press.

Glinski, Piotr. 2001. "The Ecological Movements as the Elements of Civil Society." In *Pink, Purple and Green: Women's, Religious, Environmental, and Gay/Lesbian Movements in Central Europe Today*, ed. Helena Flam. Boulder, Colo.: East European Monographs.

Gonzalez, Nancie. 1972. "The Sociology of a Dam." *Human Organization* 31:353–60.

Goodale, Jane C. 1971. *Tiwi Wives: A Study of the Women of Melville Island, North Australia*. American Ethnological Society Monographs, no. 51. Seattle: University of Washington Press.

Goodwin, Jeff, James M. Jasper, and Francesca Polleta, eds. 2001. *Passionate Politics: Emotions and Social Movements*. Chicago: University of Chicago Press.

Gottlieb, Roger. 2006. *A Greener Faith: Religious Environmentalism and Our Planet's Future*. New York: Oxford University Press.

Grant, Bruce. 1995. *In the Soviet House of Culture*. Princeton, N.J.: Princeton University Press.

Gray, Patty A. 2003. *The Predicament of Chukotka's Indigenous Movement: Post-Soviet Activism in the Russian Far North*. Cambridge: Cambridge University Press.

Groves, Julian. 2001. "Animal Rights and the Politics of Emotion: Folk Constructions of Emotion in the Animal Rights Movement." In *Passionate Politics: Emotions and Social Movements*, ed. Jeff Goodwin, James M. Jasper, and Francesca Polleta, 212–32. Chicago: University of Chicago Press.

Grunberg, Laura. 2000. "Women's NGOs in Romania." In *Reproducing Gender: Politics, Publics, and Everyday Life after Socialism*, ed. Susan Gal and Gail Kligman, 307–36. Princeton, N.J.: Princeton University Press.

Hagan, John, Hans Merkens, and Klaus Boehnke. 1995. "Deliquency and Disdain: Social Capital and the Control of Right-Wing Extremism among East and West Berlin Youth." *American Journal of Sociology* 100(4):1028–52.

Hall, Edward. 1973. *The Silent Language.* New York: Anchor Books.

Halpern, Joel M., and B. Kerewsky-Halpern. 1972. *A Serbian Village in Historical Perspective.* New York: Holt, Rinehart and Winston.

Hann, Chris M. 1980. *Tazlar: A Village in Hungary.* Cambridge: Cambridge University Press.

Haraszti, Miklos. 1990. "The Beginnings of Civil Society: The Independent Peace Movement and the Danube Movement." In *In Search of Civil Society: Independent Peace Movements in the Soviet Bloc*, ed. Vladimir Tismaneanu. London: Routledge.

Harper, Krista. 2005. "'Wild Capitalism' and 'Ecocolonialism': A Tale of Two Rivers." *American Anthropologist* 107(2):221–33.

Havel, Vaclav. 1987. "The Power of the Powerless." In *Vaclav Havel*, or *Living in Truth*, ed. Ján Vladislav. London: Faber and Faber.

Havlíček, Roman. 2000. "Destruction of Rural Communities as an Inseparable Part of the Construction of Large Dams in Slovakia." World Commission on Dams.

Hayden, Cori. 2003. *When Nature Goes Public: The Making and Unmaking of Bioprospecting in Mexico.* Princeton, N.J.: Princeton University Press.

Hays, Samuel P. 1958. *Conservation and the Gospel of Efficiency: The Progressive Conservation Movement, 1890–1920.* Cambridge: Cambridge University Press.

———. 1987. *Beauty, Health, and Permanence.* Cambridge: Cambridge University Press.

Hicks, Barbara. 1996. *Environmental Politics in Poland.* New York: Columbia University Press.

Hobsbawm, Eric, and T. Ranger, eds. 1982. *The Invention of Tradition.* Cambridge: Cambridge University Press.

Hockenos, Paul. 1993. *Free to Hate.* New York: Routledge.

Huba, Mikuláš. 2003. "The Development of the Environmental Non-governmental Movement in Slovakia." In *Local Communities and Post-Communist Transition: Czechoslovakia, the Czech Republic and Slovakia*, ed. Simon Smith, 91–104. London: Routledge.

Hughes, David. 2005. "Third Nature: Making Space and Time in the Great Limpopo Conservation Area." *Cultural Anthropology* 20(2):157–84.

Hymes, Dell. 1986 [1972]. "Models of Interaction of Language and Social Life." In *Directions in Sociolinguistics: The Ethnography of Communication*, ed. John J. Gumperz and Dell Hymes, 35–71. New York: Basil Blackwell.

International Herald Tribune. 2007. "Czech President Says EU Membership Brought Little to Czech Republic, Slovakia." January 11.

Jancar-Webster, Barbara. 1993. "The East European Environmental Movement and the Transformation of East European Society." In *Environmental Action in Eastern Europe*, ed. Jancar-Webster, 192–219. Armonk, N.Y.: M. E. Sharpe, Inc.

Jehlicka, Petr, and Thomas Kostelecky. 1992. "The Development of the Czecho-Slovak Green Party since the 1990 Elections." *Environmental Politics* 1(1):72–94.

Jehlicka, Petr, and Joe Smith. n.d. "Out of the Woods and Into the Lab: Exploring the Strange Marriage of American Woodcraft and Soviet Ecology in Czech Environmentalism." Manuscript.

Joppke, Christian. 1995. *East German Dissidents and the Revolution of 1989: Social Movement in a Leninist Regime*. New York: New York University Press.

Keane, John. 1988. *Civil Society and the State*. London: Verso.

Kenney, Padraic. 2003. *A Carnival of Revolution: Central Europe 1989*. Princeton, N.J.: Princeton University Press.

Khator, Renu. 1991. *Environment, Development and Politics in India*. Lanham, Md.: University Press of America.

Kideckel, David A. 1976. "The Social Organization of Production on a Romanian Cooperative Farm." *Dialectical Anthropology* 1(3):267–76.

———. 1993. *The Solitude of Collectivism: Romanian Villagers to the Revolution and Beyond*. Ithaca, N.Y.: Cornell University Press.

Kilburn, Michael, and Miroslav Vanek. 2004. "The Ecological Roots of a Democracy Movement." *Environmental Rights*, Carnegie Council on Ethics and International Affairs Human Rights Dialogue, http://www.cceia.org//resources/publications/dialogue/2_11/section_1/4443.html (accessed October 13, 2004.

Kirschbaum, Stanislav. 2005. *A History of Slovakia: The Struggle for Survival*. 2d edition. New York: Palgrave MacMillan.

Kitschelt, Herbert. 1989. *The Logistics of Party Formation*. Ithaca, N.Y.: Cornell University Press.

———. 1992. "The Formation of Party Systems in East Central Europe." *Politics and Society* 20(1):7–50.

Kligman, Gail. 1998. *The Politics of Duplicity: Controlling Reproduction in Ceausescu's Romania*. Berkeley: University of California Press.

Komaromi, Ann. 2004. "The Material Existence of Soviet Samizdat." *Slavic Review* 63(3):597–618.

Konrad, Gyorg. 1984. *Antipolitics*. New York: Harcourt Brace Jovanovich.

Konrad, Gyorg, and Ivan Szelenyi. 1979. *The Intellectuals on the Road to Class Power*. New York: Harcourt.

Konvicka, L., and J. Kavan. 1994. "Youth Movements and the Velvet Revolution." *Communist and Post-Communist Studies* 27(2):160–76.

Ladd, A. E., T. C. Hood, and K. Van Liere. 1983. "Ideological Themes in the Anti-Nuclear Movement." *Sociological Inquiry* 8:252–72.

Lampland, Martha. 1991. "Pigs, Party Secretaries and Private Lives." *American Ethnologist* 18(3):459–79.

Lave, Jean, and Etienne Wenger. 1991. *Situated Learning: Legitimate Peripheral Participation.* Cambridge: Cambridge University Press.

Lee, Martha F. 1995. *Earth First! Environmental Apocalypse.* Syracuse: Syracuse University Press.

Lee, Richard B. 1979. *The !Kung San: Men, Women and Work in a Foraging Society.* Cambridge: Cambridge University Press.

Leff, Carol Skalnik. 1997. *The Czech and Slovak Republics: Nation Versus State.* Boulder, Colo.: Westview Press.

Lévi-Strauss, Claude. 1963. *Structural Anthropology.* New York: Basic Books.

Liefferink, Duncan, and Mikael Skou Andersen. 1998. "Greening the EU: National Positions in the Run-up to the Amsterdam Treaty." *Environmental Politics* 7(3):66–93.

Liehm, Antonin J., ed. 1973. *The Politics of Culture.* New York: Grove Publishing.

Lovenduski, Joni, and Jean Woodall. 1987. *Politics and Society in Eastern Europe.* Bloomington: Indiana University Press.

Lowe, Philip, G. Cox, M. MacEwen, T. O'Riordan, and M. Winter. 1985. *The Politics of Farming, Forestry and Conservation.* London: Gower.

Lowe, Philip, and M. Goyder. 1983. *Environmental Groups in Politics.* London: George Allen and Unwin.

Lowe, Philip, and Wolfgang Rudig. 1986. "Political Ecology and the Social Sciences." *British Journal of Political Science* 16:513–50.

Luke, Timothy. 1997. "On Environmentality, Geo-power and Eco-knowledge in the Discourse of Contemporary Environmentalism." *Cultural Critique* 31:57–81.

Lynch, Barbara Deutsch. 1993. "The Garden and the Sea: U.S.-Latino Environmental Discourses and Mainstream Environmentalism." *Social Problems* 40(1): 108–24.

Maday, B. C., and M. Hollos. 1983. *New Hungarian Peasants: An East Central European Experience with Collectivization.* New York: Columbia University Press.

Malinowski, Bronislaw. 1984[1922]. *Argonauts of the Western Pacific.* Prospect Heights, Ill.: Waveland Press.

Mandel, Ruth, and Caroline Humphrey, eds. 2002. *Markets and Moralities: Ethnographies of Post-Socialism.* Oxford: Berg Publishers.

Markowitz, Lisa. 2001. "Finding the Field Notes on the Ethnography of NGOs." *Human Organization* 60(1):40–46.

Marshall, Patrick G. 1991. "The Greening of Eastern Europe." *Congressional Quarterly Researcher*, November 15, 851–71.

Mateosian, Greg. 1993. *Reproducing Rape: Domination Through Talk in the Coutroom.* Chicago: University of Chicago Press.

Mayer, Zald, and John McCarthy. 1979. *The Dynamics of Social Movements.* Cambridge, Mass.: Winthrop Publishers.

Mazur, A. 1975. "Opposition to Technological Innovation." *Minerva* 13:58–81.

McAdam, Doug, and David A. Snow, eds. 2007. *Social Movements: Readings on their Emergence, Mobilization, and Dynamics.* New York: Oxford University Press.

McAdam, Doug, Sidney Tarrow, and Charles Tilly. 2001. *Dynamics of Contention.* Cambridge: Cambridge University Press.

Milosz, Czeslaw. 2001. *The Captive Mind.* New York: Penguin Classics.

Milton, Kay. 1993. *Environmentalism: The View from Anthropology.* London: Routledge.

———. 1996. *Environmentalism and Cultural Theory.* London: Routledge.

Moore, Sally Falk. 1987. "Explaining the Present: Theoretical Dilemmas in Processual Anthropology." *American Ethnologist* 14(4):727–36.

Muller-Rommel, F. 1982. "Ecology Parties in Western Europe." *West European Politics* 68:68–74.

Nader, Laura. 1972. "Up the Anthropologist: Perspective Gained from Studying Up." In *Reinventing Anthropology*, ed. Dell Hymes, 284–311. New York: Pantheon Books.

Naess, Arne. 1989. *Ecology, Community and Lifestyle.* Cambridge: Cambridge University Press.

Nagengast, Carole. 1991. *Reluctant Socialists, Rural Entrepreneurs: Class, Culture and the Polish State.* Boulder, Colo.: Westview Press.

Nash, June C., ed. 2005. *Social Movements: An Anthropological Reader.* Malden, Mass.: Blackwell.

Netting, Robert McC. 1981. *Balancing on an Alp: Ecological Change and Continuity in a Swiss Mountain Community.* New York: Cambridge University Press.

Obrebski, Jozef. 1976. *The Changing Peasantry of Eastern Europe.* Edited by B. Kerewsky-Halpern and J. M. Halpern. Cambridge, Mass.: Schenkman.

Obrman, Ján. 1993. *RFE/RL Research Report* 2(19):31–32.

Oelschlaeger, Max. 1989. *The Idea of Wilderness.* New Haven: Yale University Press.

Olivo, Christiane. 2001. *Creating a Democratic Civil Society in Eastern Germany: The Case of the Citizen Movements and Alliance 90.* New York: Praeger.

Ortner, Sherry B. 1974. "Is Female to Male as Nature Is to Culture?" In Michelle Zimbalist Rosaldo and Louise Lamphere, eds., *Woman, Culture, and Society*, 68–87. Stanford, Calif.: Stanford University Press.

Pardo-Kaplan, Deborah. 2005. "EEN Urges Christians to Embrace the Earth." *Science and Technology News*, March.

Peet, Richard, and Michael Watts, eds. 1996. *Liberation Ecologies: Environment, Development and Social Movements.* London: Routledge.

Pehe, Jiři. 1988. *The Prague Spring.* New York: University Press of America.

———. 1992. *RFE/RL Research Report* 1(39).

Peña, Devon G. 2005. *Mexican Americans and the Environment: Tierra Y Vida.* Tucson: University of Arizona Press.

Pilcher, William. 1972. *The Portland Longshoremen: A Dispersed Urban Community.* New York: Holt, Rinehart and Winston.

Piven, Frances F., and Richard A. Cloward. 1977. *Poor People's Movements: Why They Succeed, How They Fail.* New York: Pantheon Books.

Podoba, Juraj. 1998. "Rejecting Green Velvet: Transition, Environment and Nationalism in Slovakia." *Environmental Politics*7(1):129–44.

Pollack, Detlef, and Jan Wielgohs, eds. 2004. *Dissent and Opposition in Communist Eastern Europe: Origins of Civil Society and Democratic Transition.* New York: Ashgate.

Pollak, Janet. 1991. "The Nuclear Power Plant Accidents at Jaslovkse Bohunice, Czecho-slovakia: Reaction and Response." Paper presented at the meeting of the Middle States Anthropology Association, April.

Poznanski, Kazimierz, ed. 1992. *Constructing Capitalism: The Reemergence of Civil Society and Liberal Economy in the Post-Communist World.* Boulder, Colo.: Westview Press.

Priban, Jiri. 2004. "Reconstituting Paradise Lost: Temporality, Civility, and Ethnicity in Post-Communist Constitution-Making." *Law and Society Review* 38(3):407–31.

Ramet, Sabrina P. 1995. *Social Currents in Eastern Europe.* Durham, N.C.: Duke University Press.

Rangan, Haripriya. 2001. *Of Myth and Movements: Rewriting Chipko into Himalayan History.* London: Verso.

Rappaport, Roy. 1984. *Pigs for the Ancestors.* New Haven: Yale University Press.

Ries, Nancy. 1997. *Russian Talk: Culture and Conversation during Perestroika.* Ithaca, N.Y.: Cornell University Press.

Rubin, Charles. 1994. *The Green Crusade: Rethinking the Roots of Environmentalism.* New York: Free Press.

Rudig, Wolfgang. 1986. "A Comparison of Anti-Nuclear Movements in the United States, Britain, France and West Germany." In *Public Acceptance of New Technology*, ed. R. Williams and S. Mills, 364–417. London: Croom Helm.

———. 1991. "Green Party Politics around the World." *Environment* 33(8):7–31.

Ruggs, Dean S. 1985. *Eastern Europe.* Essex, UK: Longman Group.

Sahlins, Marshall. 1985. *Islands of History.* Chicago: University of Chicago Press.

Sale, Kirkpatrick. 1993. *The Green Revolution: The American Movement, 1962–1992.* New York: Hill and Wang.

Salzmann, Zdenek, and V. Scheuffler. 1974. *Komarov: A Czech Farming Village.* New York: Holt, Rinehart and Winston.

Sampson, Steven. 1982. *The Planners and the Peasants: An Anthropological Study of Urban Development in Romania.* South Jutland, Denmark: University Center.

Scott, Alan. 1990. *Ideology and the New Social Movements.* London: Unwin Hyman.

Scott, James. 1985. *Weapons of the Weak: Everyday Forms of Peasant Resistance.* New Haven: Yale University Press.

———. 1998. *Seeing Like a State: How Certain Schemes to Improve the Human Condition Have Failed.* New Haven: Yale University Press.

Seiler, Cotten. 2006. "'So That We as a Race Might Have Something Authentic to Travel By': African American Automobility and Cold-War Liberalism." *American Quarterly* 58(4):1091–17.

Sessions, George. 1995. *Deep Ecology for the Twenty-First Century.* Boston: Shambhala Publications.

Siegelbaum, Lewis, and Andrei Sokolov. 2000. *Stalinism as a Way of Life: A Narrative in Documents.* New Haven: Yale University Press.

Simic, Andrei. 1973. *The Peasant Urbanites.* New York: Seminar Press.

Simonian, Ligia. 2005. "Political Organization among Indigenous Women of the Brazilian State of Roraima: Constraints and Prospects." In *Social Movements: An Anthropological Reader,* ed. June C. Nash, 285–303. Malden, Mass.: Blackwell.

Sivaramakrishnan, K. 1999. *Modern Forests: Statemaking and Environmental Change in Colonial East India.* Stanford: Stanford University Press.

Smith, P. J., ed. 1975. *The Politics of Physical Resources.* Harmondsworth, UK: Penguin.

Snajdr, Edward. 1998. "The Children of the Greens: New Ecological Activism in Post-Socialist Slovakia." *Problems of Post-Communism* 45(1):54–62.

———. 1999. "Green Intellectuals in Slovakia." In *Intellectuals and Politics in Central Europe,* ed. Andras Bozoki, 207–26. Budapest: Central European University Press.

———. 2007. "Ethnicizing the Subject: Domestic Violence and the Politics of Primordialism in Kazakhstan." *Journal of the Royal Anthropological Institute* 13:603–20.

Spivak, Gayatri. 1988. "Can the Subaltern Speak?" In *Marxism and the Interpretation of Culture,* ed. Carry Nelson and Lawrence Grossberg, 271–313. Urbana, Ill.: University of Illinois Press.

Stone, Daniel. 2005. "The Cable Car at Kasprowy Wierch: An Environmental Debate." *Slavic Review* 64(3):601–24.

Stokes, Gale. 1993. *The Walls Came Tumbling Down.* Oxford: Oxford University Press.

Sturges, P., and Anna Vojtech. 1996. *Marushka and the Month Brothers.* New York: North-South Publishing.

Szalai, Julia. 2000. "From Informal Labor to Paid Occupations: Marketization from Below in Hungarian Women's Work." In *Reproducing Gender: Politics,*

Publics, and Everyday Life after Socialism, ed. Susan Gal and Gail Kligman, 200–204. Princeton, N.J.: Princeton University Press.

Taylor, Bron Raymond, ed. 1995. *Ecological Resistance Movements*. Albany: State University of New York Press.

Taylor, Diana. 1994. "Performing Gender: Las Madras de la Plaza del Mayo." In *Negotiating Performance: Gender, Sexuality and Theatricality in Latina/o America*, ed. Diana Taylor and Juan Villejas, 275–305. Durham, N.C.: Duke University Press.

Thomas, K. 1983. *Man and the Natural World: Changing Attitudes in England, 1500–1800*. London: Allen Lane.

Thompson, Jon. 1991. "East Europe's Dark Dawn." *National Geographic* 179(6):36–63.

Tilly, Charles. 2004. *Social Movements, 1768–2004*. Boulder, Colo.: Paradigm Publishers.

Time-Life. 1987. *Eastern Europe*. Alexandria, Va.: Time-Life Books.

Tismaneanu, Vladimir. 1990. "Eastern Europe: The Story the Media Missed." *Bulletin of the Atomic Scientists*, 17–20. March.

Toth, James. 2005. "Local Islam Gone Global: The Roots of Religious Militancy in Egypt and Its Transnational Transformation." In *Social Movements: An Anthropological Reader*, ed. June C. Nash, 117–45. Malden, Mass.: Blackwell.

Touraine, Alain. 1981. *The Voice and the Eye: An Analysis of Social Movements*. Cambridge: Cambridge University Press.

———. 2000. *Can We Live Together? Equality and Difference*. Stanford, Calif.: Stanford University Press.

Trubiniova, Lubica. 1991. *SZ Archives*. Bratislava.

Tsing, Anna Lowenhaupt. 2001. "Nature in the Making." In *New Directions in Anthropology and Environment*, ed. Carole Crumley, 3–23. New York: Alta Mira Press.

Turnbull, Colin. 1968. *The Forest People*. New York: Simon and Schuster Inc.

Turner, Nancy. 2005. *The Earth's Blanket: Traditional Teachings for Sustainable Living*. Seattle: University of Washington Press.

Turner, Victor. 1967. *The Forest of Symbols: Aspects of Ndembu Ritual*. Ithaca, N.Y.: Cornell University Press.

Verdery, Katherine. 1983. *Transylvanian Villagers*. Berkeley: University of California Press.

———. 1993. "Nationalism and Nationalist Sentiment in Post-Socialist Romania." *Slavic Review* 52(2):179–203.

———. 1996. *What Was Socialism and What Comes Next?* Princeton, N.J.: Princeton University Press.

———. 1999. *The Political Lives of Dead Bodies*. New York: Columbia University Press.

Viola, Eduardo J. 1988. "The Ecologist Movement in Brazil (1974–1986)." *International Journal of Urban and Regional Research* 12:123–28.

Wali, Alaka. 1989. *Kilowatts and Crisis: Hydroelectric Power and Social Dislocation in Eastern Panama*. Boulder, Colo.: Westview Press.

Waller, Michael. 1989. "The Ecology Issue in Eastern Europe: Protests and Movements." *Journal of Communist Studies* 5(3):303–28.

———. 1992. "Profile: The Dams on the Danube." *Environmental Politics* 1(1):121–43.

———. 1994. *Parties, Trade Unions and Society in East-Central Europe*. London: Routledge.

Wapner, Paul. 1996. *Environmental Activism and World Civic Politics*. Albany, N.Y.: State University of New York Press.

Warner, Michael. 2000. *The Trouble with Normal: Sex, Politics and the Ethics of Queer Life*. Cambridge, Mass.: Harvard University Press.

Warner, William Lloyd. 1958. *A Black Civilization: A Study of an Australian Tribe*. Rev. ed. New York: Harper and Brothers.

Weber, Max. 1978. *Economy and Society*. Edited by G. Roth and C. Wittich. Berkeley: University of California Press.

Weigle, Marcia A., and Jim Butterfield. 1992. "Civil Society in Reforming Communist Regimes: The Logic of Emergence." *Comparative Politics* 25(1): 1–23.

Weiner, Douglas. 1988. *Models of Nature: Ecology, Conservation and Cultural Revolution in Soviet Russia*. Bloomington: Indiana University Press.

———. 2002. *A Little Corner of Freedom: Russian Nature Protection from Stalin to Gorbachev*. Berkeley: University of California Press.

Wenger, Etienne. 1999. *Communities of Practice: Learning, Meaning and Identity*. Cambridge: Cambridge University Press.

Wheaton, Bernard, and Zdenek Kavan. 1992. *The Velvet Revolution: Czechoslovakia, 1988–1991*. Boulder, Colo.: WestviewBIBPress.

White, Lynn, Jr. 1967. "The Historical Roots of Our Ecological Crisis." *Science*, March 10, 1203–7.

White, Stephen. 2001. *Communism and Its Collapse: Making of the Contemporary World*. New York: Routledge.

Whittier, Nancy. 2001. "Emotional Strategies: The Collective Reconstruction and Display of Oppositional Emotions in the Movement against Child Sexual Abuse." In *Passionate Politics: Emotions and Social Movements*, ed. Jeff Goodwin, James M. Jasper, and Francesca Polleta, 233–50. Chicago: University of Chicago Press.

Williams, Kieran. 1997. *The Prague Spring and Its Aftermath: Czechoslovak Politics, 1968–70*. Cambridge: Cambridge University Press.

Williams, Melvin D. 1981. *On the Street Where I Lived*. New York: Holt, Rinehart and Winston.

Winner, I. P. 1972. *A Slovenian Village: Zerovnica*. Providence, R.I.: Brown University Press.

Worster, Donald. 1973. *American Environmentalism: The Formative Period, 1860–1915*. New York: Wiley.

———. 1977. *Nature's Economy: The Roots of Ecology*. San Francisco: Sierra Club.

Yearley, Steven. 1996. *Sociology, Environmentalism, Globalization*. London: Sage.

INTERVIEWS

Budaj 1995. Ján Budaj, February 28, Bratislava

Eva 1995. Eva (pseudonym), March 12, Bratislava

Filková 1995. Maria Filková, April 24, Bratislava

Halama 1994. Igor Halama, October 12, Bratislava

Hladký 1995. Milan Hladký, July 9, Bratislava

Huba 1995. Mikuláš Huba, March 4, Bratislava

Luboš 1995. Luboš (pseudonym), July 10, Bratislava

Mesík 1995. Juraj Mesik, June 27, Banská Bystrica

Podoba 1994. Juraj Podoba, October 9, Bratislava

Pokorný 1995. Jozef Pokorný, June 22, Bratislava

Šremer 1995. Pavel Šremer, September 16, Bratislava

Šimončičová 1995. Katka Šimončičová, June 25, Bratislava

INDEX

Adamec, Vladimir, 90, 202n8

African continent, 170

Age of Ecology, 18

Agrawal, Arun, 5, 14–15, 23, 196n5

Agricultural Land Protection Act, 30

Air Purity Law (the chimney law), 30, 31

aktivista, 200n9

Amazon Basin, 141

Anderson, Eugene, 10

András, Peter, 167, 169

Antall, Jozef, 103

anthropology: of East Europe, 196n8; and ethnographic method, 8–9; nature and, 10; political ecology and, 10–15; social movements and, 11–13

anti-elites, 50, 64–68, 73

anti-politicians, 66

anti-Semitism, 170–73, 192

architecture: folk, as cultural monuments, 56; peasant, 199n6, 200n9; preservation of, 51–55; private life and, 32–35; socialism and, 25–27. *See also* Huba, Mikuláš; zo 6

Armenia, 141

Association of Nature Protection, 37

atheism (Marxist), 48

Austria, 61, 98, 106, 135, 206n5; environmental organizations in, 109. *See also* Eurochain; Global 2000

Austrians, 123

automobility, 15

Bailey, F. G., 18

Balkans, 103

Ball, Jim, 209n4

Banská Bystrica: demonstrations during Velvet Revolution, 89; origin of *Eko-trend*, 45; public transportation in, 28; site of new Slovak capital, 125, 200n12, 205n2

basic organization (*základná orginazácia*, zo), 43

Bateson, Gregory, 204n8

Belgrade, 198n3

Berlin Wall, 3

Bernolak, Antonin, 102, 124, 203n3

Bicyba, 83

Binder, Julius, 107, 108, 185, 203n5

bioprospecting, 15

Black Triangle (Bohemia), 59

Blumer, Herbert, 11

Bohemia, 40, 91, 93, 101, 113; and pollution, 16, 59

books (Western), 123. *See also* censorship; *samizdat*

in, 74; transition from socialism and freedom in, 98; vacations in, 157; Velvet Revolution and, 87

East European environmentalists, 105

East European Reporter, 199n2

East Germans, 157

East Germany, 87; dissident movement in, 199n1; Lutherans in, 191; peace movement in, 5, 191

ecological activism: in Latin America and Asia, 14; Slovakia's new generation of, 126. *See also* environmentalism; environmentalists

ecological devastation, 15

ecological harmony, 57

ecology, 6; defined, 18; ethnic discourse of, 121; immigration ecology, 191; of poverty, 34, 198n8; praetorian surrogate, 17; religion and, 191–92; science of, 49. *See also* post-ecology

ecology club (student), 45. *See also* Ekotrend

ecology of poverty, 34

ecology party, 91–92

economic centralization, 29

Economic Ministry, 31

ecotourism, 159

Eduscho, 181

Ekofilm, 161

Ekopanorama, 132, 136

ekotabor (ecology camp), 148

Ekotrend, 45–46, 86, 89, 137, 200n12

elections, 96

Ely, Christopher, 208n7

emotions, in social movements, 12

English, 121

environment (*životné prostredie*), 47

environmental horror stories, 16

environmental impact assessment (EIA), 128, 129

environmentalism: classification of nature, 197n13; development projects and public perceptions of, 197n15;

in North America, 13, 197n14; in post-industrial culture, 14; recreation and, 73

environmentalists: defined, 10; in opposition to communism in Czech Lands, 195n3; social movements and, 12–13

environmentality, 15; alternative definition of, 196n5; communist (state socialist) 23, 46, 183; in context of Eastern Europe, 5; defined, 5; new models of, 16, 187–89; post-ecology and, 189–92

environmental laws (of Czechoslovakia), 29–31

Environmental Partnership for Central Europe, 137

ethnicity: and membership in conservation groups, 199n11; as target of socialism, 27

ethnicization, 126

ethnic violence, 103

ethnographic landscape (defined), 8

ethnography, 13

Ethnology Institute (of the Slovak Academy of Sciences), 9, 128

Eurochain, 106, 110

Europe, 15–18

European Bank for Reconstruction and Development (EBRD), 142, 154

European Council, 161

European Parliament, 204n6

European Union (EU), 8, 19, 153, 162, 171; delayed entry into, 125; membership in, 188

Evangelical community, American, 191, 209n4

Evangelical Environmental Network, 209n4

Fairhead, James, 14, 18, 189

farming, peasant, 24, 164

Fatra Mountains, 157

fauna, 32

independent state, 7, 12, 102, 116; media in, 8; origins of Slovaks, 196n6; peasant culture, 33, 164; post-ecological condition, 6; relations with Hungary, 103; separation from Czech Republic, 7, 100, 174; society, 7; transition from communism, 125; wartime independent state of, 101, 196n7

Slovak Institute for the Care of Historical Monuments (CHMNC), 31, 32,

Slovak language, 102, 120, 203n3. *See also* Matica Act

Slovak National Council, 96, 111, 116, 120, 152

Slovak National Party (SNS), 102, 111, 112, 115, 125, 132, 151

Slovak National Theater, 87

Slovak National Uprising, 55, 124

Slovak National Uprising (SNP) Square, 88

Slovak Rivers Network, 127, 138, 142, 150, 203n4

Slovaks, 7

Slovak Union of Nature and Landscape Protectors. *See* SZOPK

Slovak Writers' Union, 65, 83

Slovenia, 103

Slovenská Republika (Slovak Republic), 10, 184–85

Slovnaft, 29, 59, 77

Sme (We Are), 10, 182

Smena, 203n4

Smežiansky, Peter, 166

Smith, Joe, 37

Snow, David, 196n11

socialism: benefits of, 28; environmentality of, 28–31; industrialization, 29; use of term, 195n2

socialist city, 56–57, 198n3

Socialist Federation (of Czechoslovakia), 42

socialist landscape, 24

Socialist Union of Youth (SZM), 41, 85

social movements: anthropology and, 11–12; discursive aspects of, 11–12; history of, 96n11; new and old, 11; positionality of, 13; post-ecology and, 189–92

Society for Sustainable Living (STUŽ), 165, 142; creation of, 13; Huba's leadership of, 155; *ochranárstvo* and, 166; sustainability, 141; translation of European Council documents, 161–62; Vavroušek memorial, 192

Sokol, Ján, 84

Solidarity (Poland), 3, 4, 17, 87

South Asian guest workers, 125

sovereignty (Slovak), 109, 113, 204n7

Soviet tanks, 29

Soviet Union, 3, 22, 74, 195n2

Spain, tourists from, 167

speech communities, 11

Stalinist-style mega projects, 152, 178, 184

Stankovaný, 163

State Nature Protection Act, 31

state-owned department store, 123

state property, 33

state socialism, 195n2

Stockholm Conference on the Environment in Europe, 41

Stokes, Gale, 200n14

Stop Nicotin!, 83

Strana Zelených (Green Party, SZ), 91

Strana Zelených Slovensko (SZS), 118–119, 204n9

Stražovke Mountains, 43

street musicians (Bolivian), 171, 176

street names, 124

Strom Života (Tree of Life), 41, 42, 85, 139, 199n11. *See also* Brontosaurus

structure of the conjuncture, 178–79

St. Sylvester's Day, 100

students: 17; Appeal of Slovak Students, 174; demonstrations during socialism, 88; in Greenpeace and Za Matku Zem, 143–44; response to *Bratislava/nahlas*, 80–81